As Miss Beelzebub Likes

matoba

volume 3

Translation: Lisa Coffman
Lettering: Lorina Mapa

This book is a work of fiction. Names, characters, places, and incidents are the product of the author's imagination or are used fictitiously. Any resemblance to actual events, locales, or persons, living or dead, is coincidental.

BEELZEBUB-JO NO OKINIMESU MAMA. Vol. 3
©2016 matoba/SQUARE ENIX CO., LTD.
First published in Japan in 2016 by SQUARE ENIX CO., LTD. English translation rights arranged with SQUARE ENIX CO., LTD. and Yen Press, LLC through Tuttle-Mori Agency, Inc., Tokyo.

English translation ©2018 by SQUARE ENIX CO., LTD.

Yen Press
1290 Avenue of the Americas
New York, NY 10104

Visit us at yenpress.com
facebook.com/yenpress   yenpress.tumblr.com
twitter.com/yenpress   instagram.com/yenpress

First Yen Press Edition: September 2018

Yen Press is an imprint of Yen Press, LLC.
The Yen Press name and logo are trademarks of Yen Press, LLC.

The publisher is not responsible for websites (or their content) that are not owned by the publisher.

Library of Congress Control Number: 2017963582

ISBNs: 978-0-316-44775-1 (paperback)
978-0-316-44776-8 (ebook)

D0035871

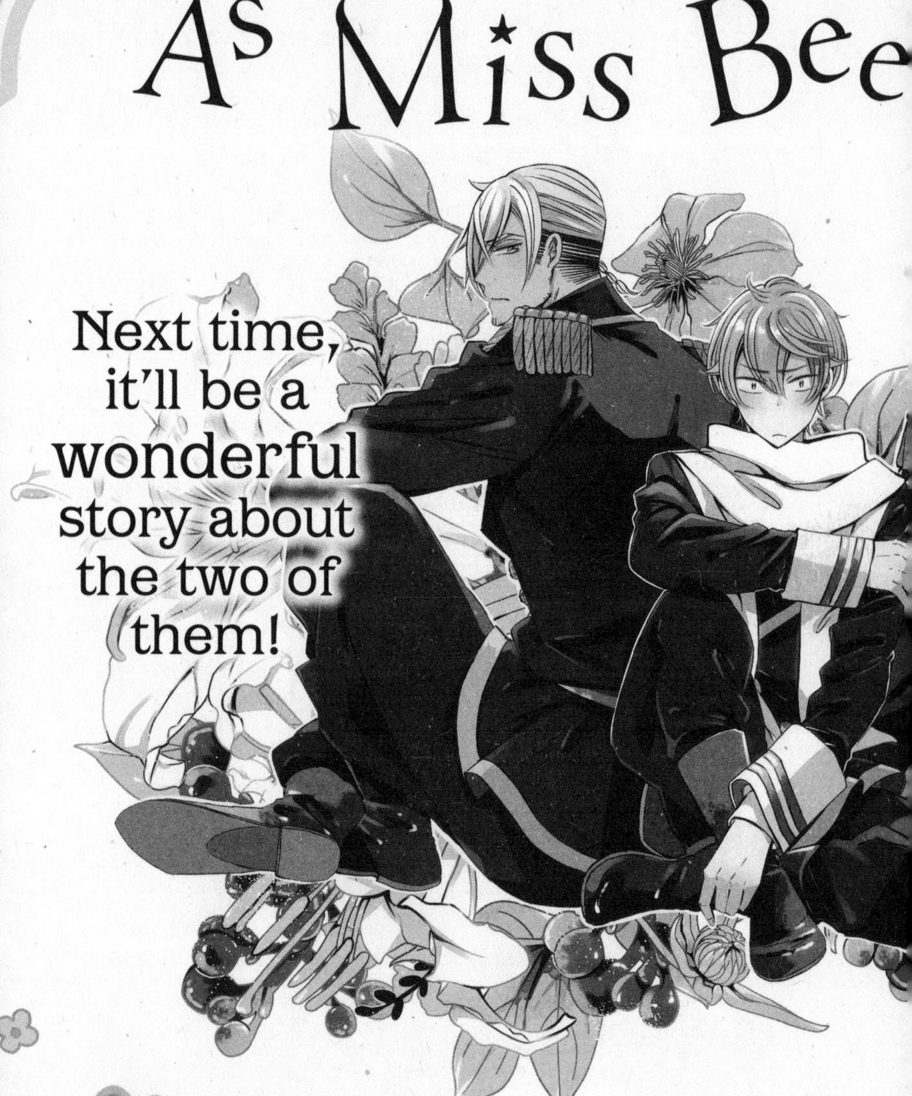
As Miss Bee
Next time, it'll be a wonderful story about the two of them!

AS MISS BEELZEBUB LIKES VOL. 4

CHAPTER 15

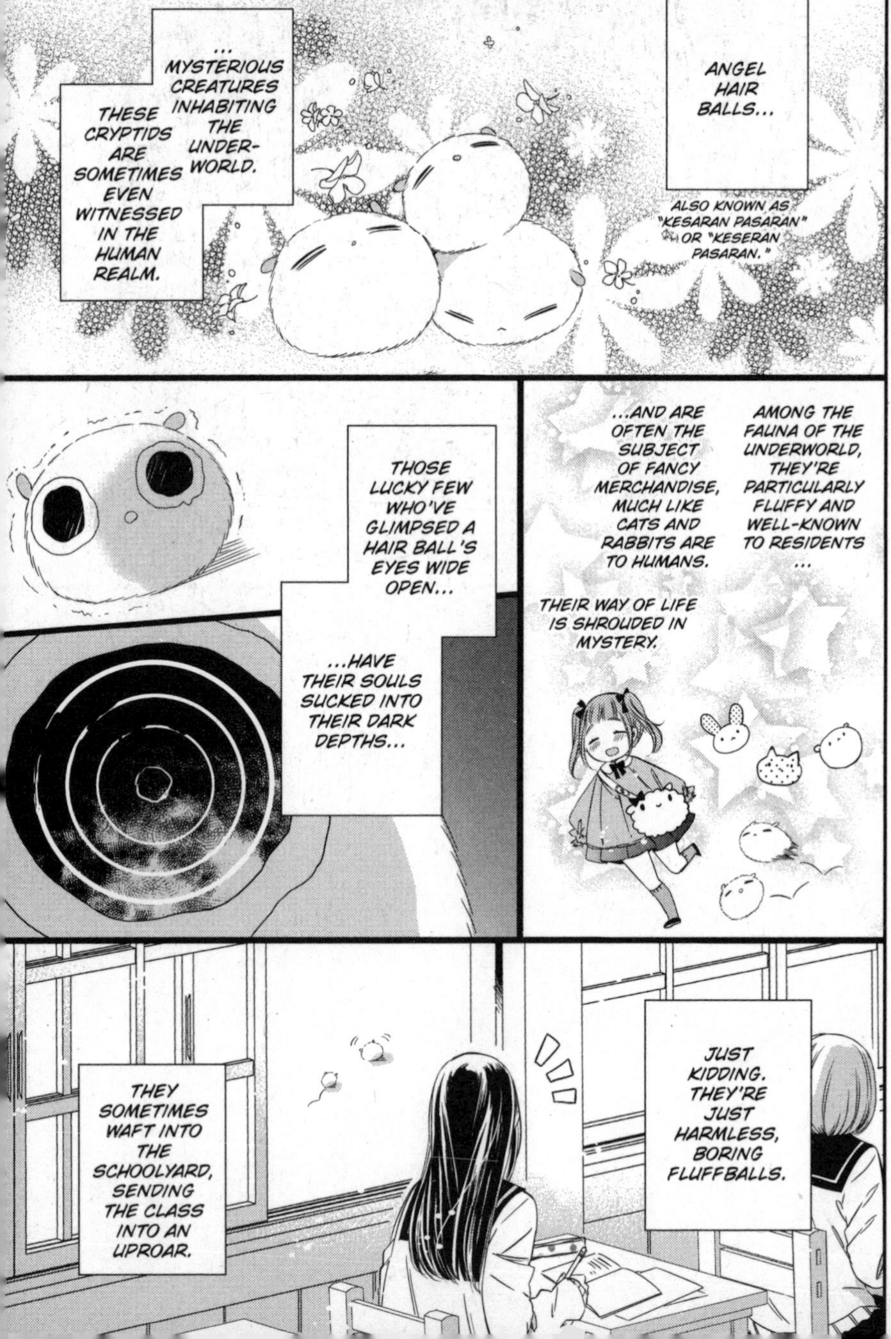
ANGEL HAIR BALLS…
ALSO KNOWN AS "KESARAN PASARAN" OR "KESERAN PASARAN."
…MYSTERIOUS CREATURES INHABITING THE UNDERWORLD.
THESE CRYPTIDS ARE SOMETIMES EVEN WITNESSED IN THE HUMAN REALM.
AMONG THE FAUNA OF THE UNDERWORLD, THEY'RE PARTICULARLY FLUFFY AND WELL-KNOWN TO RESIDENTS…
…AND ARE OFTEN THE SUBJECT OF FANCY MERCHANDISE, MUCH LIKE CATS AND RABBITS ARE TO HUMANS.
THEIR WAY OF LIFE IS SHROUDED IN MYSTERY.
THOSE LUCKY FEW WHO'VE GLIMPSED A HAIR BALL'S EYES WIDE OPEN…
…HAVE THEIR SOULS SUCKED INTO THEIR DARK DEPTHS…
JUST KIDDING. THEY'RE JUST HARMLESS, BORING FLUFFBALLS.
THEY SOMETIMES WAFT INTO THE SCHOOLYARD, SENDING THE CLASS INTO AN UPROAR.

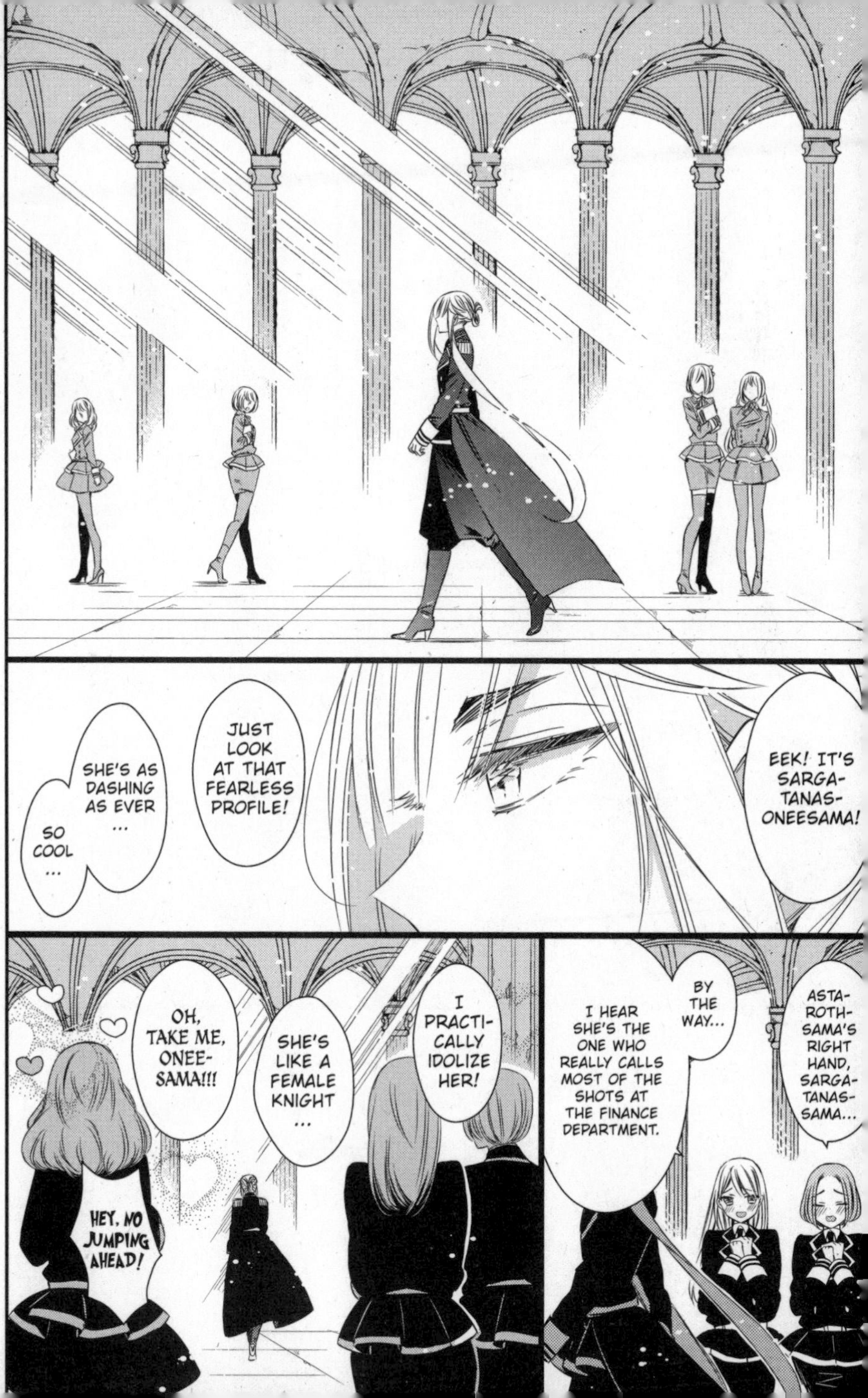
EEK! IT'S SARGA-TANAS-ONEESAMA!
JUST LOOK AT THAT FEARLESS PROFILE!
SHE'S AS DASHING AS EVER ...
SO COOL ...
ASTA-ROTH-SAMA'S RIGHT HAND, SARGA-TANAS-SAMA...
BY THE WAY...
I HEAR SHE'S THE ONE WHO REALLY CALLS MOST OF THE SHOTS AT THE FINANCE DEPARTMENT.
I PRACTI-CALLY IDOLIZE HER!
SHE'S LIKE A FEMALE KNIGHT ...
OH, TAKE ME, ONEE-SAMA!!!
HEY, NO JUMPING AHEAD!

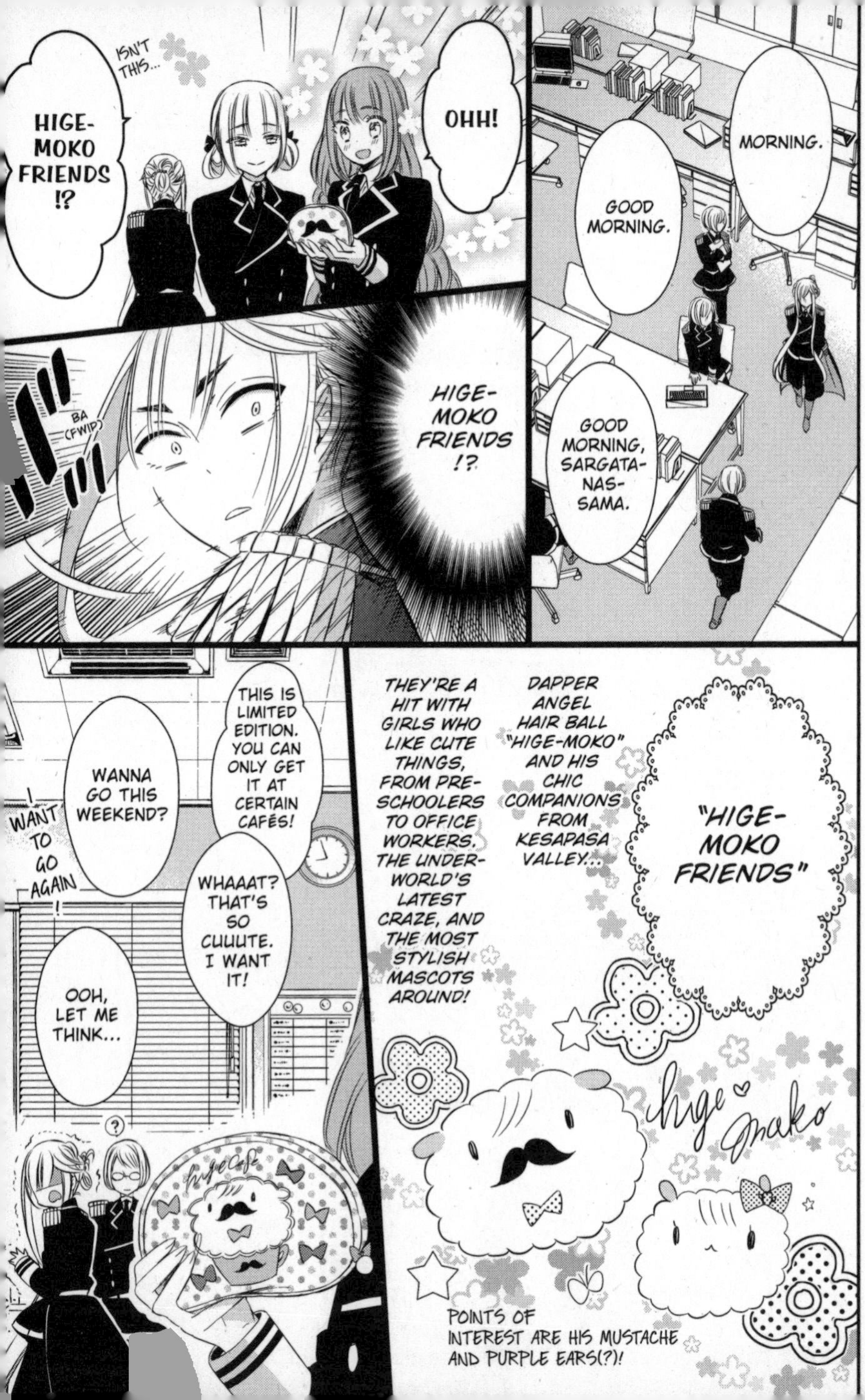
MORNING.
GOOD MORNING.
GOOD MORNING, SARGATANAS-SAMA.
OHH!
ISN'T THIS...
HIGE-MOKO FRIENDS!?
HIGE-MOKO FRIENDS!?
BA (FWIP)
"HIGE-MOKO FRIENDS"
DAPPER ANGEL HAIR BALL "HIGE-MOKO" AND HIS CHIC COMPANIONS FROM KESAPASA VALLEY...
THEY'RE A HIT WITH GIRLS WHO LIKE CUTE THINGS, FROM PRE-SCHOOLERS TO OFFICE WORKERS. THE UNDERWORLD'S LATEST CRAZE, AND THE MOST STYLISH MASCOTS AROUND!
hige moko
POINTS OF INTEREST ARE HIS MUSTACHE AND PURPLE EARS(?)!
THIS IS LIMITED EDITION. YOU CAN ONLY GET IT AT CERTAIN CAFÉS!
WANNA GO THIS WEEKEND?
WHAAAT? THAT'S SO CUUUTE. I WANT IT!
I WANT TO GO AGAIN!
OOH, LET ME THINK...
?
higeCafe

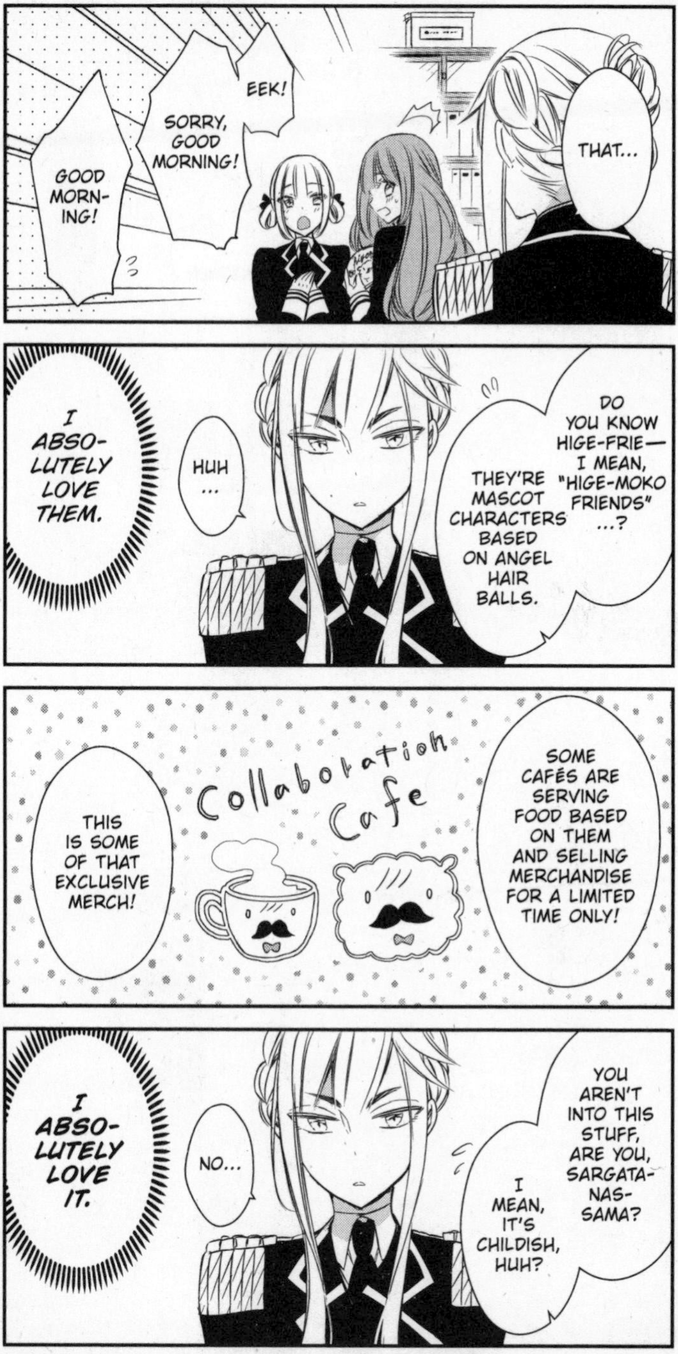
THAT...
EEK!
SORRY, GOOD MORNING!
GOOD MORNING!
DO YOU KNOW HIGE-FRIE— I MEAN, "HIGE-MOKO FRIENDS" ...?
THEY'RE MASCOT CHARACTERS BASED ON ANGEL HAIR BALLS.
HUH ...
I ABSOLUTELY LOVE THEM.
SOME CAFÉS ARE SERVING FOOD BASED ON THEM AND SELLING MERCHANDISE FOR A LIMITED TIME ONLY!
Collaboration Cafe
THIS IS SOME OF THAT EXCLUSIVE MERCH!
YOU AREN'T INTO THIS STUFF, ARE YOU, SARGATANAS-SAMA?
I MEAN, IT'S CHILDISH, HUH?
NO...
I ABSOLUTELY LOVE IT.

HER CURRENT PAJAMAS ARE MOKO THEMED

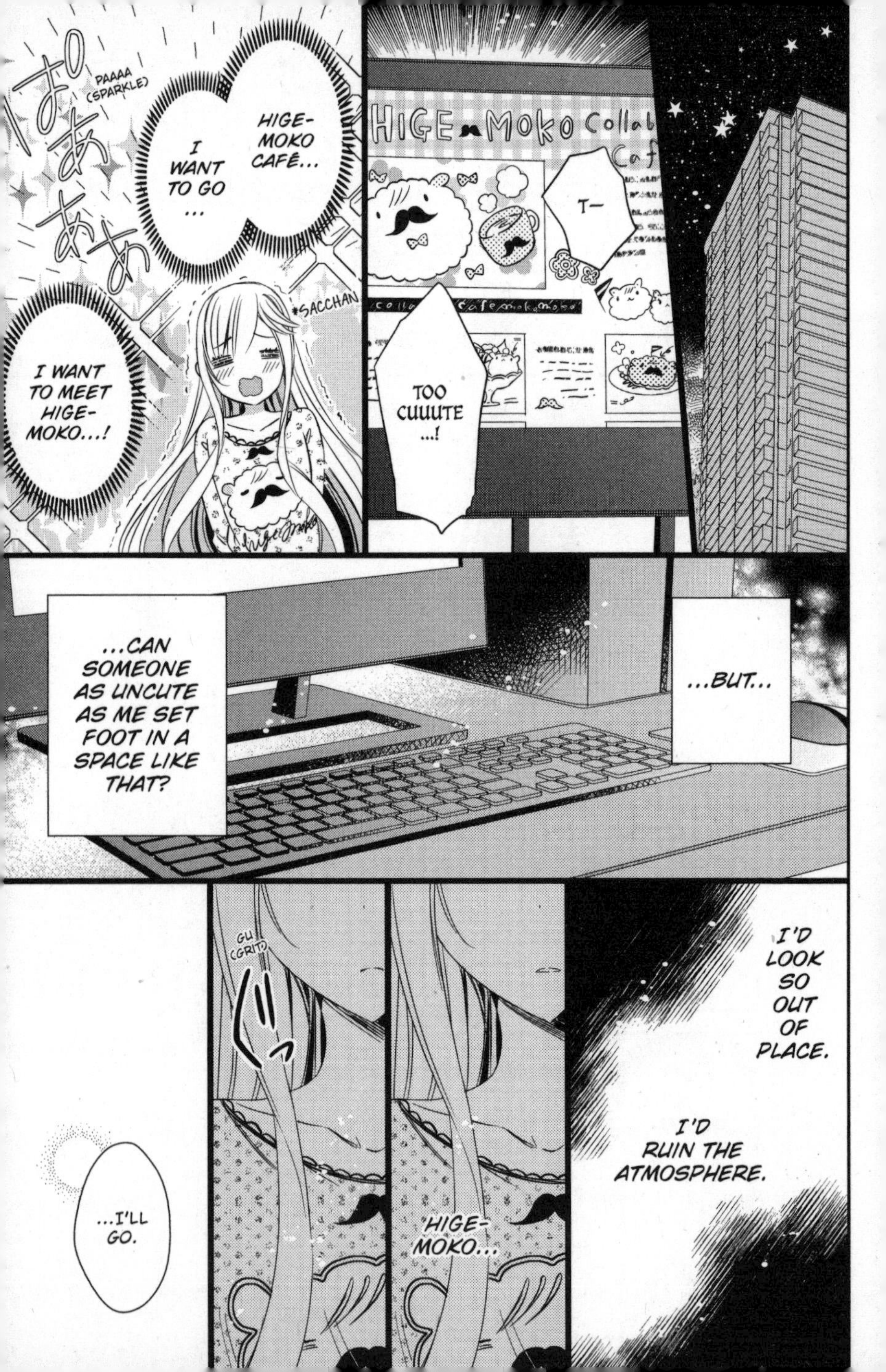

HIGE MOKO Collab Caf
T—
TOO CUUUTE ...!
ぱあああ
PAAAA (SPARKLE)
HIGE-MOKO CAFÉ...
I WANT TO GO ...
I WANT TO MEET HIGE-MOKO...!
*SACCHAN
...BUT...
...CAN SOMEONE AS UNCUTE AS ME SET FOOT IN A SPACE LIKE THAT?
I'D LOOK SO OUT OF PLACE.
I'D RUIN THE ATMOSPHERE.
HIGE-MOKO...
ぐっ
GU (GRIT)
...I'LL GO.

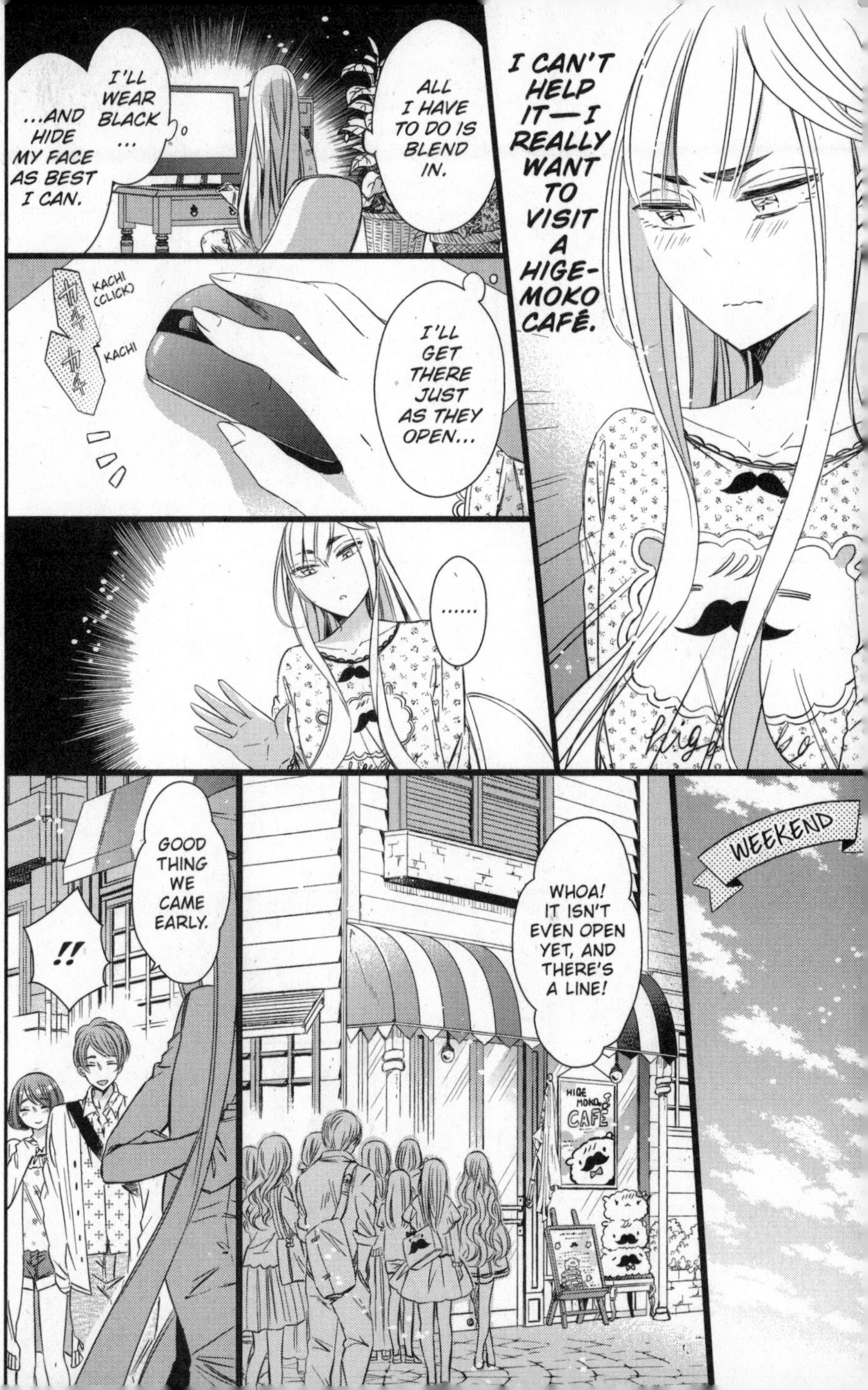
I CAN'T HELP IT—I REALLY WANT TO VISIT A HIGE-MOKO CAFÉ.
ALL I HAVE TO DO IS BLEND IN.
I'LL WEAR BLACK...
...AND HIDE MY FACE AS BEST I CAN.
I'LL GET THERE JUST AS THEY OPEN...
KACHI (CLICK)
KACHI
......
WEEKEND
WHOA! IT ISN'T EVEN OPEN YET, AND THERE'S A LINE!
HIGE MOKO CAFÉ
GOOD THING WE CAME EARLY.
!!

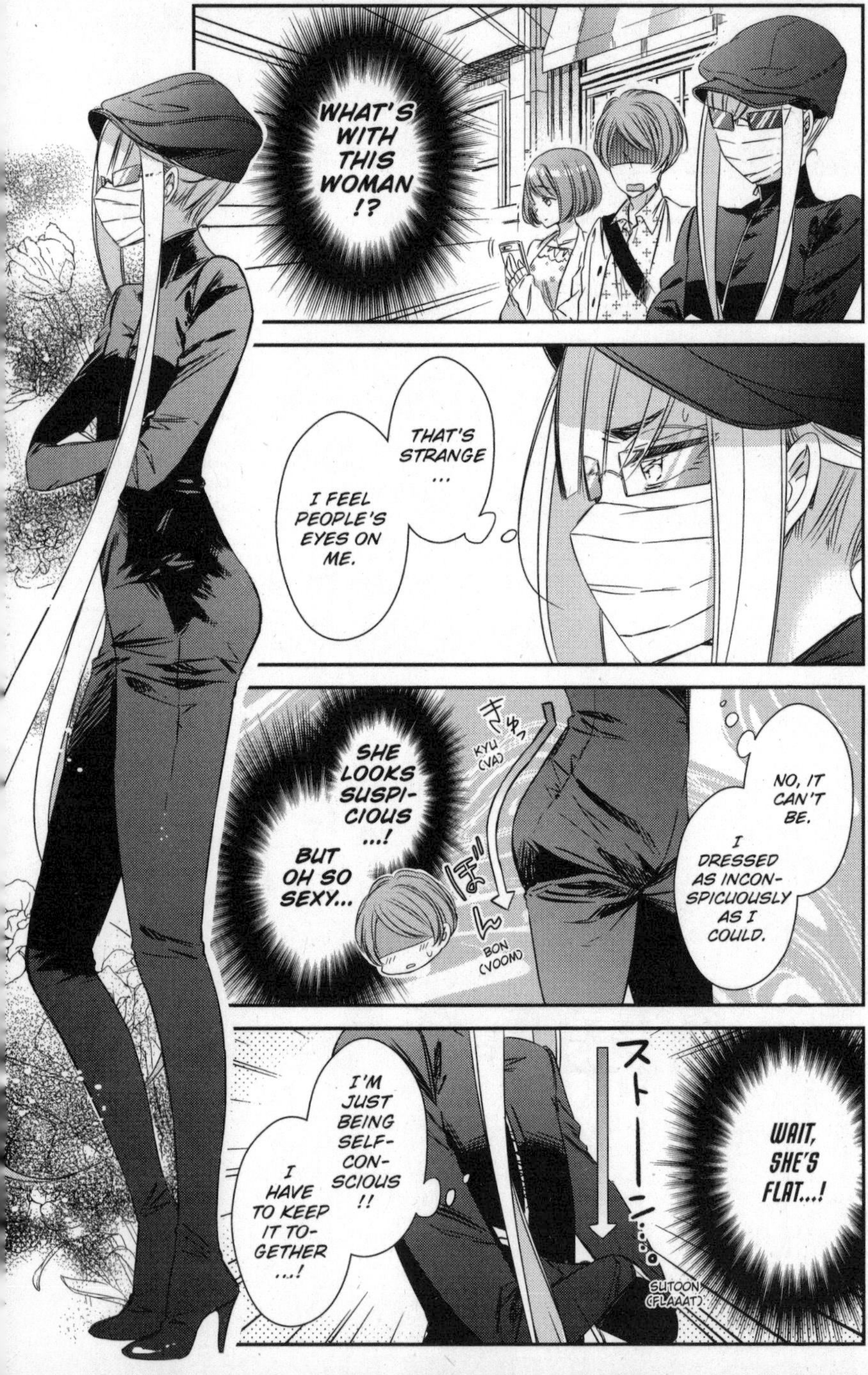
WHAT'S WITH THIS WOMAN!?
THAT'S STRANGE...
I FEEL PEOPLE'S EYES ON ME.
NO, IT CAN'T BE.
I DRESSED AS INCON-SPICUOUSLY AS I COULD.
きゅっ
KYU (VA)
SHE LOOKS SUSPI-CIOUS...!
BUT OH SO SEXY...
ぼん
BON (VOOM)
WAIT, SHE'S FLAT...!
ストーン
SUTOON (FLAAAT)
I'M JUST BEING SELF-CON-SCIOUS!!
I HAVE TO KEEP IT TO-GETHER...!

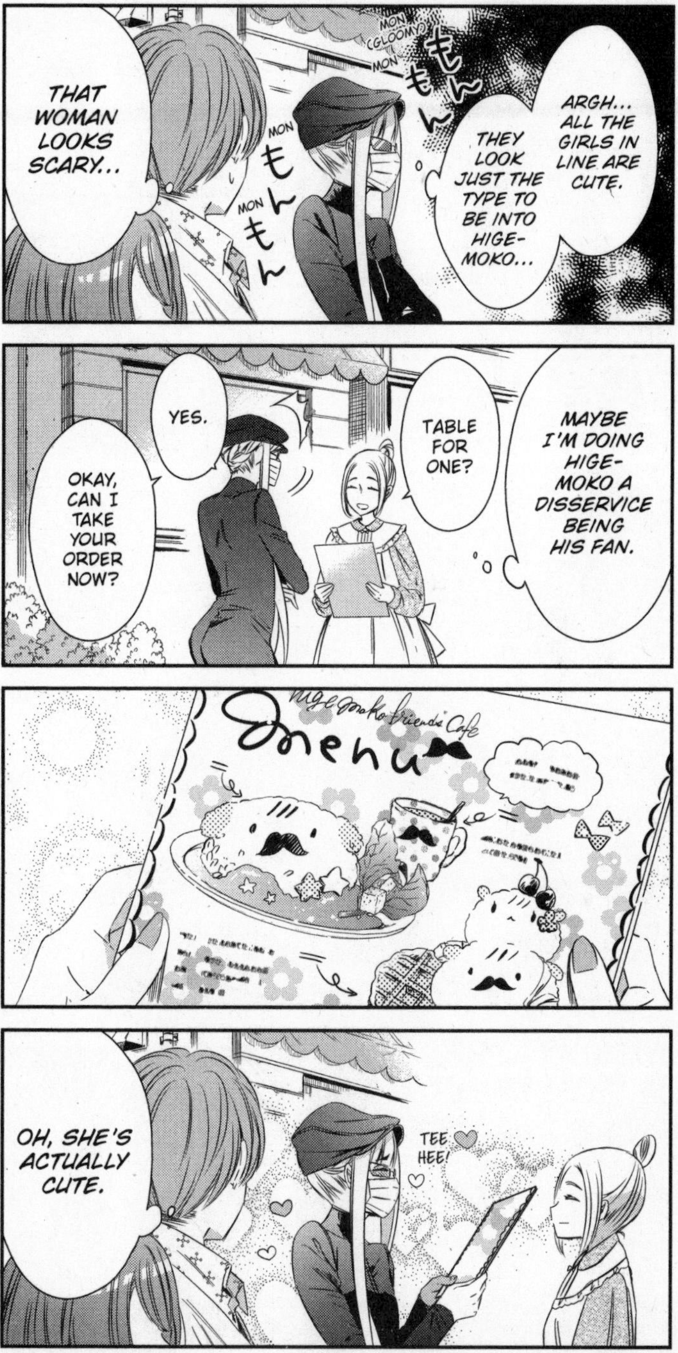
ARGH... ALL THE GIRLS IN LINE ARE CUTE.
THEY LOOK JUST THE TYPE TO BE INTO HIGE-MOKO...
MON (GLOOMY) MON もんもん
MON もん
MON もん
THAT WOMAN LOOKS SCARY...
MAYBE I'M DOING HIGE-MOKO A DISSERVICE BEING HIS FAN.
TABLE FOR ONE?
YES.
OKAY, CAN I TAKE YOUR ORDER NOW?
Hige moko friends Cafe
menu
TEE HEE!
OH, SHE'S ACTUALLY CUTE.

THOUGH SHE'S SLEEP-DEPRIVED FROM NET SURFING

WHAT KIND SERVICE

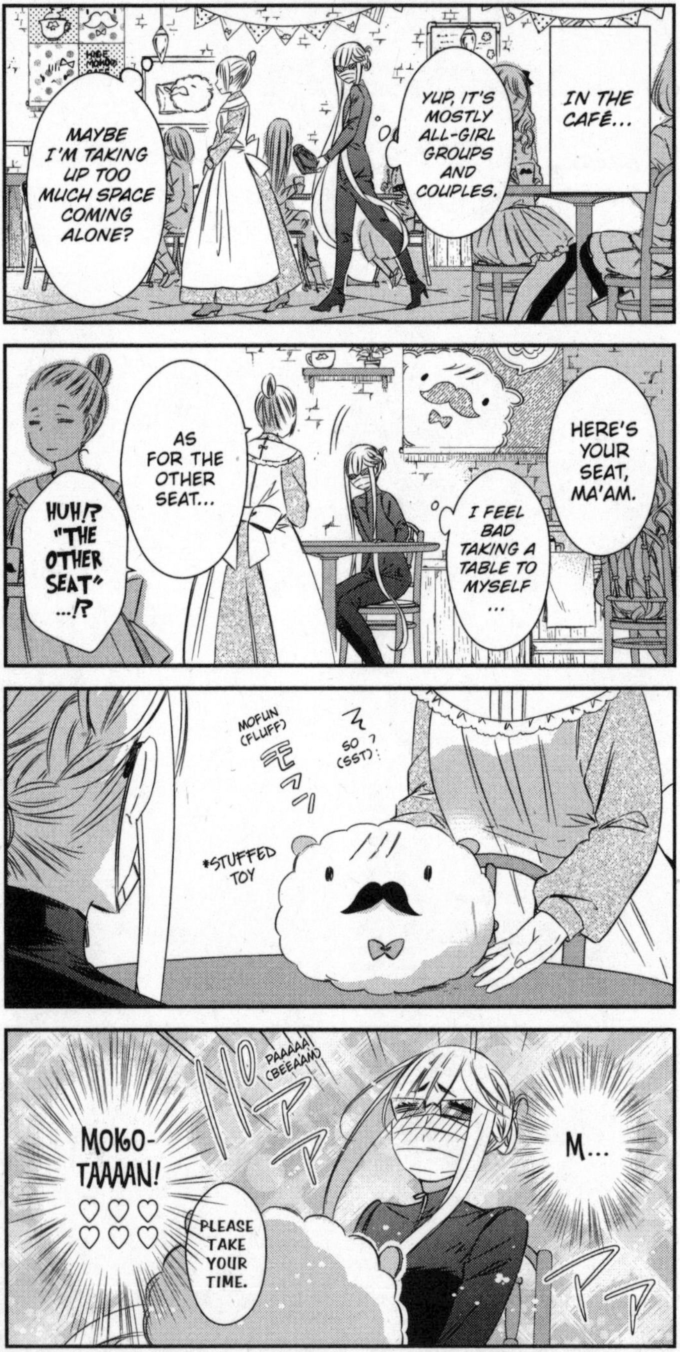
IN THE CAFÉ...
YUP, IT'S MOSTLY ALL-GIRL GROUPS AND COUPLES.
MAYBE I'M TAKING UP TOO MUCH SPACE COMING ALONE?
HERE'S YOUR SEAT, MA'AM.
I FEEL BAD TAKING A TABLE TO MYSELF...
AS FOR THE OTHER SEAT...
HUH!? "THE OTHER SEAT" ...!?
SO (SST)
MOFUN (FLUFF)
*STUFFED TOY
M...
PAAAAA (BEEAAAM)
PLEASE TAKE YOUR TIME.
MOKO-TAAAAN! ♡♡♡ ♡♡♡

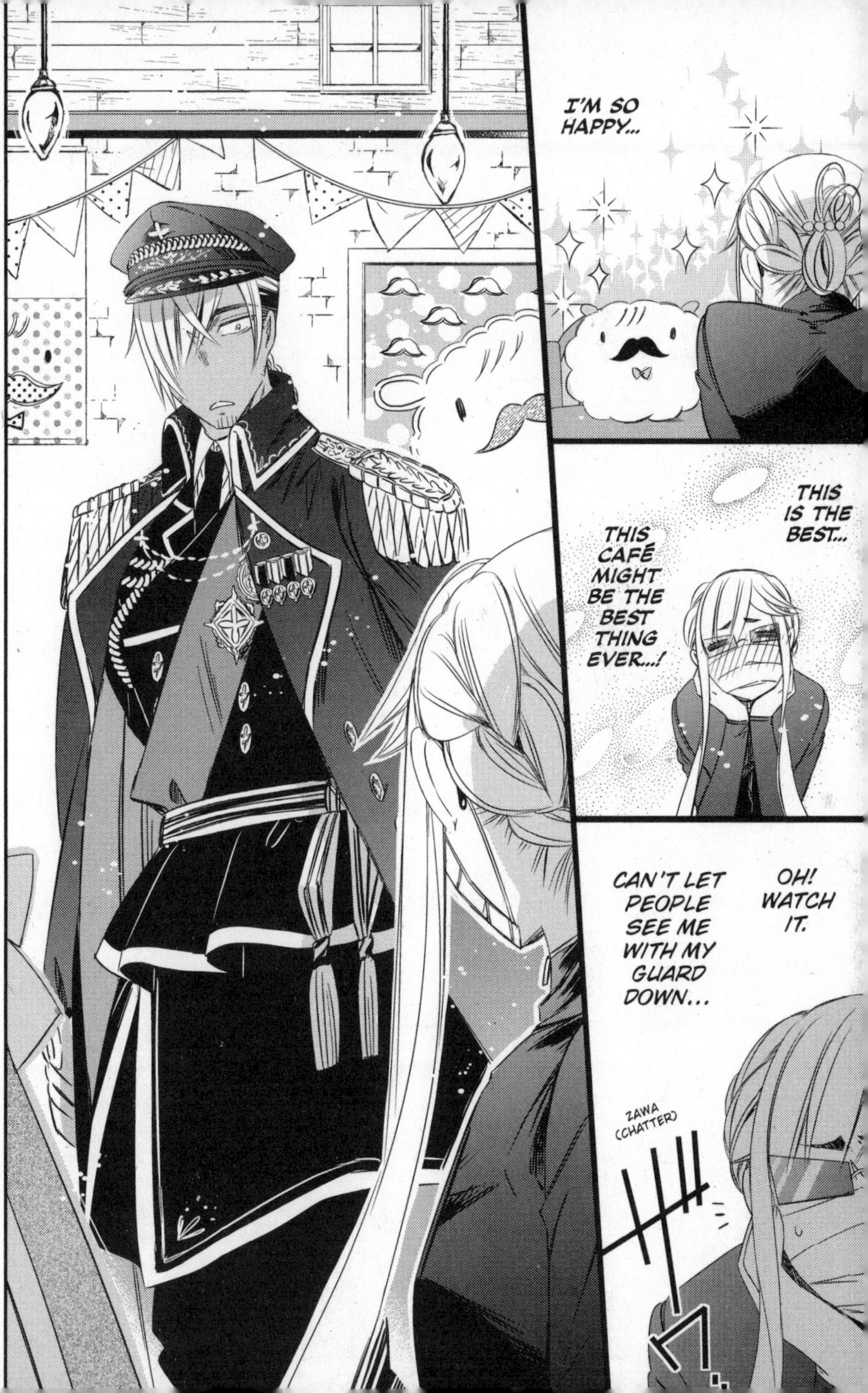
I'M SO HAPPY...
THIS IS THE BEST...
THIS CAFÉ MIGHT BE THE BEST THING EVER...!
OH! WATCH IT.
CAN'T LET PEOPLE SEE ME WITH MY GUARD DOWN...
ZAWA (CHATTER)

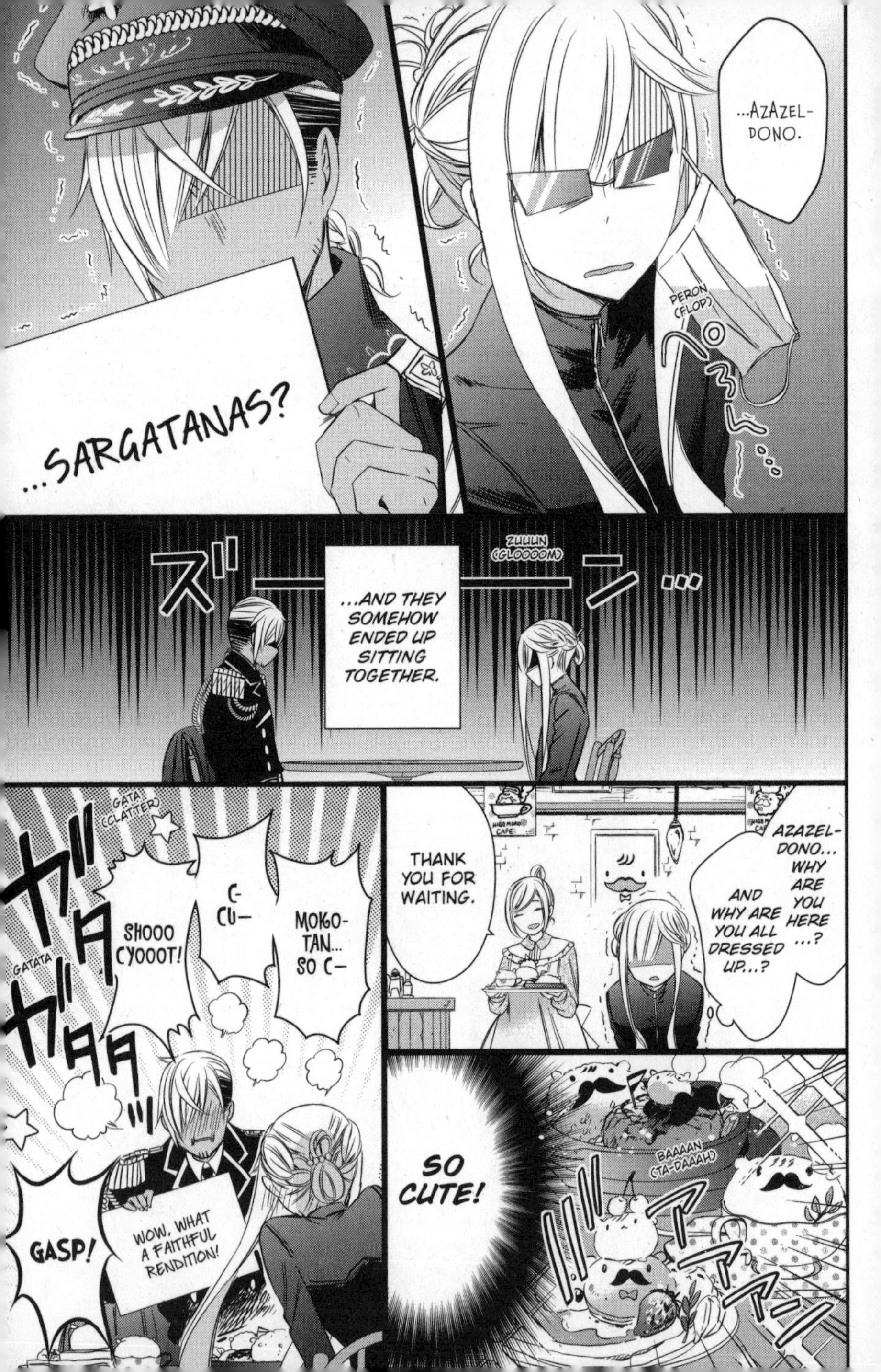

...AZAZEL-DONO.
PERON (FLOP)
...SARGATANAS?
ZUUUN (GLOOOOM)
...AND THEY SOMEHOW ENDED UP SITTING TOGETHER.
AZAZEL-DONO... WHY ARE YOU HERE ...?
AND WHY ARE YOU ALL DRESSED UP...?
HIGE MOKO CAFE
THANK YOU FOR WAITING.
BAAAAN (TA-DAAAH)
SO CUTE!
GATA (CLATTER)
MOKO-TAN... SO C—
C-CU—
SHOOO CYOOOT!
GATATA
GASP!
WOW, WHAT A FAITHFUL RENDITION!

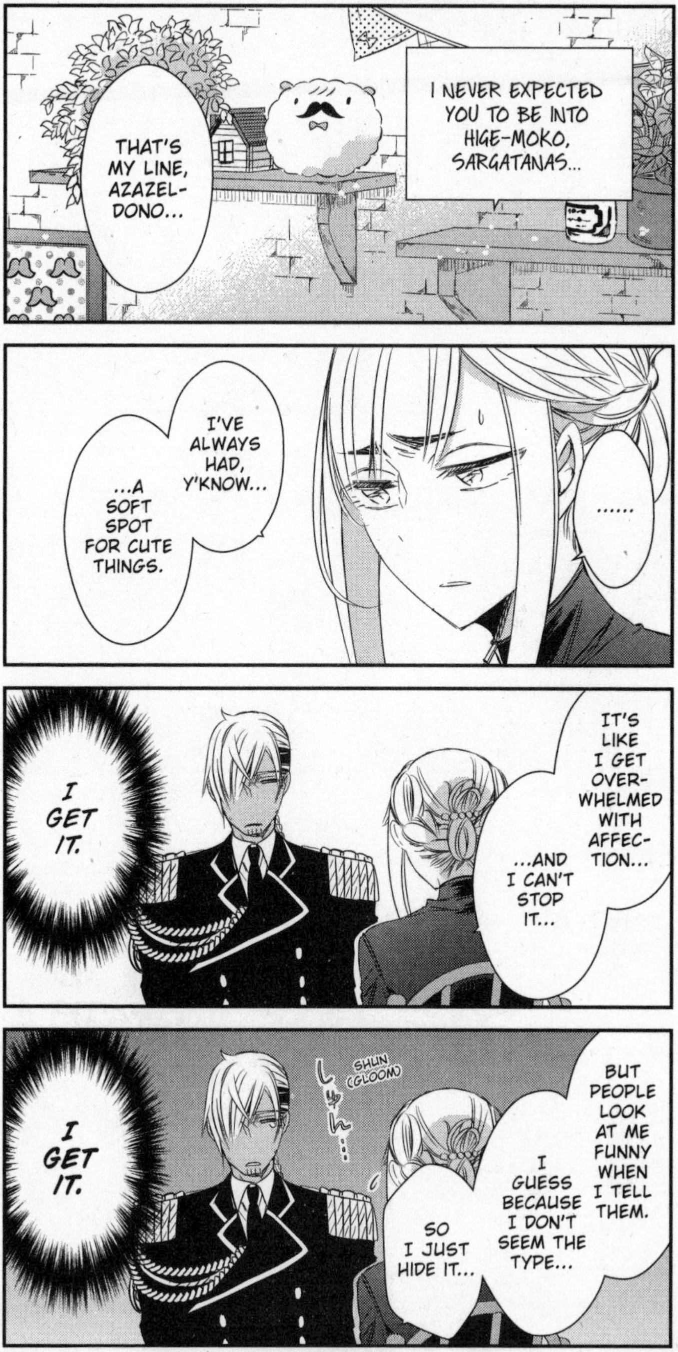
I NEVER EXPECTED YOU TO BE INTO HIGE-MOKO, SARGATANAS...
THAT'S MY LINE, AZAZEL-DONO...
......
I'VE ALWAYS HAD, Y'KNOW...
...A SOFT SPOT FOR CUTE THINGS.
IT'S LIKE I GET OVER-WHELMED WITH AFFEC-TION...
...AND I CAN'T STOP IT...
I GET IT.
BUT PEOPLE LOOK AT ME FUNNY WHEN I TELL THEM.
I GUESS BECAUSE I DON'T SEEM THE TYPE...
SO I JUST HIDE IT...
しゅん…
SHUN (GLOOM)
I GET IT.

I GET IT

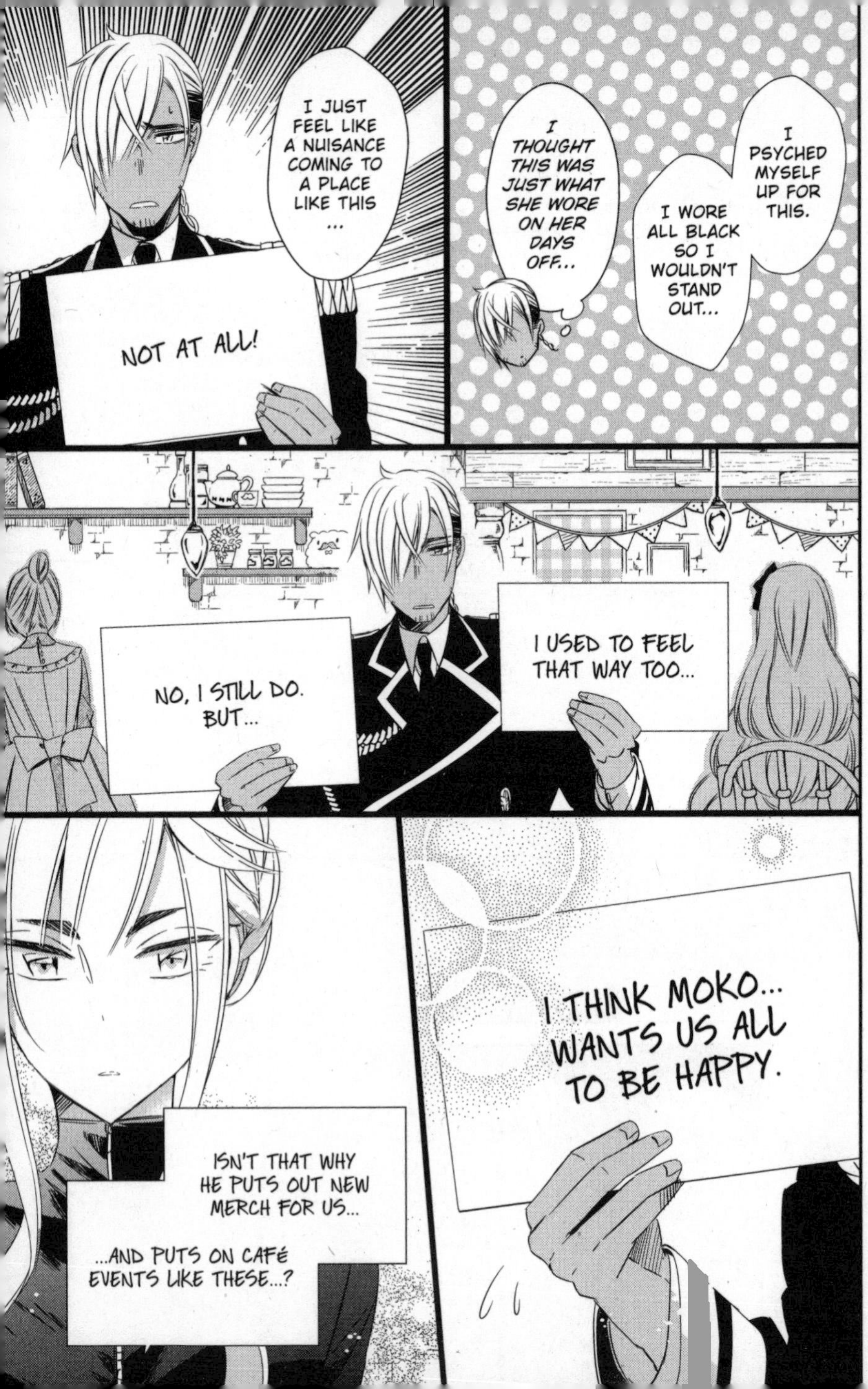
I PSYCHED MYSELF UP FOR THIS.
I WORE ALL BLACK SO I WOULDN'T STAND OUT...
I THOUGHT THIS WAS JUST WHAT SHE WORE ON HER DAYS OFF...
I JUST FEEL LIKE A NUISANCE COMING TO A PLACE LIKE THIS ...
NOT AT ALL!
I USED TO FEEL THAT WAY TOO...
NO, I STILL DO. BUT...
I THINK MOKO... WANTS US ALL TO BE HAPPY.
ISN'T THAT WHY HE PUTS OUT NEW MERCH FOR US...
...AND PUTS ON CAFÉ EVENTS LIKE THESE...?

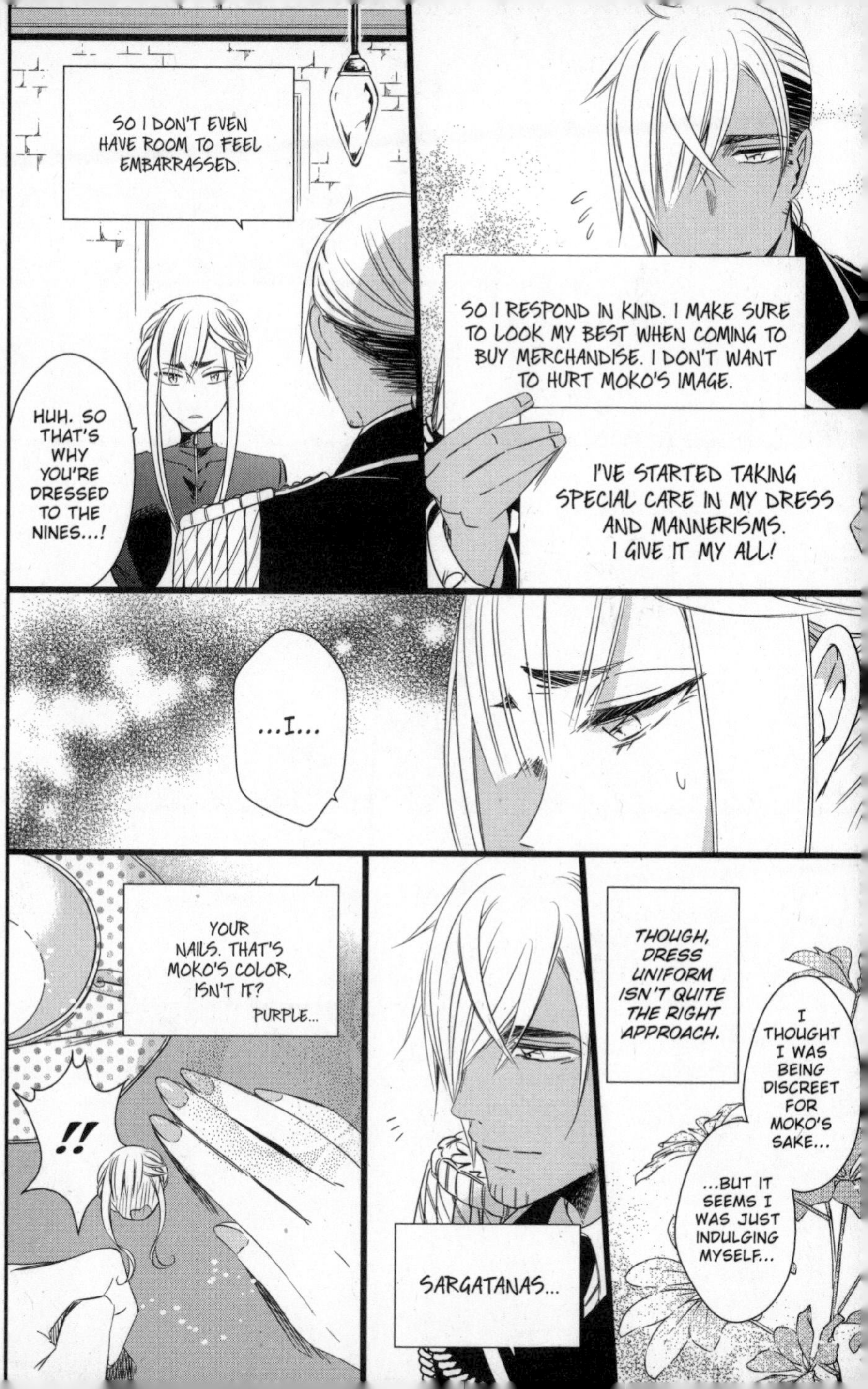
SO I RESPOND IN KIND. I MAKE SURE TO LOOK MY BEST WHEN COMING TO BUY MERCHANDISE. I DON'T WANT TO HURT MOKO'S IMAGE.
I'VE STARTED TAKING SPECIAL CARE IN MY DRESS AND MANNERISMS. I GIVE IT MY ALL!
SO I DON'T EVEN HAVE ROOM TO FEEL EMBARRASSED.
HUH. SO THAT'S WHY YOU'RE DRESSED TO THE NINES...!
...I...
THOUGH, DRESS UNIFORM ISN'T QUITE THE RIGHT APPROACH.
I THOUGHT I WAS BEING DISCREET FOR MOKO'S SAKE...
...BUT IT SEEMS I WAS JUST INDULGING MYSELF...
SARGATANAS...
YOUR NAILS. THAT'S MOKO'S COLOR, ISN'T IT?
PURPLE...
!!

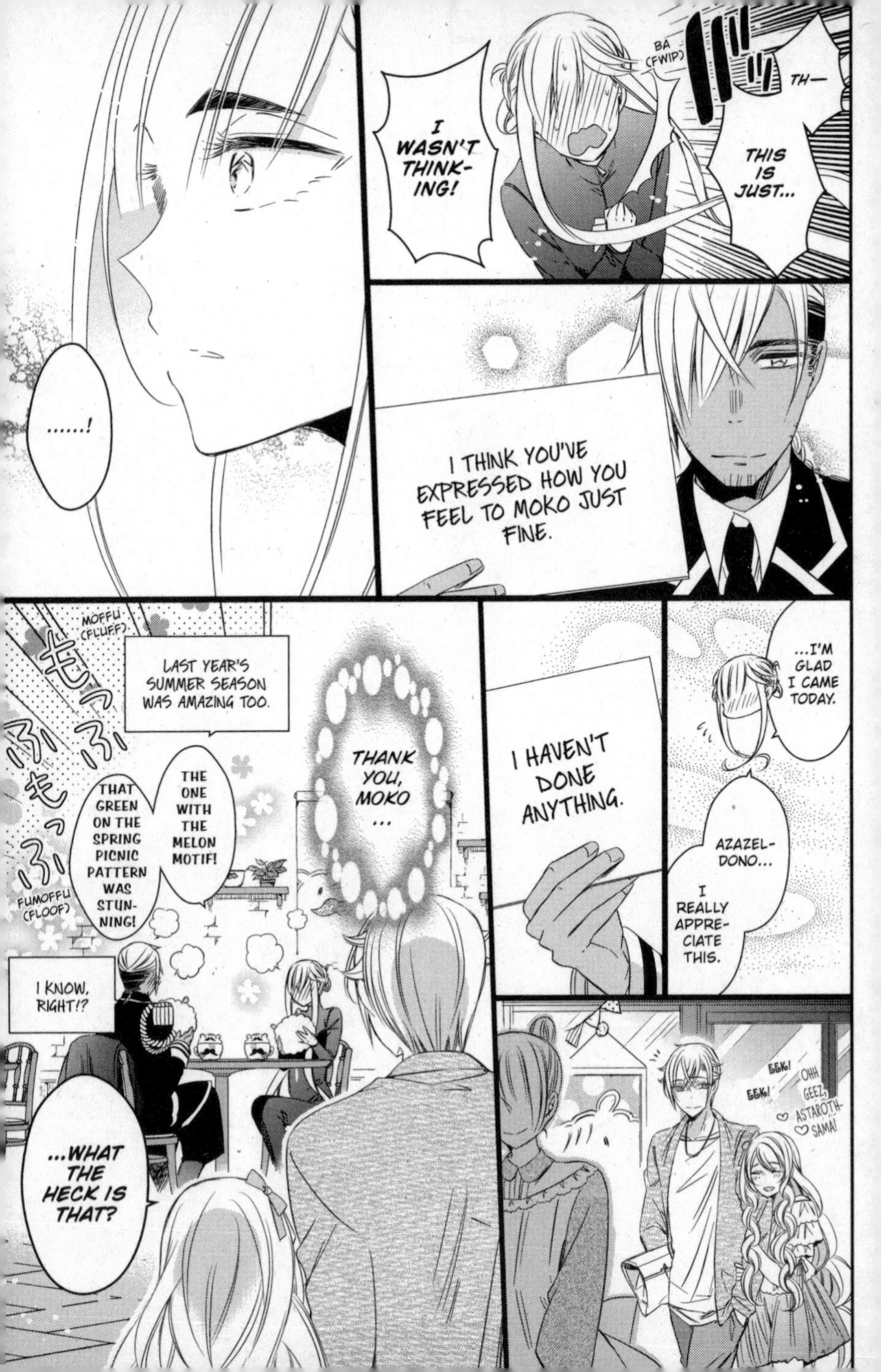
TH—
THIS IS JUST...
BA (FWIP)
I WASN'T THINKING-ING!
I THINK YOU'VE EXPRESSED HOW YOU FEEL TO MOKO JUST FINE.
......!
...I'M GLAD I CAME TODAY.
AZAZEL-DONO...
I REALLY APPRECIATE THIS.
I HAVEN'T DONE ANYTHING.
OHH GEEZ, ASTAROTH-SAMA!
EEK!
EEK!
THANK YOU, MOKO...
MOFFU (FLUFF)
LAST YEAR'S SUMMER SEASON WAS AMAZING TOO.
THE ONE WITH THE MELON MOTIF!
THAT GREEN ON THE SPRING PICNIC PATTERN WAS STUNNING!
FUMOFFU (FLOOF)
I KNOW, RIGHT!?
...WHAT THE HECK IS THAT?

As Miss
Beelzebub Likes

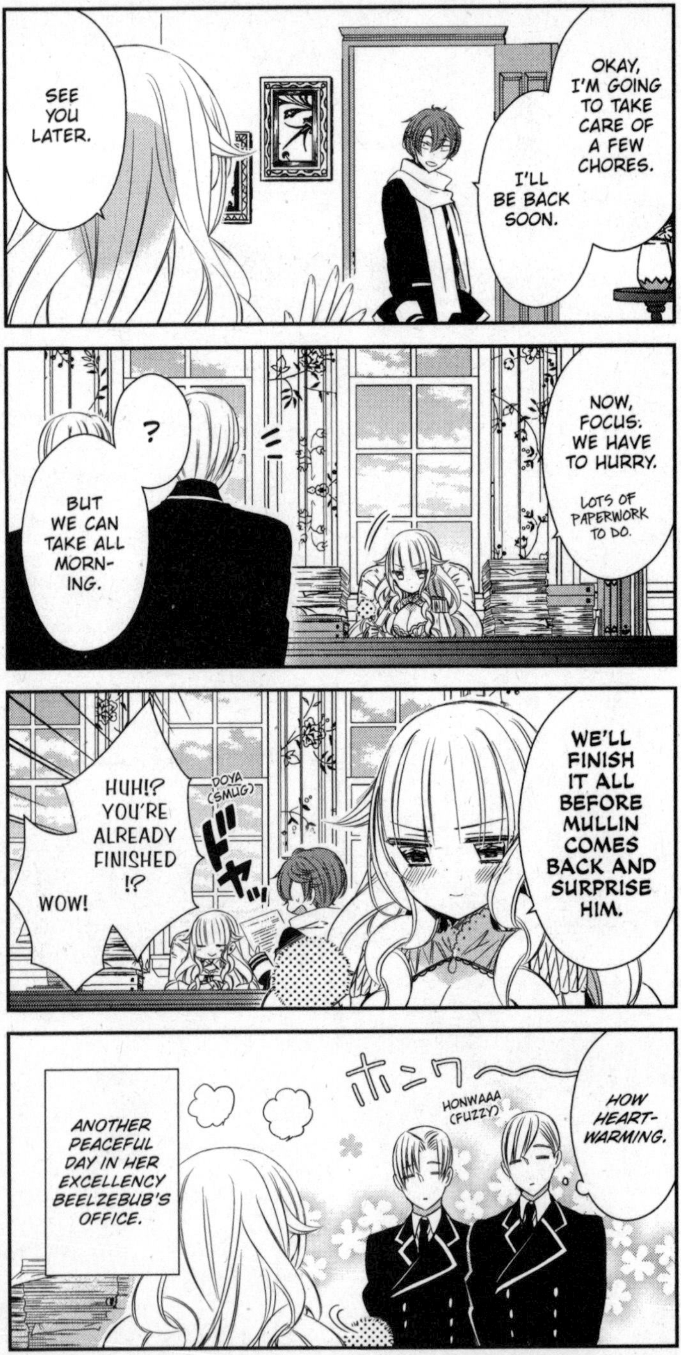
OKAY, I'M GOING TO TAKE CARE OF A FEW CHORES.
I'LL BE BACK SOON.
SEE YOU LATER.
NOW, FOCUS: WE HAVE TO HURRY.
LOTS OF PAPERWORK TO DO.
?
BUT WE CAN TAKE ALL MORN-ING.
WE'LL FINISH IT ALL BEFORE MULLIN COMES BACK AND SURPRISE HIM.
DOYA (SMUG)
HUH!? YOU'RE ALREADY FINISHED!?
WOW!
HOW HEART-WARMING.
HONWAAA (FUZZY)
ANOTHER PEACEFUL DAY IN HER EXCELLENCY BEELZEBUB'S OFFICE.

INSPIRED

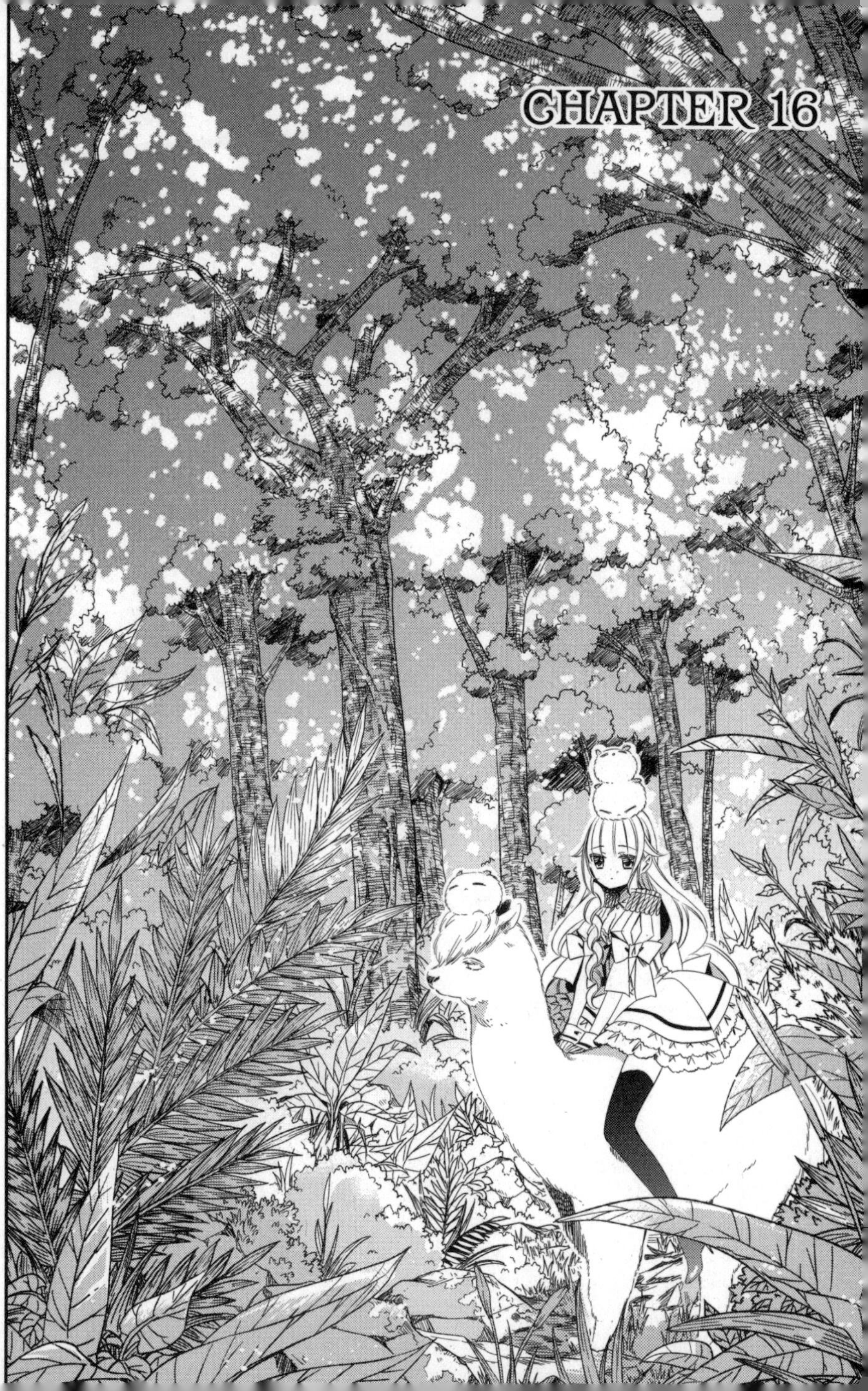
CHAPTER 16

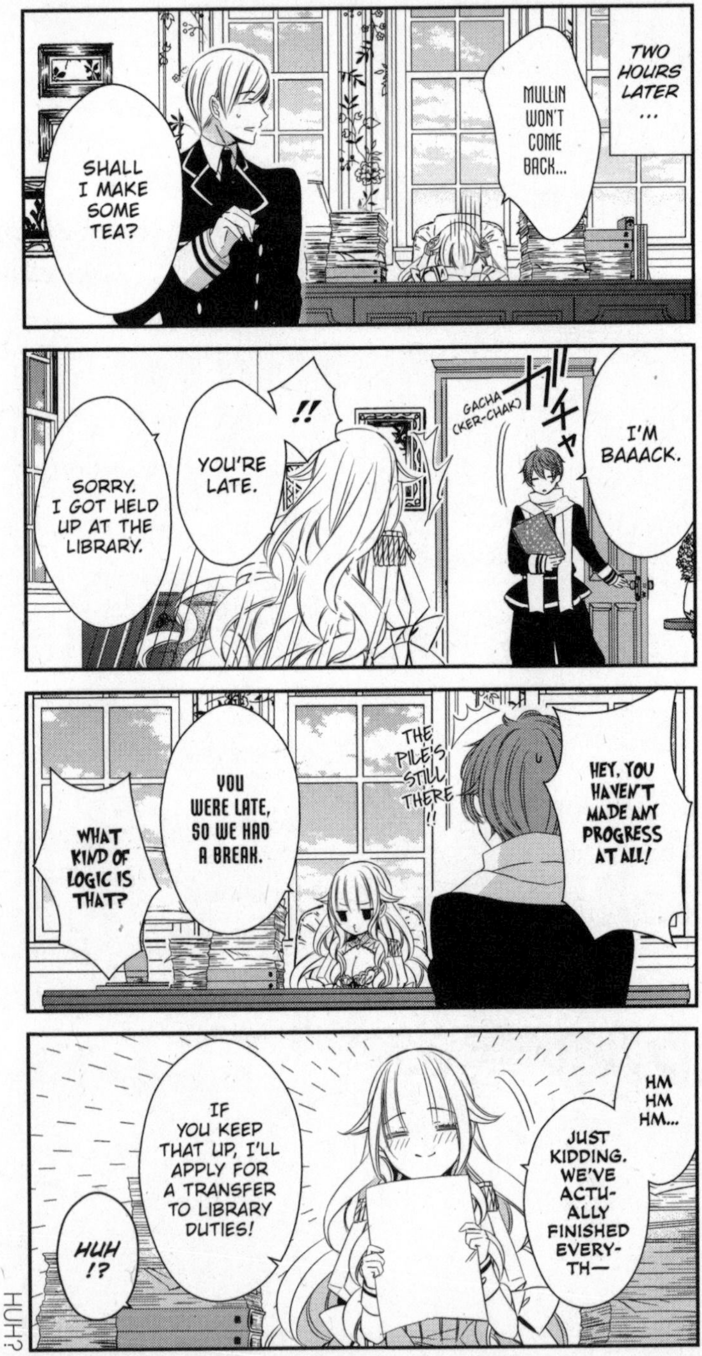
TWO HOURS LATER ...
MULLIN WON'T COME BACK...
SHALL I MAKE SOME TEA?
I'M BAAACK.
GACHA (KER-CHAK)
!!
YOU'RE LATE.
SORRY. I GOT HELD UP AT THE LIBRARY.
HEY, YOU HAVEN'T MADE ANY PROGRESS AT ALL!
THE PILE'S STILL THERE!!
YOU WERE LATE, SO WE HAD A BREAK.
WHAT KIND OF LOGIC IS THAT?
HM HM HM...
JUST KIDDING. WE'VE ACTU-ALLY FINISHED EVERY-TH—
IF YOU KEEP THAT UP, I'LL APPLY FOR A TRANSFER TO LIBRARY DUTIES!
HUH!?
HUH!?

UNEXPECTEDLY SHAKEN UP

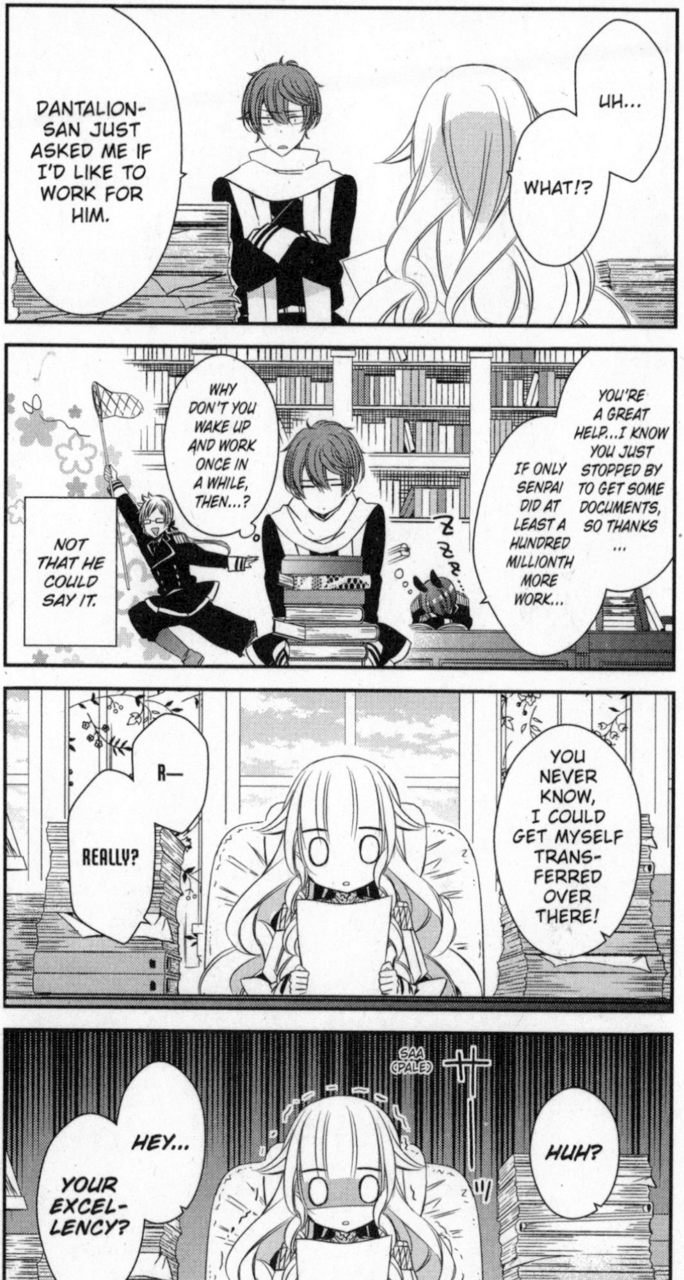
UH... WHAT!?
DANTALION-SAN JUST ASKED ME IF I'D LIKE TO WORK FOR HIM.
YOU'RE A GREAT HELP...I KNOW YOU JUST STOPPED BY TO GET SOME DOCUMENTS, SO THANKS...
IF ONLY SENPAI DID AT LEAST A HUNDRED MILLIONTH MORE WORK...
Z Z Z...
WHY DON'T YOU WAKE UP AND WORK ONCE IN A WHILE, THEN...?
NOT THAT HE COULD SAY IT.
YOU NEVER KNOW, I COULD GET MYSELF TRANS-FERRED OVER THERE!
R— REALLY?
SAA (PALE)
HUH?
HEY... YOUR EXCEL-LENCY?

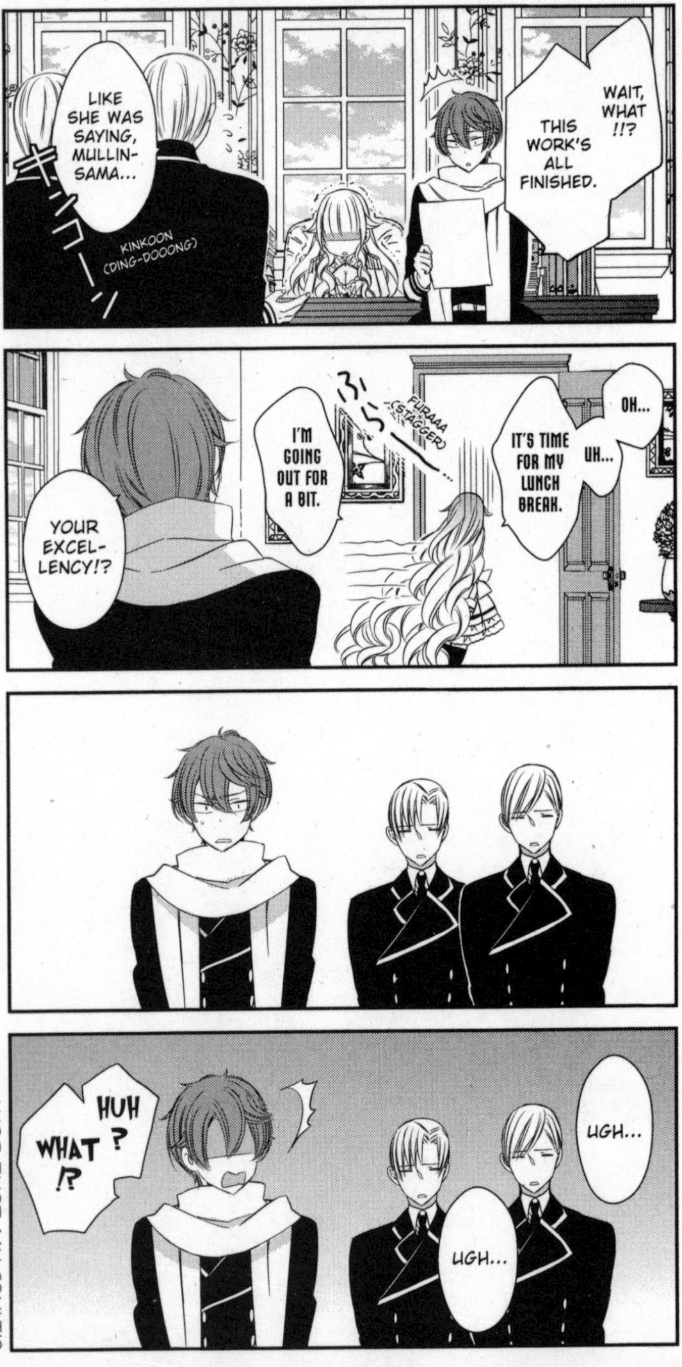
WAIT, WHAT !!?
THIS WORK'S ALL FINISHED.
LIKE SHE WAS SAYING, MULLIN-SAMA...
KINKOON (DING-DOOONG)
OH...
UH...
IT'S TIME FOR MY LUNCH BREAK.
FURAAA (STAGGER)
I'M GOING OUT FOR A BIT.
YOUR EXCEL-LENCY!?
UGH...
UGH...
HUH ?
WHAT !?

WAS THAT MY FAULT!?

GOCCHIN FOR WHEN YOU'RE FEELING DOWN

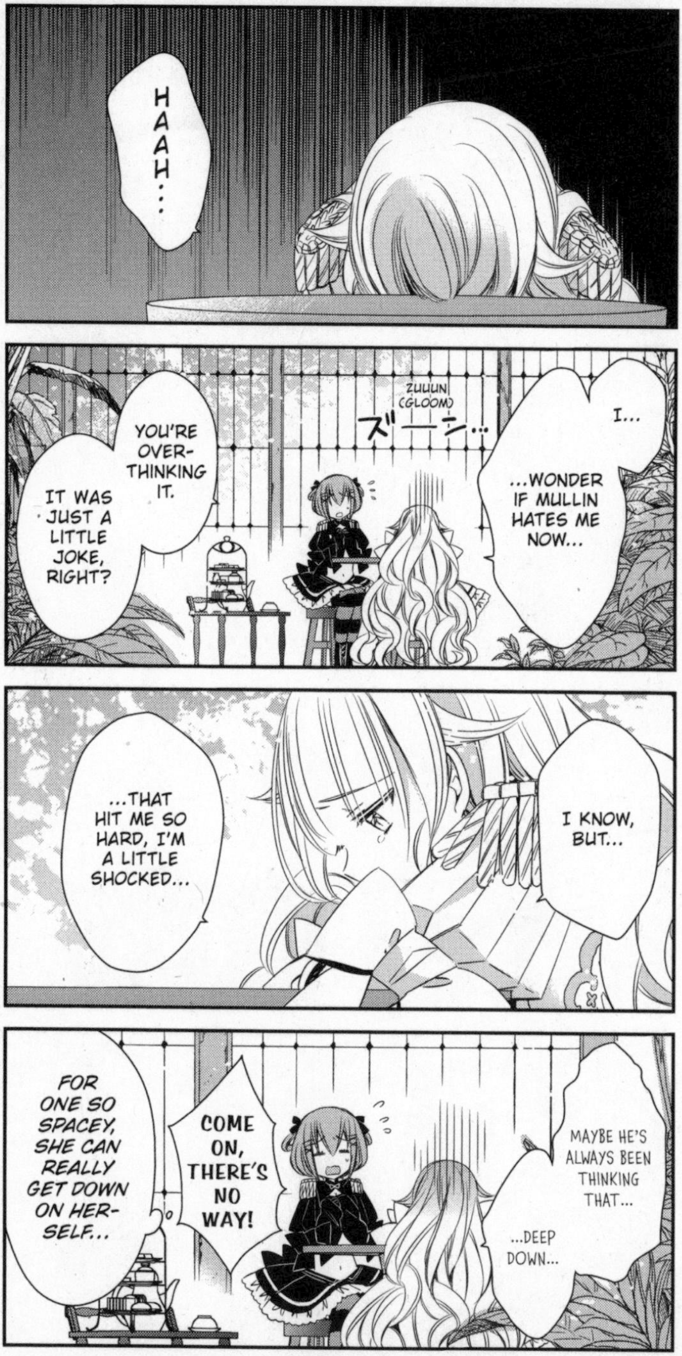
HAAAH...
I...
...WONDER IF MULLIN HATES ME NOW...
ZUUUN (GLOOM)
ズーン...
YOU'RE OVER-THINKING IT.
IT WAS JUST A LITTLE JOKE, RIGHT?
I KNOW, BUT...
...THAT HIT ME SO HARD, I'M A LITTLE SHOCKED...
MAYBE HE'S ALWAYS BEEN THINKING THAT...
...DEEP DOWN...
COME ON, THERE'S NO WAY!
FOR ONE SO SPACEY, SHE CAN REALLY GET DOWN ON HER-SELF...

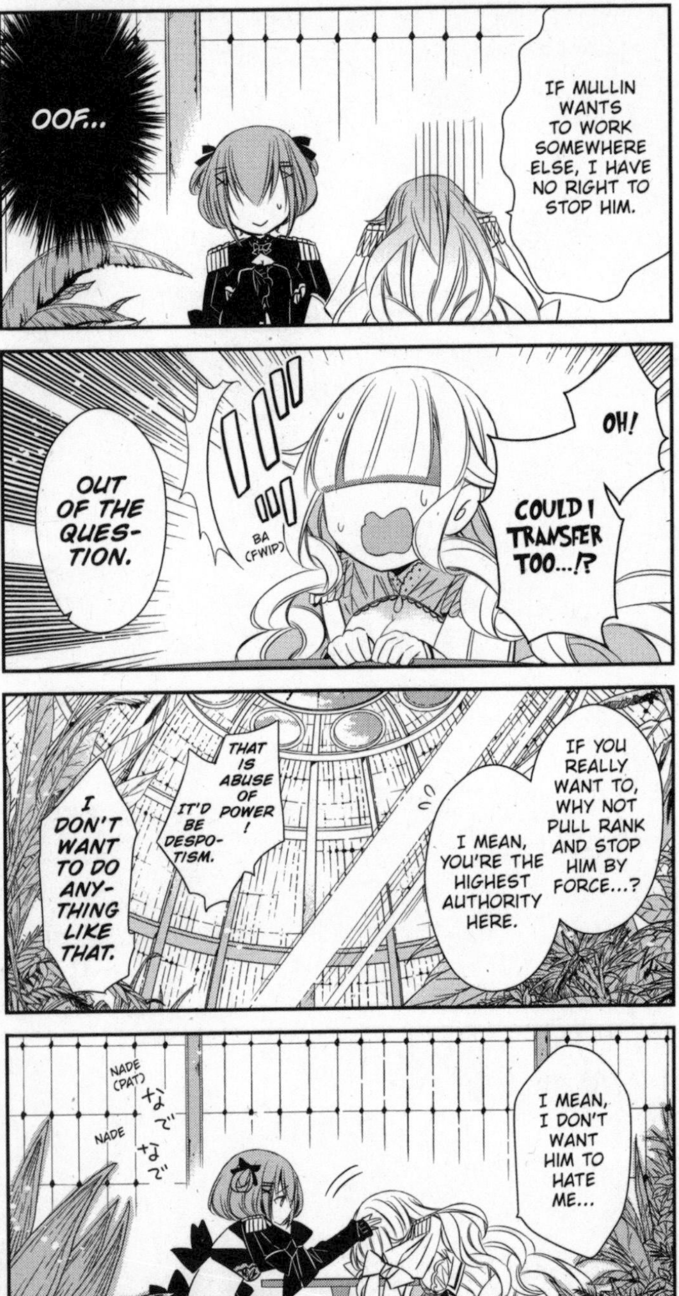
IF MULLIN WANTS TO WORK SOMEWHERE ELSE, I HAVE NO RIGHT TO STOP HIM.
OOF...
OH!
COULD I TRANSFER TOO...!?
BA (FWIP)
OUT OF THE QUES-TION.
IF YOU REALLY WANT TO, WHY NOT PULL RANK AND STOP HIM BY FORCE...?
I MEAN, YOU'RE THE HIGHEST AUTHORITY HERE.
THAT IS ABUSE OF POWER!
IT'D BE DESPO-TISM.
I DON'T WANT TO DO ANY-THING LIKE THAT.
I MEAN, I DON'T WANT HIM TO HATE ME...
NADE (PAT) なで
NADE なで

SERIOUS

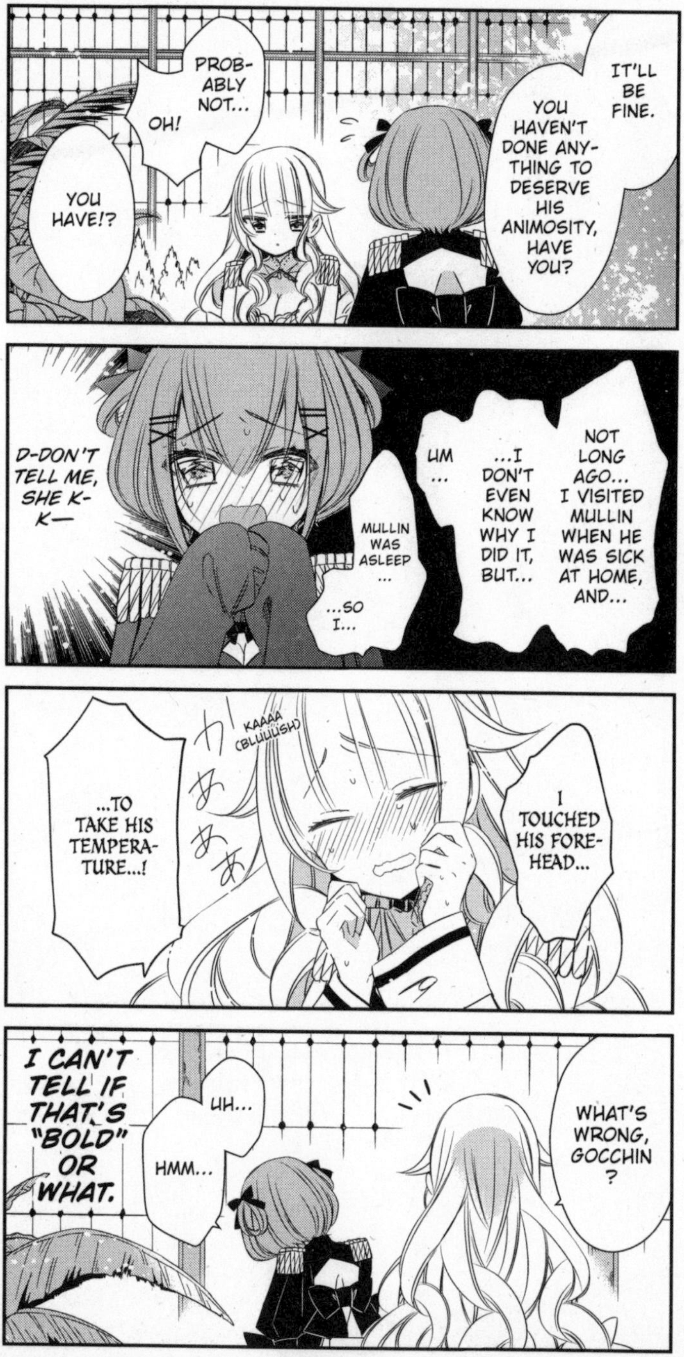
IT'LL BE FINE.
YOU HAVEN'T DONE ANYTHING TO DESERVE HIS ANIMOSITY, HAVE YOU?
PROBABLY NOT...
OH!
YOU HAVE!?
NOT LONG AGO... I VISITED MULLIN WHEN HE WAS SICK AT HOME, AND...
...I DON'T EVEN KNOW WHY I DID IT, BUT...
UM...
MULLIN WAS ASLEEP...
...SO I...
D-DON'T TELL ME, SHE K-K—
I TOUCHED HIS FOREHEAD...
KAAAA (BLUUUSH)
...TO TAKE HIS TEMPERATURE...!
WHAT'S WRONG, GOCCHIN?
UH...
HMM...
I CAN'T TELL IF THAT'S "BOLD" OR WHAT.

SHE COMPARED (THEIR FOREHEADS) BUT COULDN'T TELL WHOSE WAS HOTTER

WHAT TO DO FOR HER?

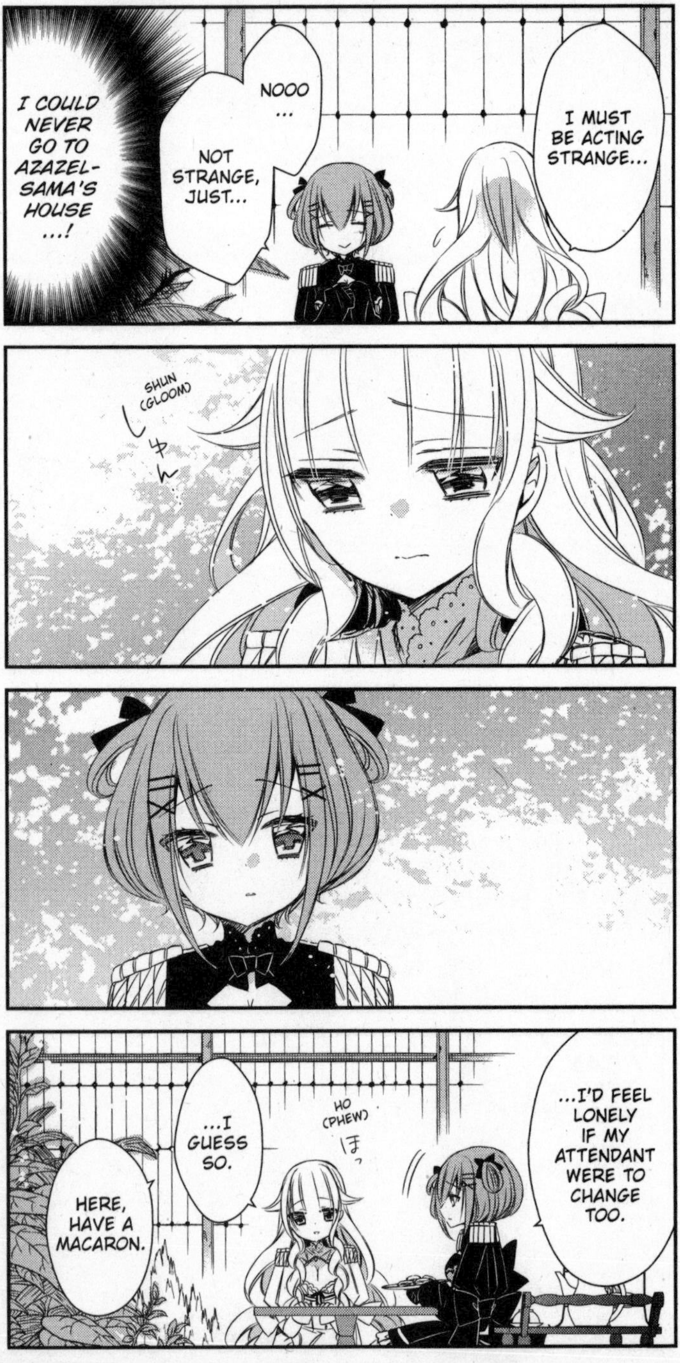
I MUST BE ACTING STRANGE...
NOOO ...
NOT STRANGE, JUST...
I COULD NEVER GO TO AZAZEL-SAMA'S HOUSE ...!
SHUN (GLOOM)
しゅん
...I'D FEEL LONELY IF MY ATTENDANT WERE TO CHANGE TOO.
HO (PHEW)
ほっ
...I GUESS SO.
HERE, HAVE A MACARON.

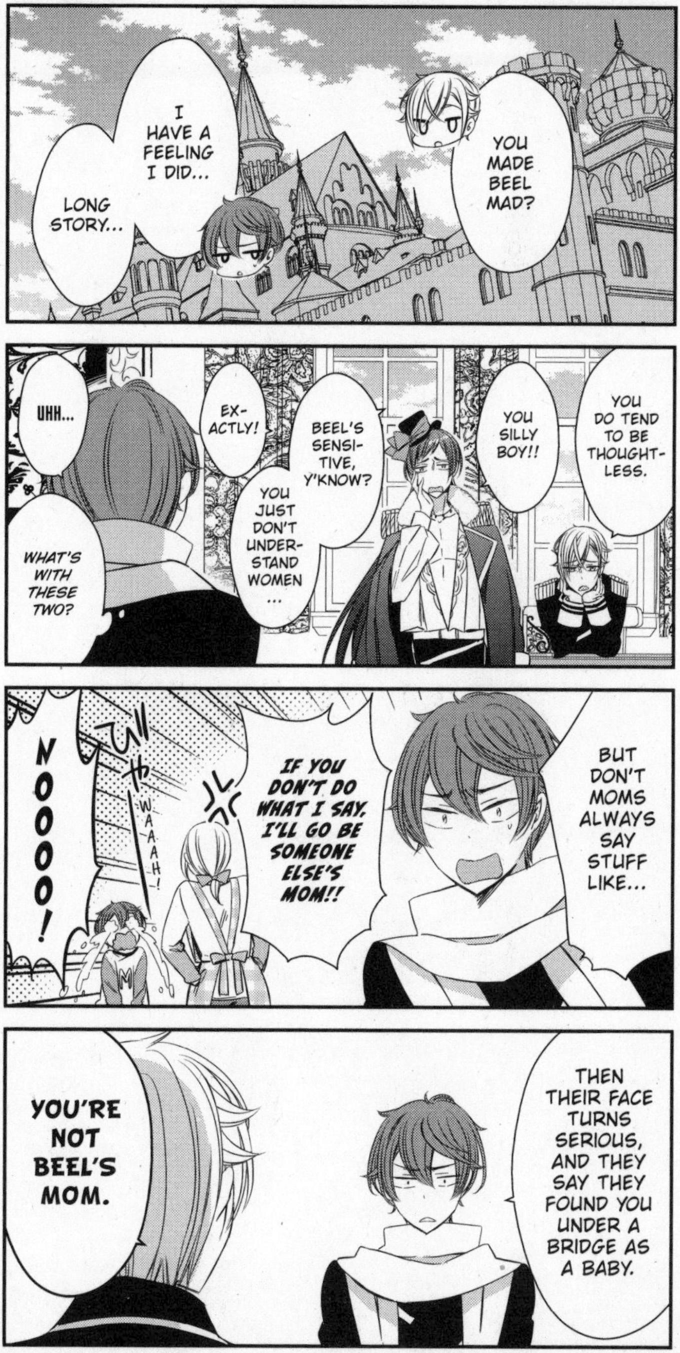
YOU MADE BEEL MAD?
I HAVE A FEELING I DID...
LONG STORY...
YOU DO TEND TO BE THOUGHTLESS.
YOU SILLY BOY!!
BEEL'S SENSITIVE, Y'KNOW?
EXACTLY!
YOU JUST DON'T UNDERSTAND WOMEN...
UHH...
WHAT'S WITH THESE TWO?
BUT DON'T MOMS ALWAYS SAY STUFF LIKE...
IF YOU DON'T DO WHAT I SAY. I'LL GO BE SOMEONE ELSE'S MOM!!
WAAAH!
NOOOOO!
THEN THEIR FACE TURNS SERIOUS, AND THEY SAY THEY FOUND YOU UNDER A BRIDGE AS A BABY.
YOU'RE NOT BEEL'S MOM.

MOMMY'S KILLER COMBO

I'M BOTH, M'DEAR

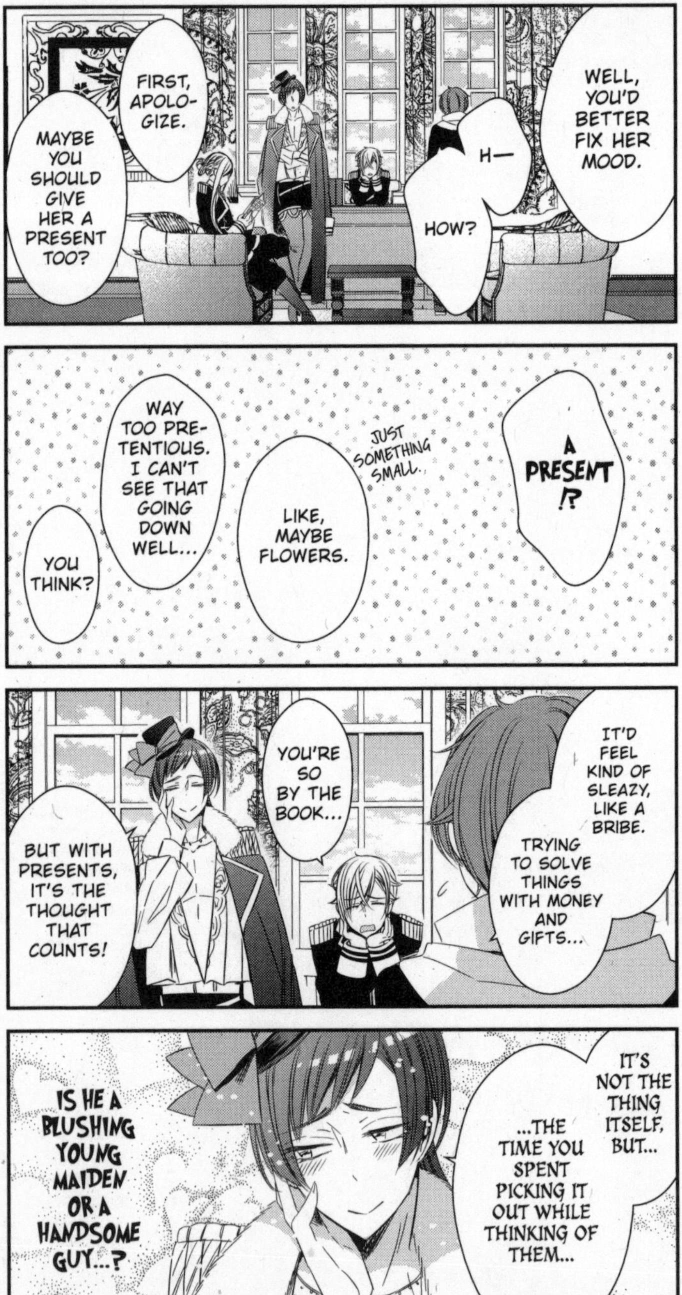
WELL, YOU'D BETTER FIX HER MOOD.
H—
HOW?
FIRST, APOLO-GIZE.
MAYBE YOU SHOULD GIVE HER A PRESENT TOO?
A PRESENT!?
JUST SOMETHING SMALL.
LIKE, MAYBE FLOWERS.
WAY TOO PRE-TENTIOUS. I CAN'T SEE THAT GOING DOWN WELL...
YOU THINK?
IT'D FEEL KIND OF SLEAZY, LIKE A BRIBE.
TRYING TO SOLVE THINGS WITH MONEY AND GIFTS...
YOU'RE SO BY THE BOOK...
BUT WITH PRESENTS, IT'S THE THOUGHT THAT COUNTS!
IT'S NOT THE THING ITSELF, BUT...
...THE TIME YOU SPENT PICKING IT OUT WHILE THINKING OF THEM...
IS HE A BLUSHING YOUNG MAIDEN OR A HANDSOME GUY...?

RIGHT IN THERE

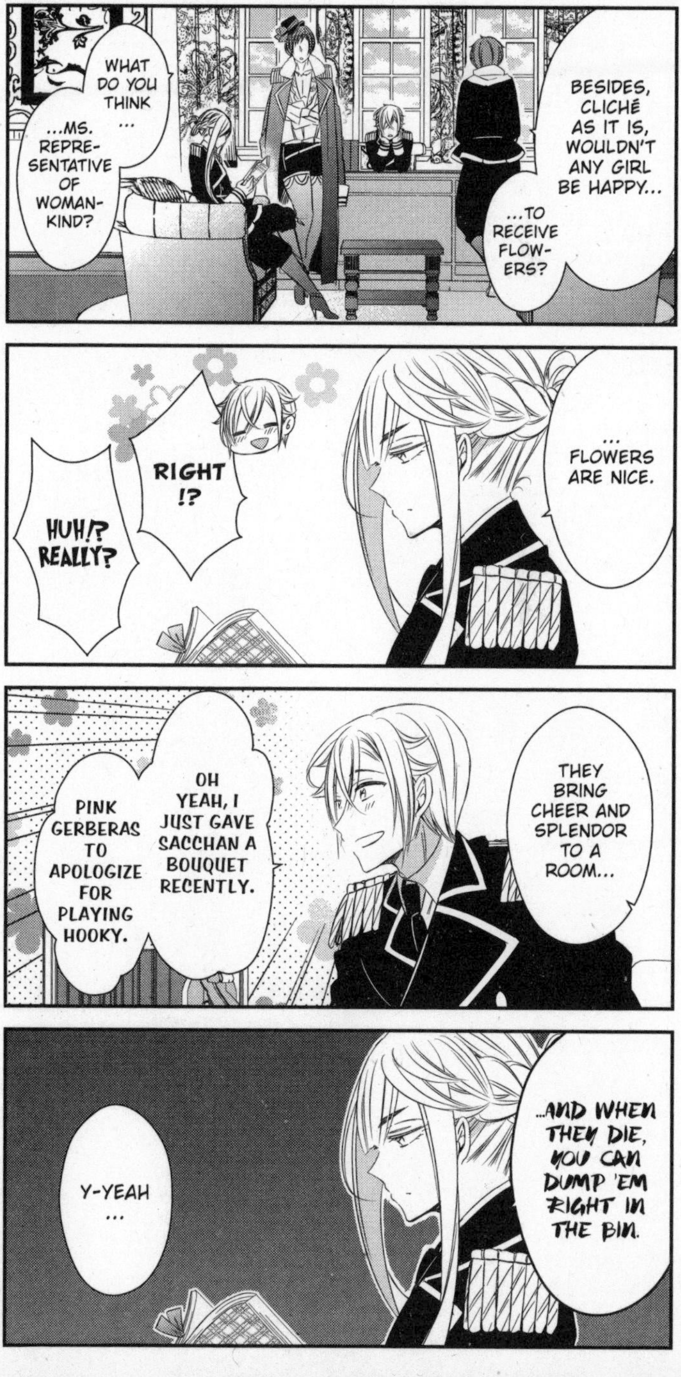
BESIDES, CLICHÉ AS IT IS, WOULDN'T ANY GIRL BE HAPPY...
...TO RECEIVE FLOWERS?
WHAT DO YOU THINK ...
...MS. REPRESENTATIVE OF WOMANKIND?
... FLOWERS ARE NICE.
RIGHT !?
HUH!? REALLY?
THEY BRING CHEER AND SPLENDOR TO A ROOM...
OH YEAH, I JUST GAVE SACCHAN A BOUQUET RECENTLY.
PINK GERBERAS TO APOLOGIZE FOR PLAYING HOOKY.
...AND WHEN THEY DIE, YOU CAN DUMP 'EM RIGHT IN THE BIN.
Y-YEAH ...

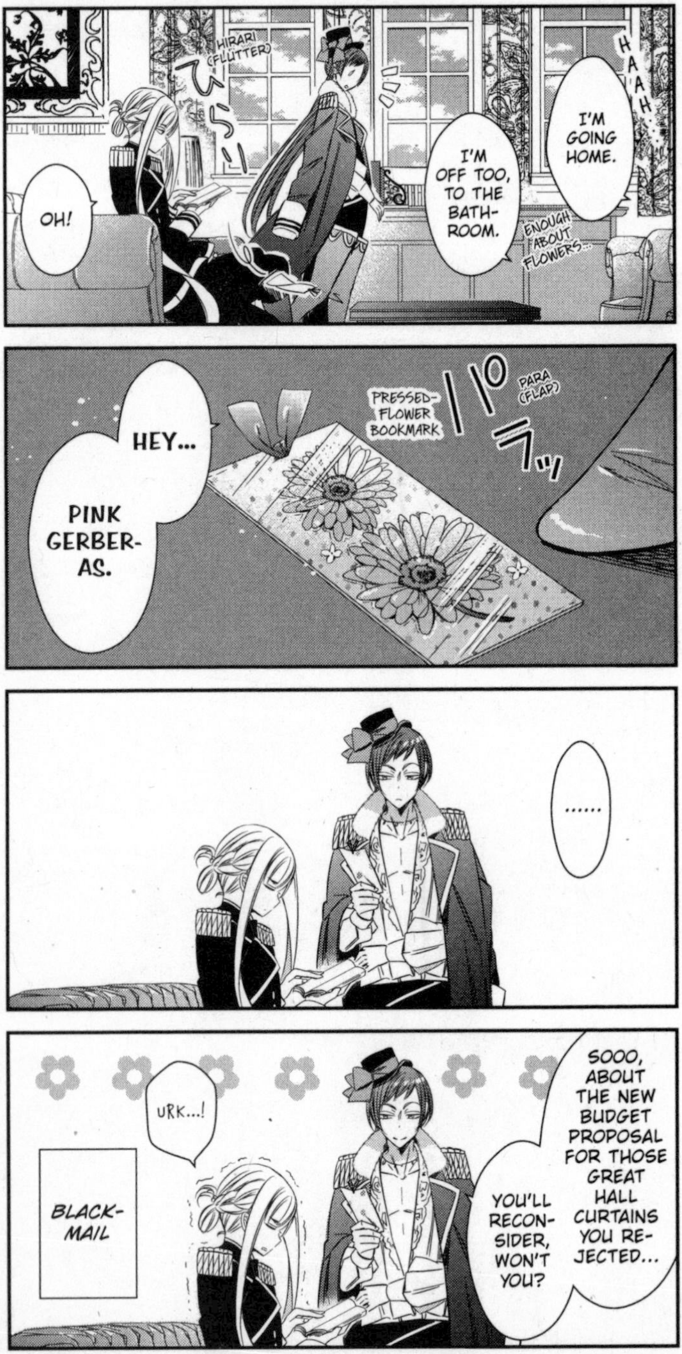
HAAAH
I'M GOING HOME.
ENOUGH ABOUT FLOWERS...
I'M OFF TOO, TO THE BATH-ROOM.
ひらっ
HIRARI (FLUTTER)
OH!
パラッ
PARA (FLAP)
PRESSED-FLOWER BOOKMARK
HEY...
PINK GERBER-AS.
......
SOOO, ABOUT THE NEW BUDGET PROPOSAL FOR THOSE GREAT HALL CURTAINS YOU RE-JECTED...
YOU'LL RECON-SIDER, WON'T YOU?
URK...!
BLACK-MAIL

SHE DIDN'T DUMP THEM AFTER ALL

WHAT!?

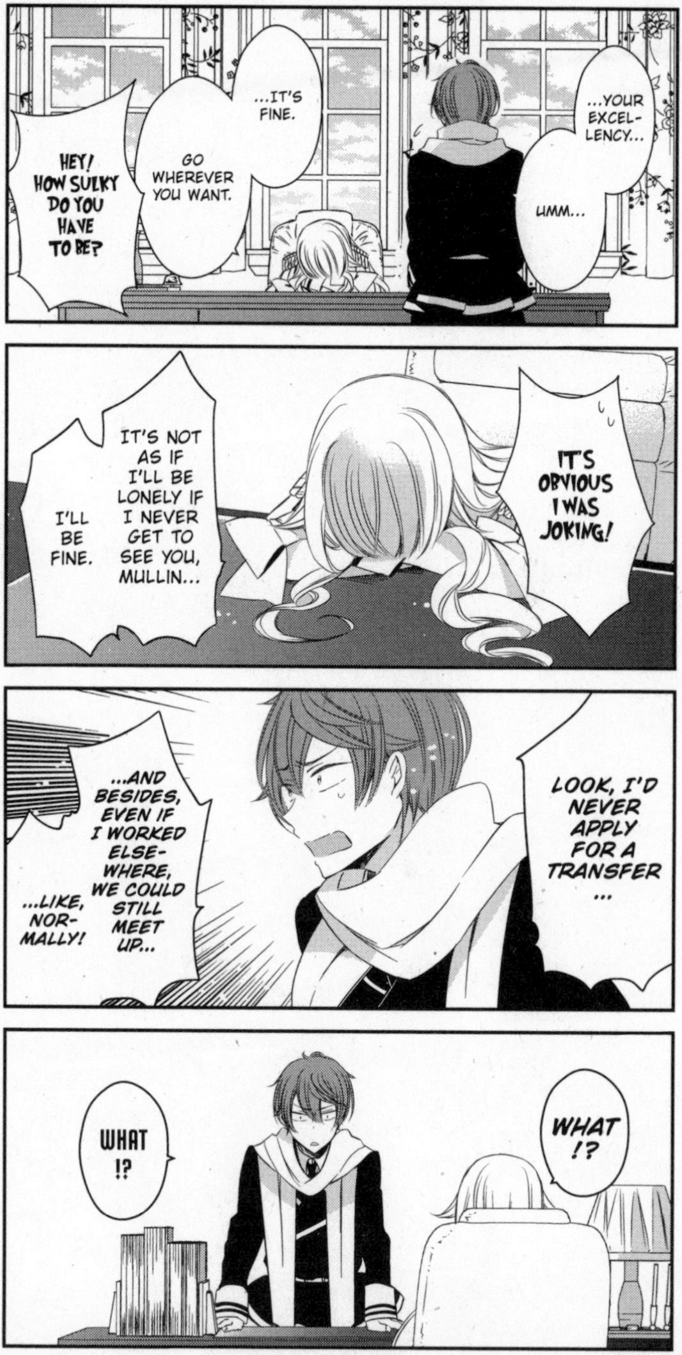
...YOUR EXCEL-LENCY...
UMM...
...IT'S FINE.
GO WHEREVER YOU WANT.
HEY! HOW SULKY DO YOU HAVE TO BE?
IT'S OBVIOUS I WAS JOKING!
IT'S NOT AS IF I'LL BE LONELY IF I NEVER GET TO SEE YOU, MULLIN...
I'LL BE FINE.
LOOK, I'D NEVER APPLY FOR A TRANSFER ...
...AND BESIDES, EVEN IF I WORKED ELSE-WHERE, WE COULD STILL MEET UP...
...LIKE, NOR-MALLY!
WHAT !?
WHAT !?

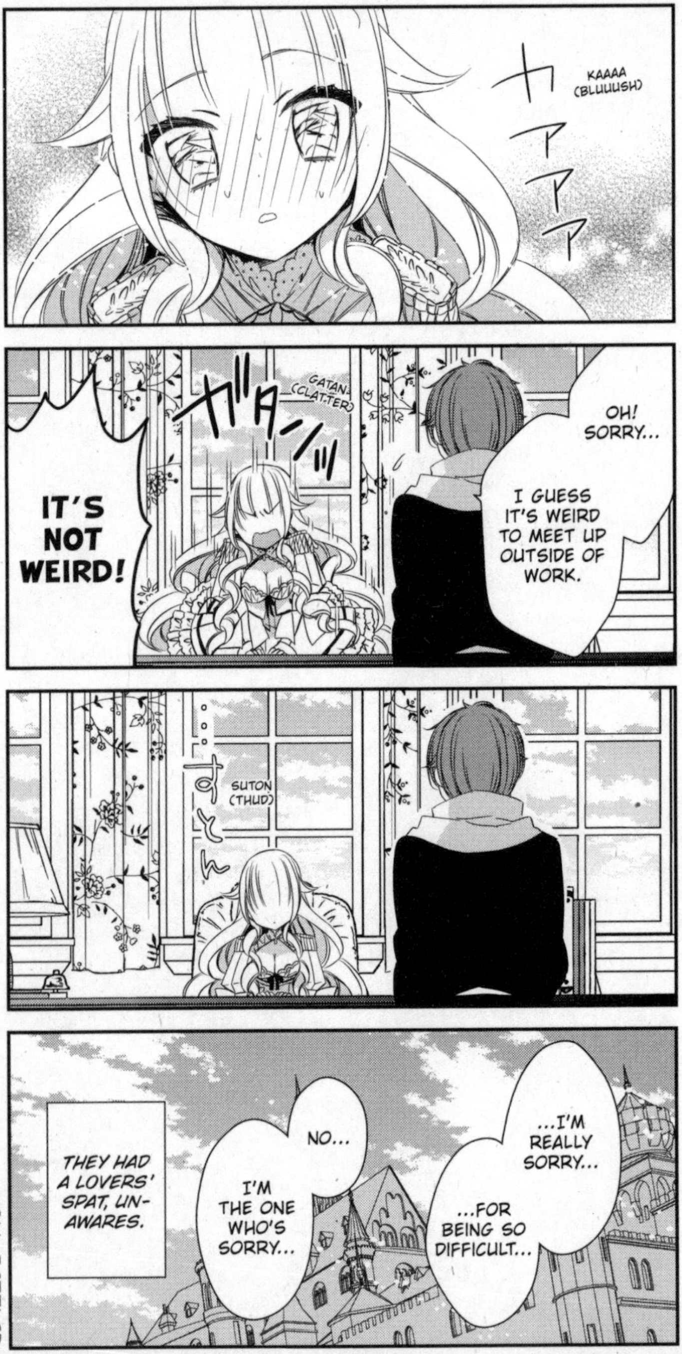
カァァァ
KAAAA (BLUUUSH)
OH! SORRY...
I GUESS IT'S WEIRD TO MEET UP OUTSIDE OF WORK.
ガタンッ
GATAN (CLATTER)
IT'S NOT WEIRD!
.....
すとん
SUTON (THUD)
...I'M REALLY SORRY...
...FOR BEING SO DIFFICULT...
NO...
I'M THE ONE WHO'S SORRY...
THEY HAD A LOVERS' SPAT, UN-AWARES.

ALL SETTLED

As Miss Beelzebub Likes

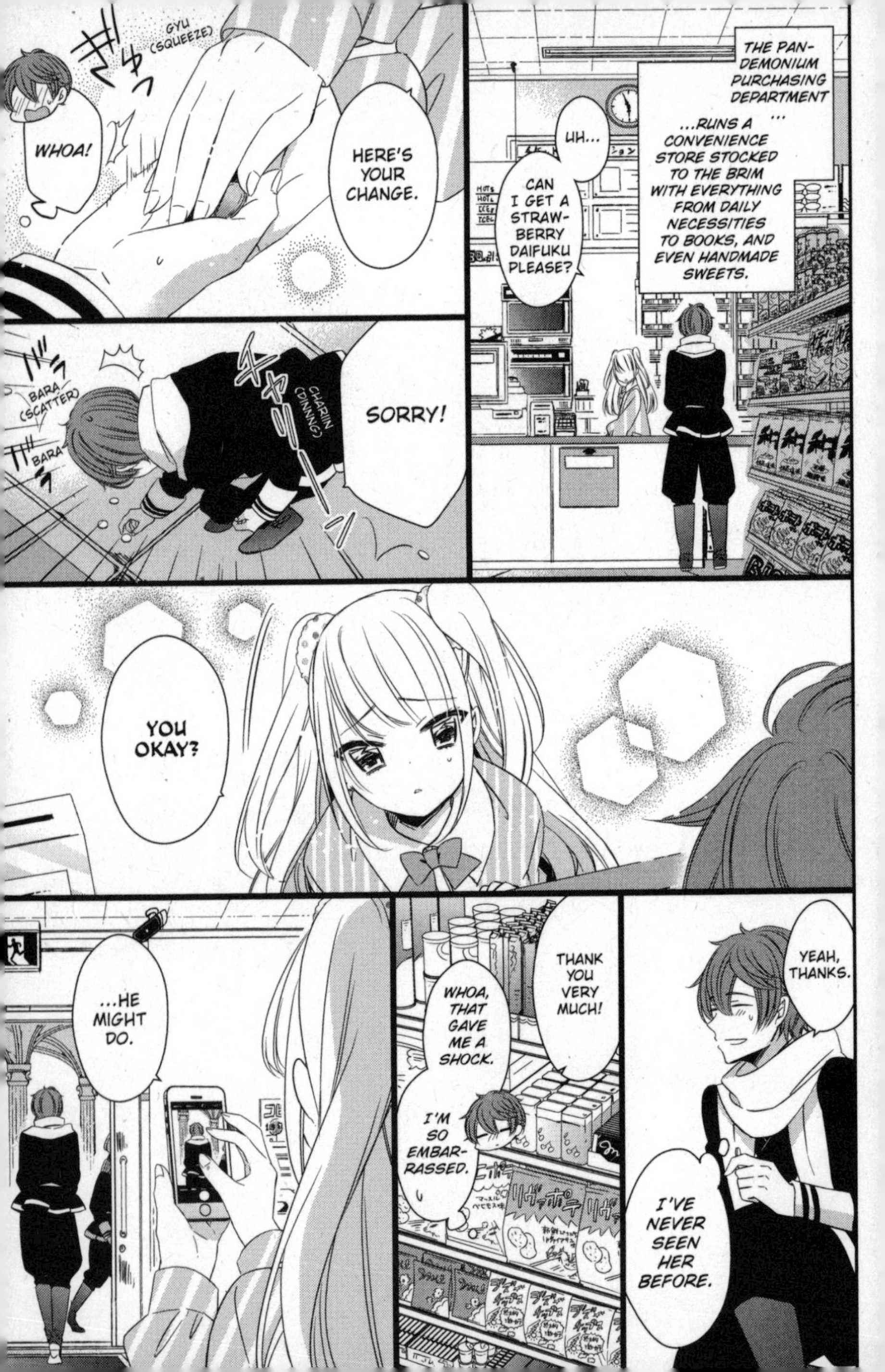
THE PAN-DEMONIUM PURCHASING DEPARTMENT...
...RUNS A CONVENIENCE STORE STOCKED TO THE BRIM WITH EVERYTHING FROM DAILY NECESSITIES TO BOOKS, AND EVEN HANDMADE SWEETS.
UH...
CAN I GET A STRAW-BERRY DAIFUKU PLEASE?
HERE'S YOUR CHANGE.
GYU (SQUEEZE)
WHOA!
BARA (SCATTER)
BARA
CHARIN (DINNING)
SORRY!
YOU OKAY?
YEAH, THANKS.
I'VE NEVER SEEN HER BEFORE.
THANK YOU VERY MUCH!
WHOA, THAT GAVE ME A SHOCK.
I'M SO EMBAR-RASSED.
...HE MIGHT DO.

CHAPTER 17

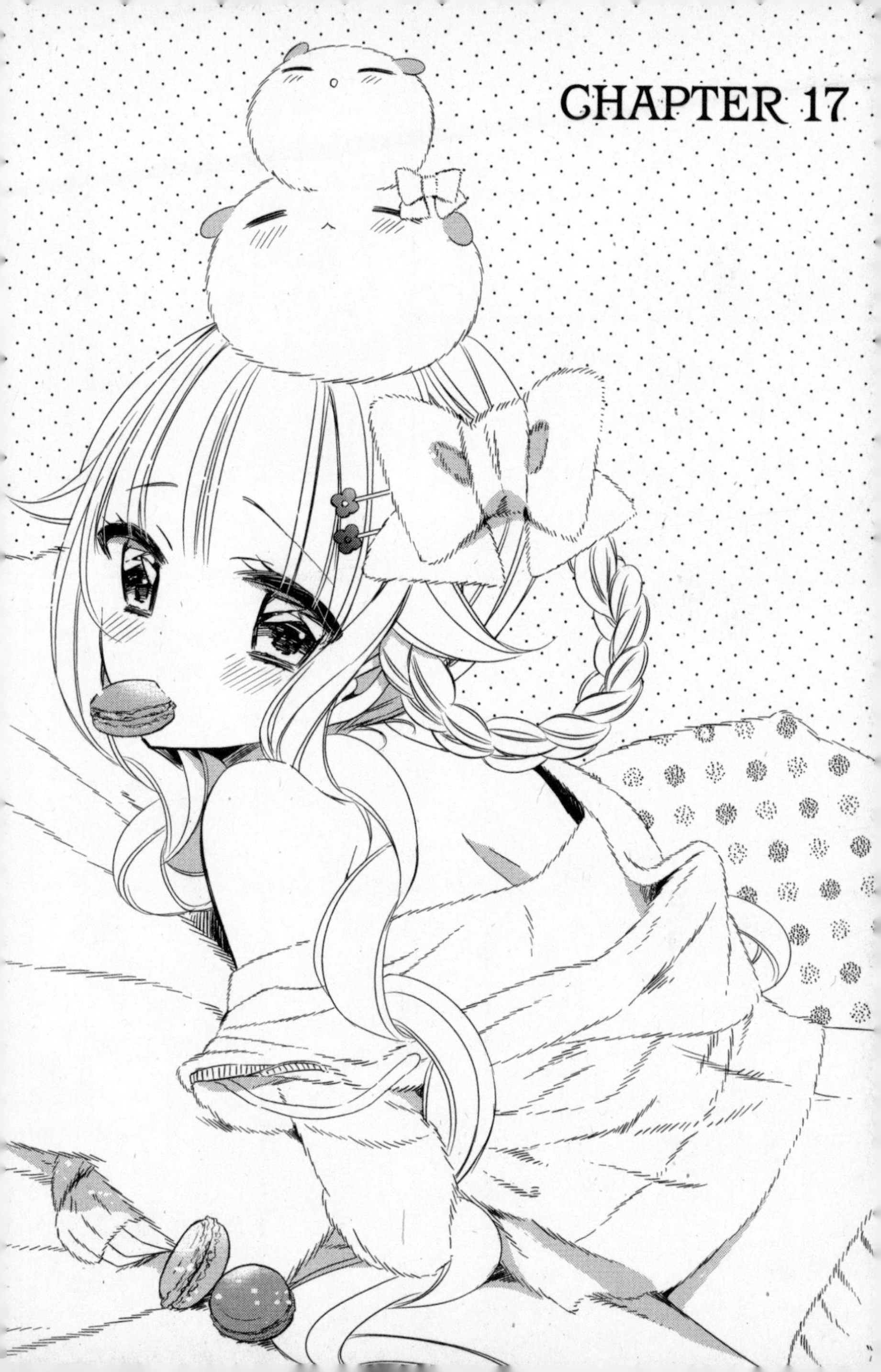

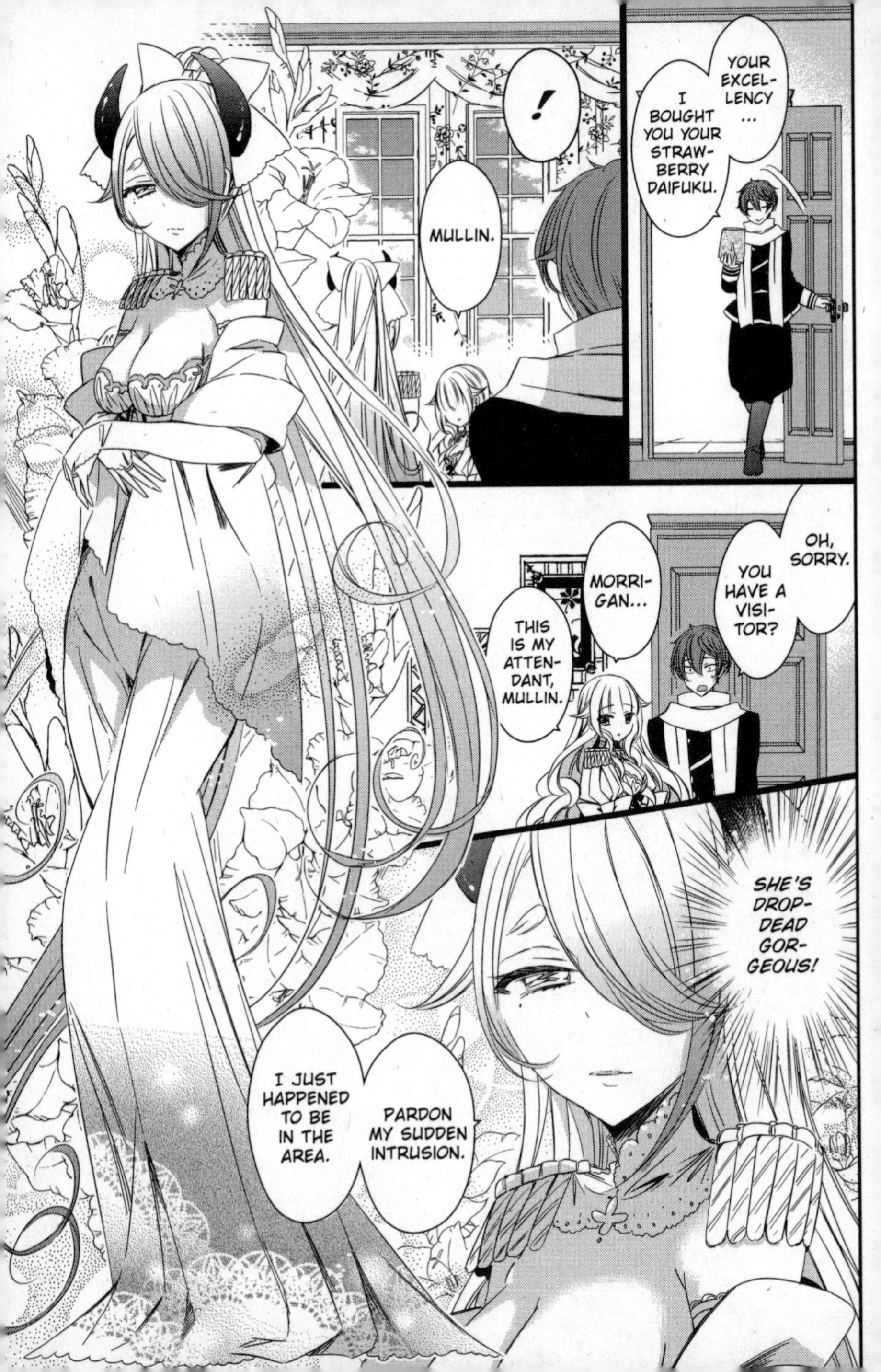
YOUR EXCELLENCY...
I BOUGHT YOU YOUR STRAWBERRY DAIFUKU.
!
MULLIN.
OH, SORRY.
YOU HAVE A VISITOR?
MORRIGAN...
THIS IS MY ATTENDANT, MULLIN.
SHE'S DROP-DEAD GORGEOUS!
PARDON MY SUDDEN INTRUSION.
I JUST HAPPENED TO BE IN THE AREA.

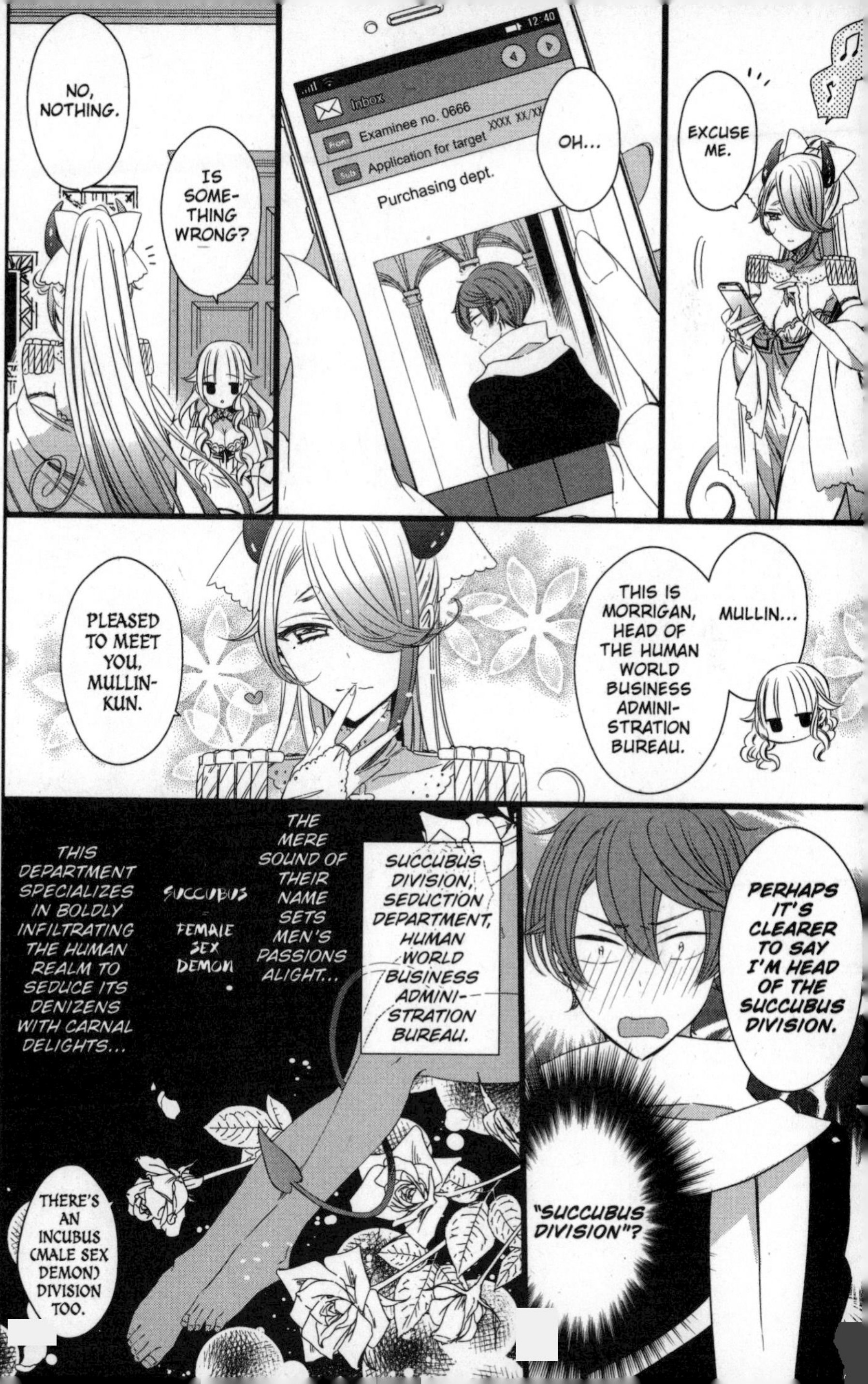

EXCUSE ME.
12:40
Inbox
Examinee no. 0666
XXXX XX/XX
Application for target
Purchasing dept.
OH...
IS SOMETHING WRONG?
NO, NOTHING.
THIS IS MORRIGAN, HEAD OF THE HUMAN WORLD BUSINESS ADMINISTRATION BUREAU.
MULLIN...
PLEASED TO MEET YOU, MULLIN-KUN.
PERHAPS IT'S CLEARER TO SAY I'M HEAD OF THE SUCCUBUS DIVISION.
"SUCCUBUS DIVISION"?
SUCCUBUS DIVISION, SEDUCTION DEPARTMENT, HUMAN WORLD BUSINESS ADMINISTRATION BUREAU.
THE MERE SOUND OF THEIR NAME SETS MEN'S PASSIONS ALIGHT...
SUCCUBUS = FEMALE SEX DEMON
THIS DEPARTMENT SPECIALIZES IN BOLDLY INFILTRATING THE HUMAN REALM TO SEDUCE ITS DENIZENS WITH CARNAL DELIGHTS...
THERE'S AN INCUBUS (MALE SEX DEMON) DIVISION TOO.

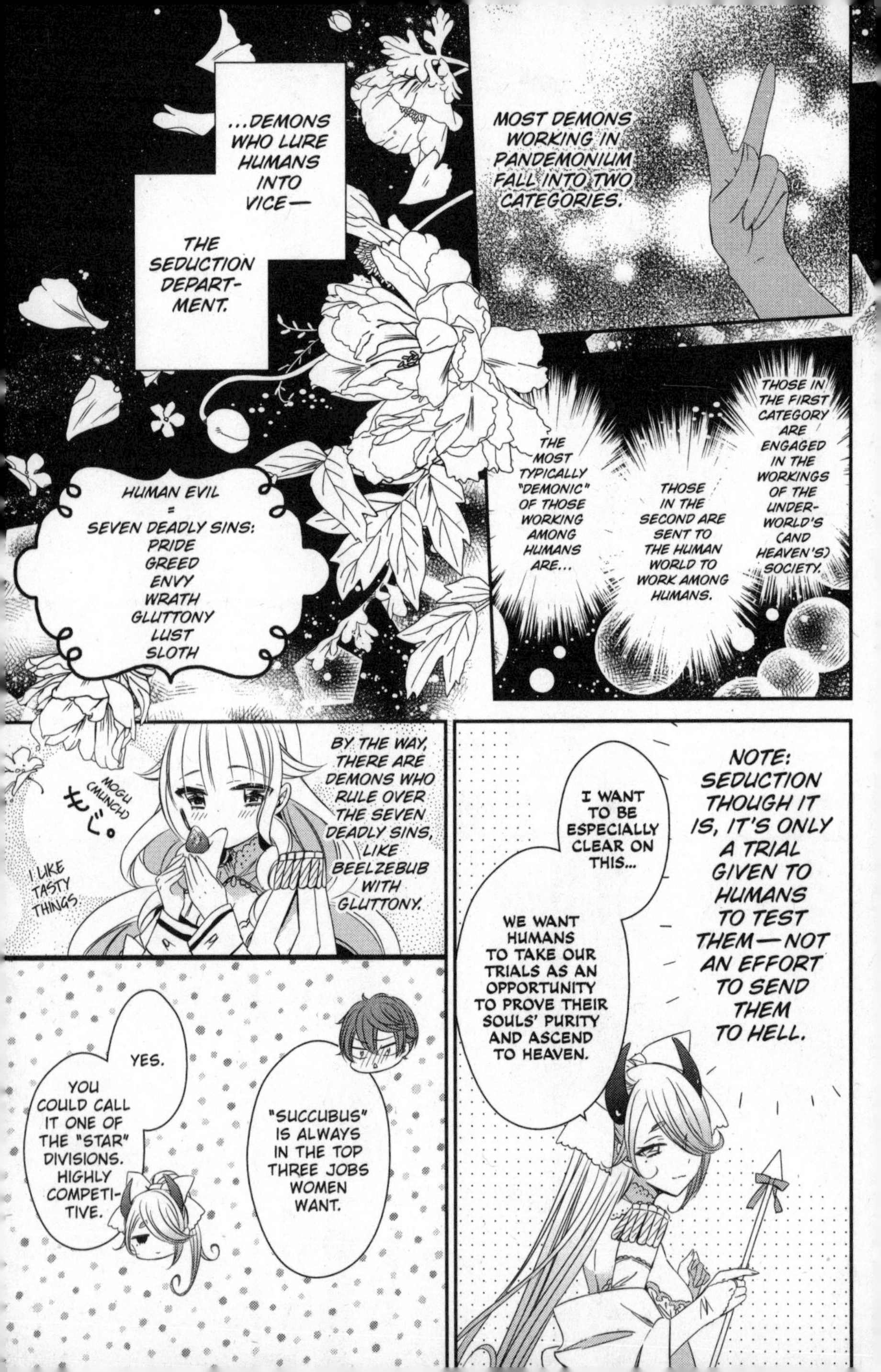
MOST DEMONS WORKING IN PANDEMONIUM FALL INTO TWO CATEGORIES.
THOSE IN THE FIRST CATEGORY ARE ENGAGED IN THE WORKINGS OF THE UNDER-WORLD'S (AND HEAVEN'S) SOCIETY.
THOSE IN THE SECOND ARE SENT TO THE HUMAN WORLD TO WORK AMONG HUMANS.
THE MOST TYPICALLY "DEMONIC" OF THOSE WORKING AMONG HUMANS ARE...
...DEMONS WHO LURE HUMANS INTO VICE—
THE SEDUCTION DEPART-MENT.
HUMAN EVIL = SEVEN DEADLY SINS: PRIDE GREED ENVY WRATH GLUTTONY LUST SLOTH
NOTE: SEDUCTION THOUGH IT IS, IT'S ONLY A TRIAL GIVEN TO HUMANS TO TEST THEM—NOT AN EFFORT TO SEND THEM TO HELL.
I WANT TO BE ESPECIALLY CLEAR ON THIS...
WE WANT HUMANS TO TAKE OUR TRIALS AS AN OPPORTUNITY TO PROVE THEIR SOULS' PURITY AND ASCEND TO HEAVEN.
BY THE WAY, THERE ARE DEMONS WHO RULE OVER THE SEVEN DEADLY SINS, LIKE BEELZEBUB WITH GLUTTONY.
MOGU (MUNCH)
もぐ。
I LIKE TASTY THINGS.
"SUCCUBUS" IS ALWAYS IN THE TOP THREE JOBS WOMEN WANT.
YES.
YOU COULD CALL IT ONE OF THE "STAR" DIVISIONS. HIGHLY COMPETI-TIVE.

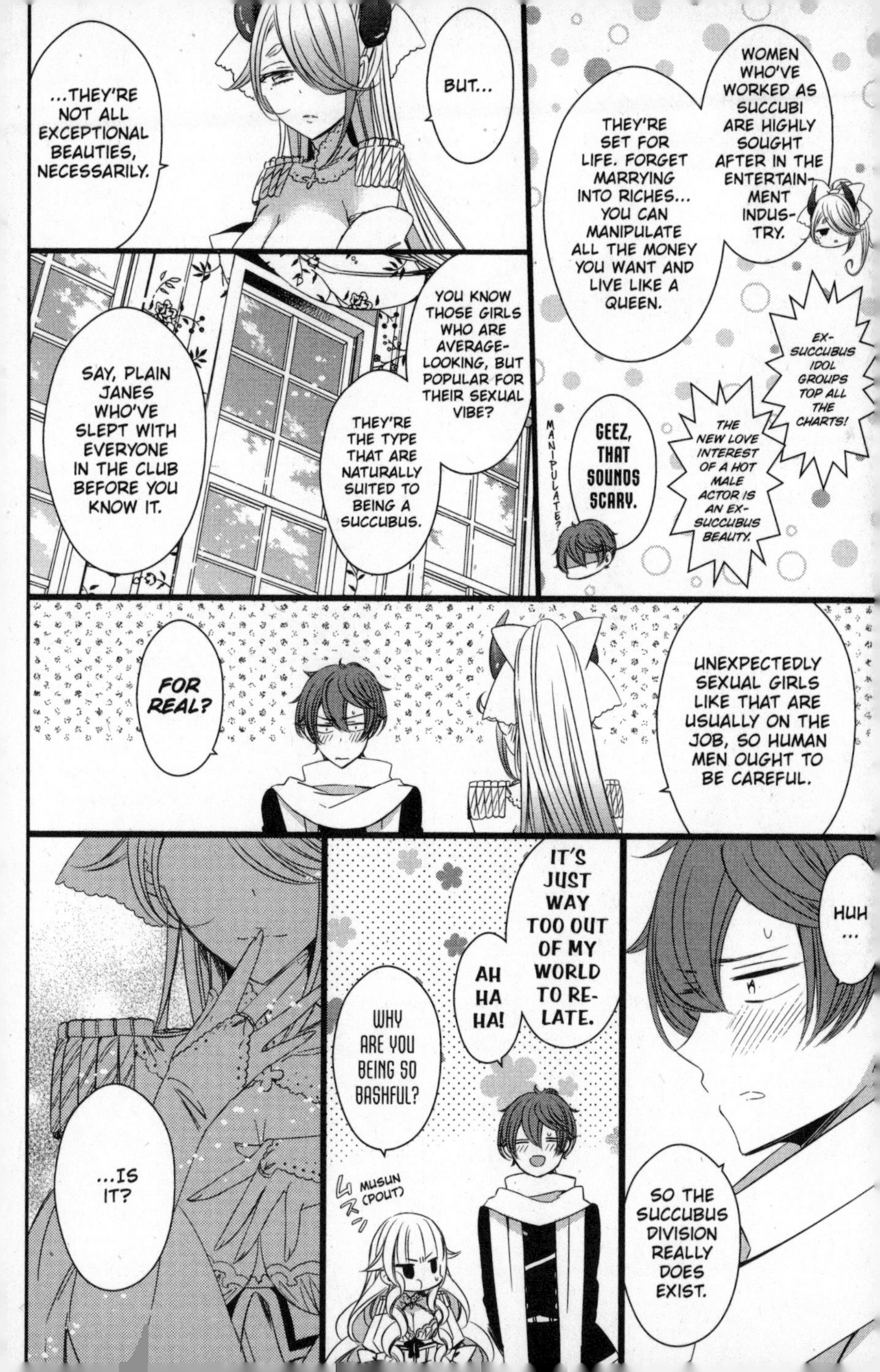
WOMEN WHO'VE WORKED AS SUCCUBI ARE HIGHLY SOUGHT AFTER IN THE ENTERTAIN-MENT INDUS-TRY.
THEY'RE SET FOR LIFE. FORGET MARRYING INTO RICHES... YOU CAN MANIPULATE ALL THE MONEY YOU WANT AND LIVE LIKE A QUEEN.
EX-SUCCUBUS IDOL GROUPS TOP ALL THE CHARTS!
THE NEW LOVE INTEREST OF A HOT MALE ACTOR IS AN EX-SUCCUBUS BEAUTY.
MANIPULATE?
GEEZ, THAT SOUNDS SCARY.
BUT...
...THEY'RE NOT ALL EXCEPTIONAL BEAUTIES, NECESSARILY.
YOU KNOW THOSE GIRLS WHO ARE AVERAGE-LOOKING, BUT POPULAR FOR THEIR SEXUAL VIBE?
THEY'RE THE TYPE THAT ARE NATURALLY SUITED TO BEING A SUCCUBUS.
SAY, PLAIN JANES WHO'VE SLEPT WITH EVERYONE IN THE CLUB BEFORE YOU KNOW IT.
UNEXPECTEDLY SEXUAL GIRLS LIKE THAT ARE USUALLY ON THE JOB, SO HUMAN MEN OUGHT TO BE CAREFUL.
FOR REAL?
HUH...
SO THE SUCCUBUS DIVISION REALLY DOES EXIST.
IT'S JUST WAY TOO OUT OF MY WORLD TO RE-LATE.
AH HA HA!
WHY ARE YOU BEING SO BASHFUL?
MUSUN (POUT)
...IS IT?

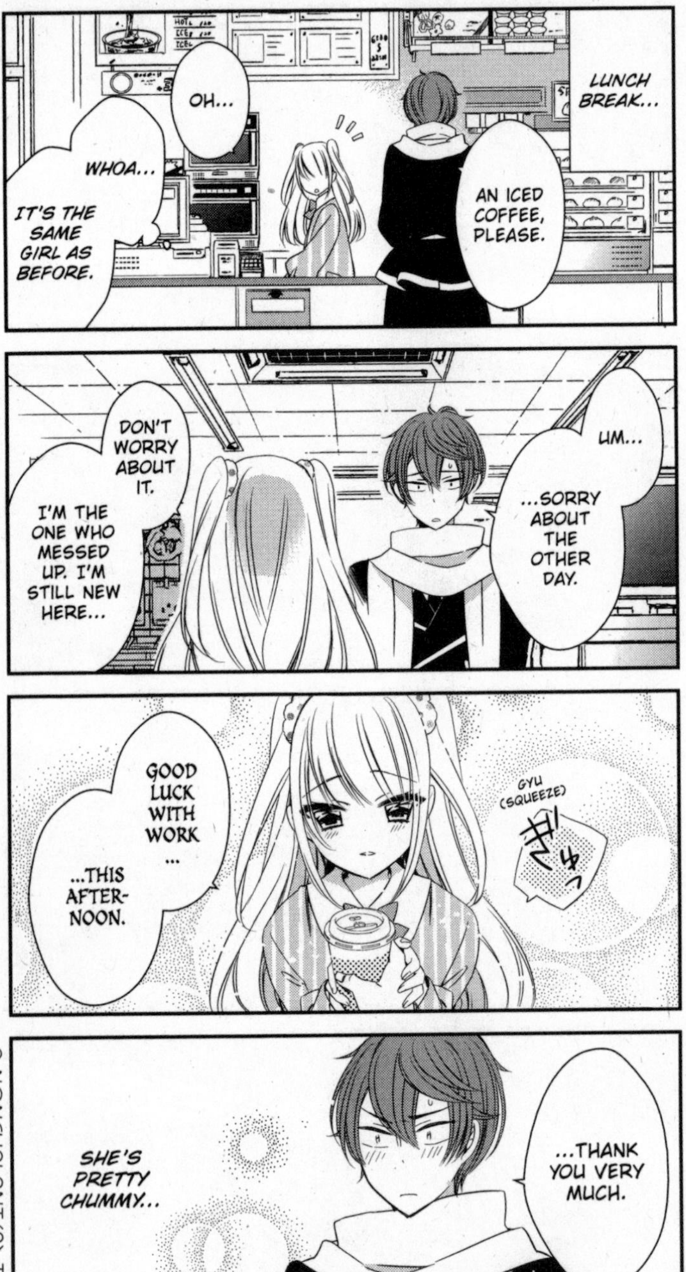
LUNCH BREAK...
AN ICED COFFEE, PLEASE.
OH...
WHOA...
IT'S THE SAME GIRL AS BEFORE.
UM...
...SORRY ABOUT THE OTHER DAY.
DON'T WORRY ABOUT IT.
I'M THE ONE WHO MESSED UP. I'M STILL NEW HERE...
GYU (SQUEEZE)
GOOD LUCK WITH WORK ...
...THIS AFTERNOON.
...THANK YOU VERY MUCH.
SHE'S PRETTY CHUMMY...

A NONCHALANT(?) TOUCH...

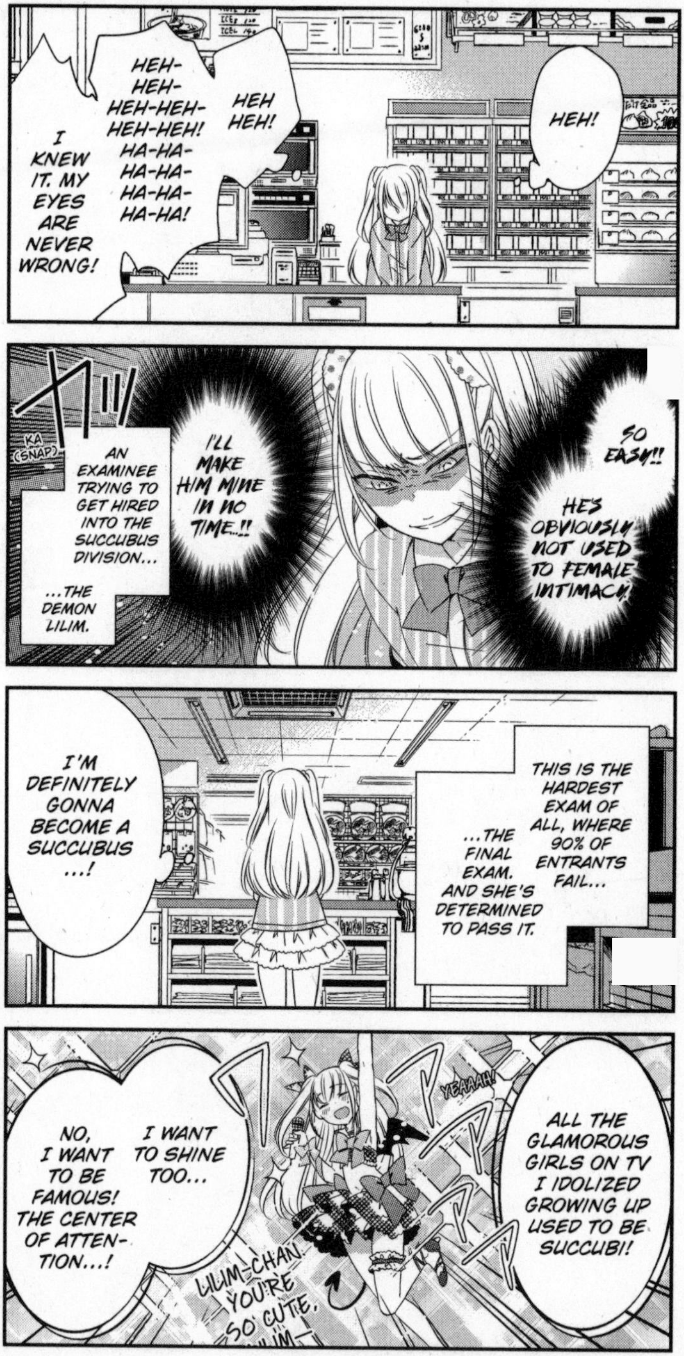
HEH!
HEH HEH!
HEH-HEH-HEH-HEH-HEH-HEH! HA-HA-HA-HA-HA-HA-HA-HA!
I KNEW IT. MY EYES ARE NEVER WRONG!
SO EASY!!
HE'S OBVIOUSLY NOT USED TO FEMALE INTIMACY!
I'LL MAKE HIM MINE IN NO TIME...!!
AN EXAMINEE TRYING TO GET HIRED INTO THE SUCCUBUS DIVISION...
...THE DEMON LILIM.
KA (SNAP)
THIS IS THE HARDEST EXAM OF ALL, WHERE 90% OF ENTRANTS FAIL...
...THE FINAL EXAM. AND SHE'S DETERMINED TO PASS IT.
I'M DEFINITELY GONNA BECOME A SUCCUBUS...!
ALL THE GLAMOROUS GIRLS ON TV I IDOLIZED GROWING UP USED TO BE SUCCUBI!
YEAAAH!
I WANT TO SHINE TOO...
NO, I WANT TO BE FAMOUS! THE CENTER OF ATTENTION...!
LILIM-CHAN, YOU'RE SO CUTE.

IMPURE MOTIVES? NO, TOTALLY INNOCENT!

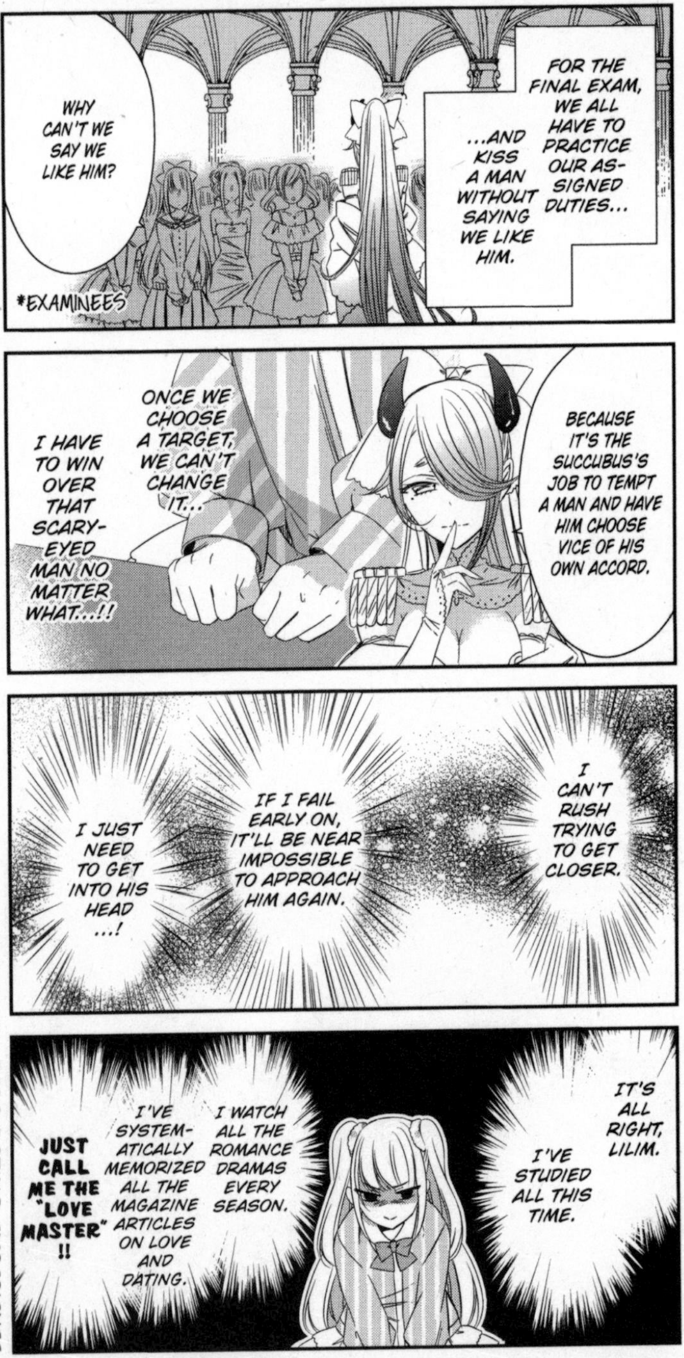
FOR THE FINAL EXAM, WE ALL HAVE TO PRACTICE OUR AS-SIGNED DUTIES...
...AND KISS A MAN WITHOUT SAYING WE LIKE HIM.
WHY CAN'T WE SAY WE LIKE HIM?
*EXAMINEES
BECAUSE IT'S THE SUCCUBUS'S JOB TO TEMPT A MAN AND HAVE HIM CHOOSE VICE OF HIS OWN ACCORD.
ONCE WE CHOOSE A TARGET, WE CAN'T CHANGE IT...
I HAVE TO WIN OVER THAT SCARY-EYED MAN NO MATTER WHAT...!!
I CAN'T RUSH TRYING TO GET CLOSER.
IF I FAIL EARLY ON, IT'LL BE NEAR IMPOSSIBLE TO APPROACH HIM AGAIN.
I JUST NEED TO GET INTO HIS HEAD ...!
IT'S ALL RIGHT, LILIM.
I'VE STUDIED ALL THIS TIME.
I WATCH ALL THE ROMANCE DRAMAS EVERY SEASON.
I'VE SYSTEM-ATICALLY MEMORIZED ALL THE MAGAZINE ARTICLES ON LOVE AND DATING.
JUST CALL ME THE "LOVE MASTER"!!

IT'S OKAY (NOT)

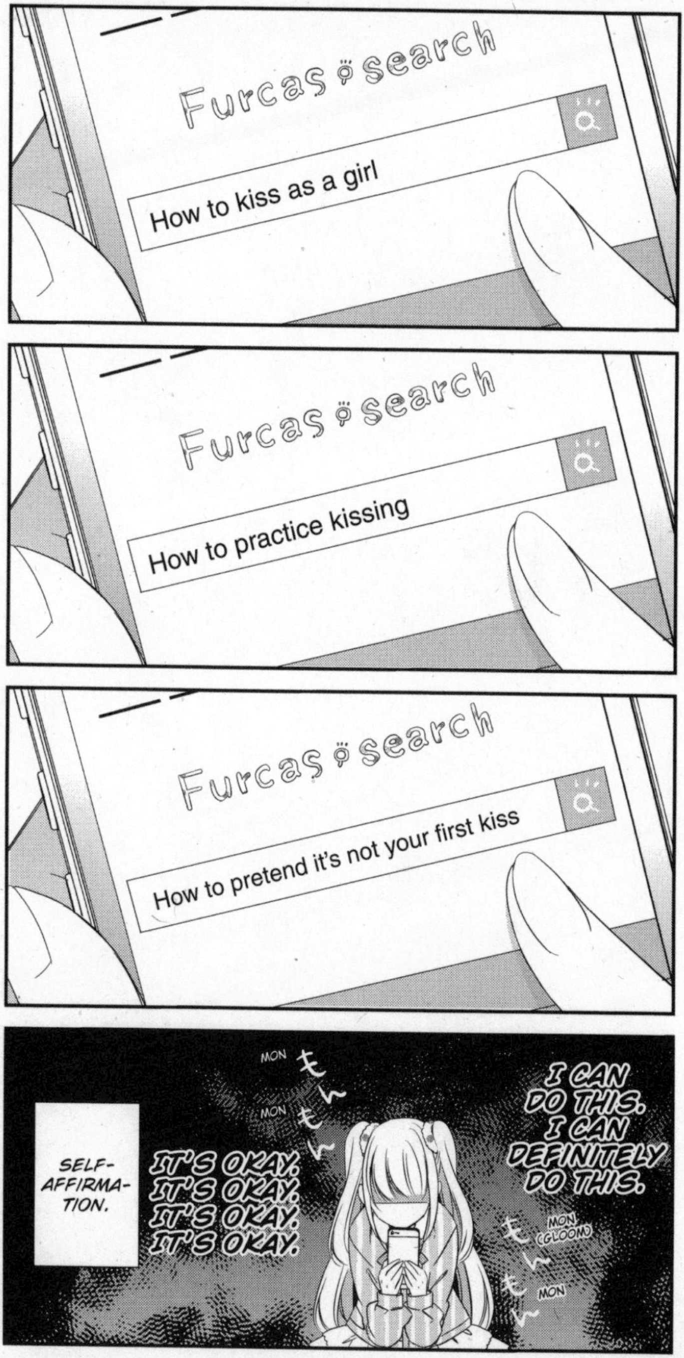
Furcas search
How to kiss as a girl
Furcas search
How to practice kissing
Furcas search
How to pretend it's not your first kiss
I CAN DO THIS. I CAN DEFINITELY DO THIS.
MON (GLOOM)
MON
MON
MON
IT'S OKAY. IT'S OKAY. IT'S OKAY. IT'S OKAY.
SELF-AFFIRMATION.

HER TRUE FEELINGS

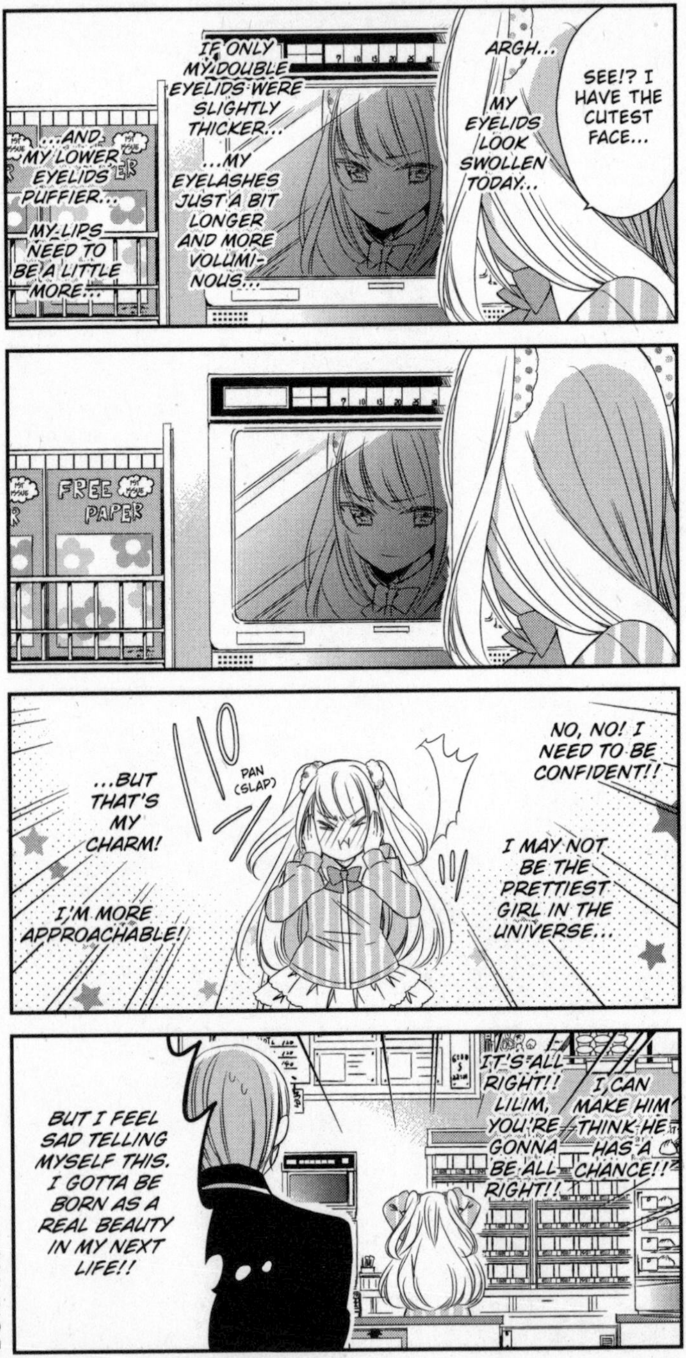
SEE!? I HAVE THE CUTEST FACE...
ARGH... MY EYELIDS LOOK SWOLLEN TODAY...
IF ONLY MY DOUBLE EYELIDS WERE SLIGHTLY THICKER...
...MY EYELASHES JUST A BIT LONGER AND MORE VOLUMI-NOUS...
...AND MY LOWER EYELIDS PUFFIER...
MY LIPS NEED TO BE A LITTLE MORE...
1ST ISSUE
FREE PAPER
NO, NO! I NEED TO BE CONFIDENT!!
I MAY NOT BE THE PRETTIEST GIRL IN THE UNIVERSE...
PAN (SLAP)
...BUT THAT'S MY CHARM!
I'M MORE APPROACHABLE!
I CAN MAKE HIM THINK HE HAS A CHANCE!!
IT'S ALL RIGHT!! LILIM, YOU'RE GONNA BE ALL RIGHT!!
BUT I FEEL SAD TELLING MYSELF THIS. I GOTTA BE BORN AS A REAL BEAUTY IN MY NEXT LIFE!!

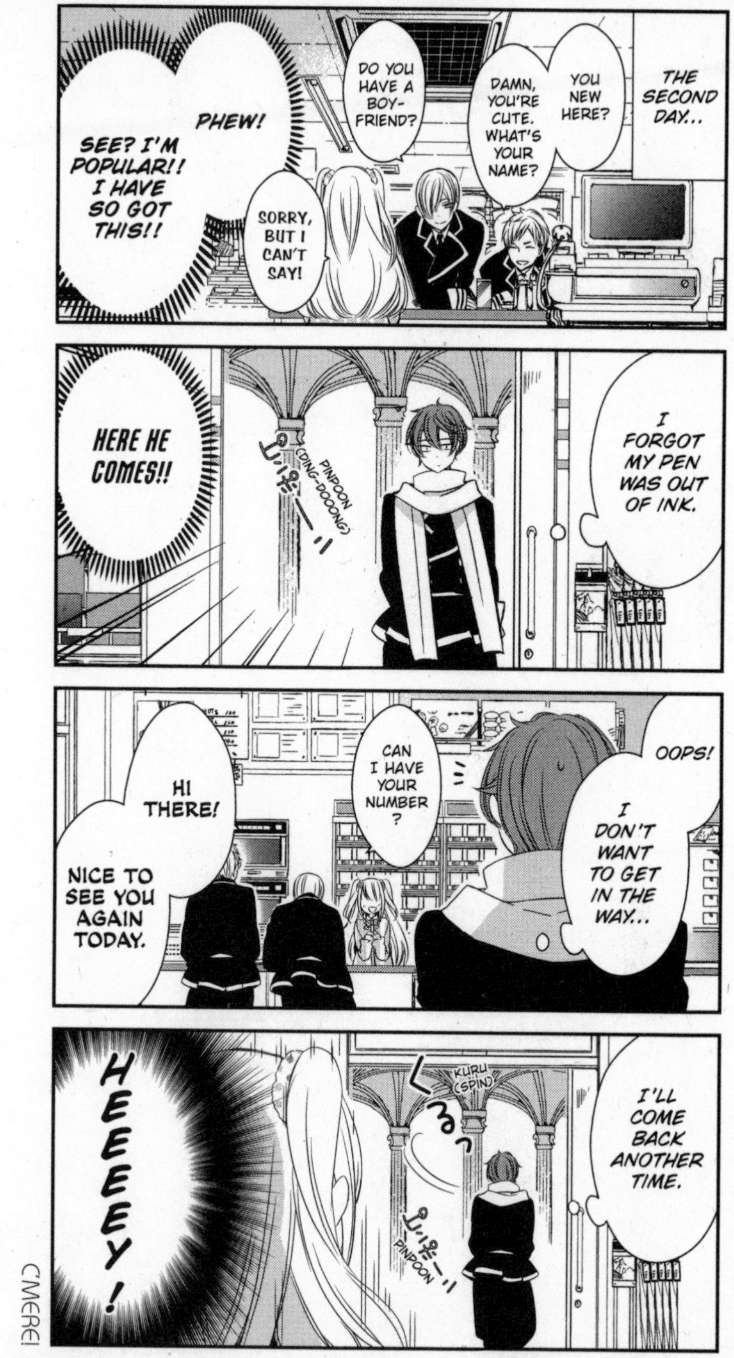
THE SECOND DAY...
YOU NEW HERE?
DAMN, YOU'RE CUTE. WHAT'S YOUR NAME?
DO YOU HAVE A BOY-FRIEND?
SORRY, BUT I CAN'T SAY!
PHEW!
SEE? I'M POPULAR!! I HAVE SO GOT THIS!!
I FORGOT MY PEN WAS OUT OF INK.
PINPOON (DING-DOOONG)
HERE HE COMES!!
OOPS!
I DON'T WANT TO GET IN THE WAY...
CAN I HAVE YOUR NUMBER?
HI THERE!
NICE TO SEE YOU AGAIN TODAY.
I'LL COME BACK ANOTHER TIME.
KURU (SPIN)
PINPOON
HEEEEY!
C'MERE!

EMPTY AT CLOSING TIME

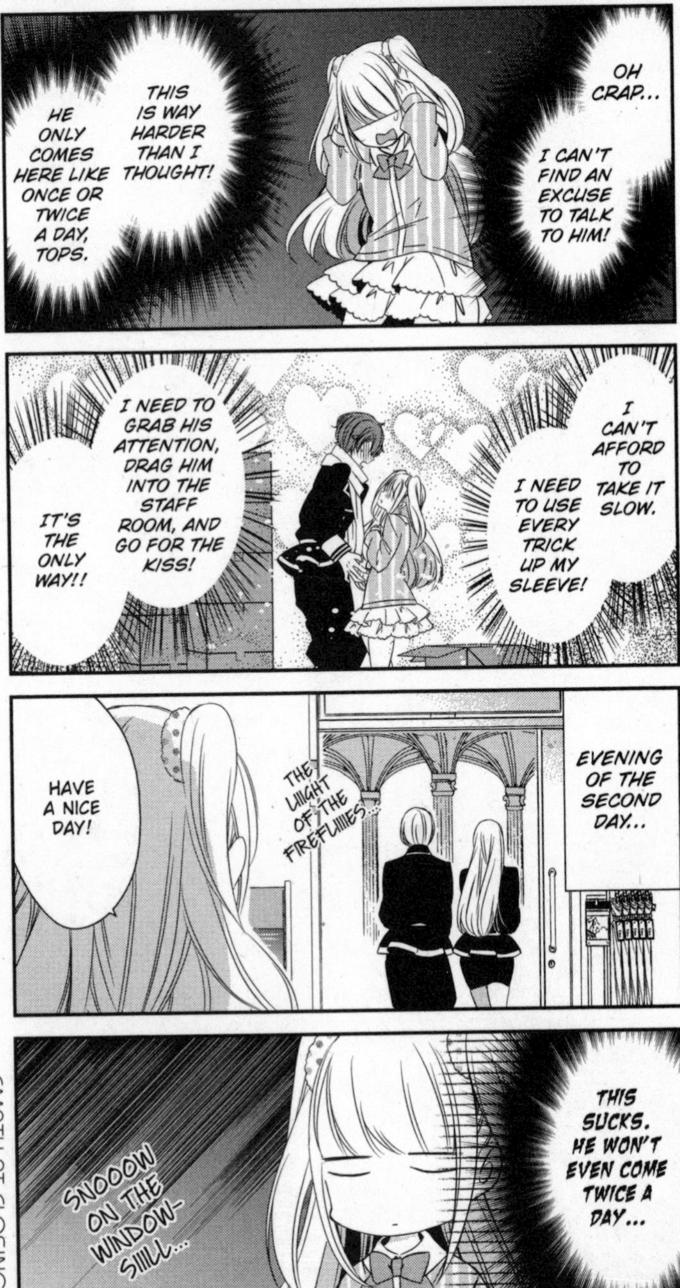
OH CRAP...
I CAN'T FIND AN EXCUSE TO TALK TO HIM!
THIS IS WAY HARDER THAN I THOUGHT!
HE ONLY COMES HERE LIKE ONCE OR TWICE A DAY, TOPS.
I CAN'T AFFORD TO TAKE IT SLOW.
I NEED TO USE EVERY TRICK UP MY SLEEVE!
I NEED TO GRAB HIS ATTENTION, DRAG HIM INTO THE STAFF ROOM, AND GO FOR THE KISS!
IT'S THE ONLY WAY!!
EVENING OF THE SECOND DAY...
THE LIIIGHT OF THE FIREFLIIIES...
HAVE A NICE DAY!
THIS SUCKS. HE WON'T EVEN COME TWICE A DAY...
SNOOOW ON THE WINDOW-SIIILL...

WHAT DO BUBBLES SMELL LIKE, ANYWAY?

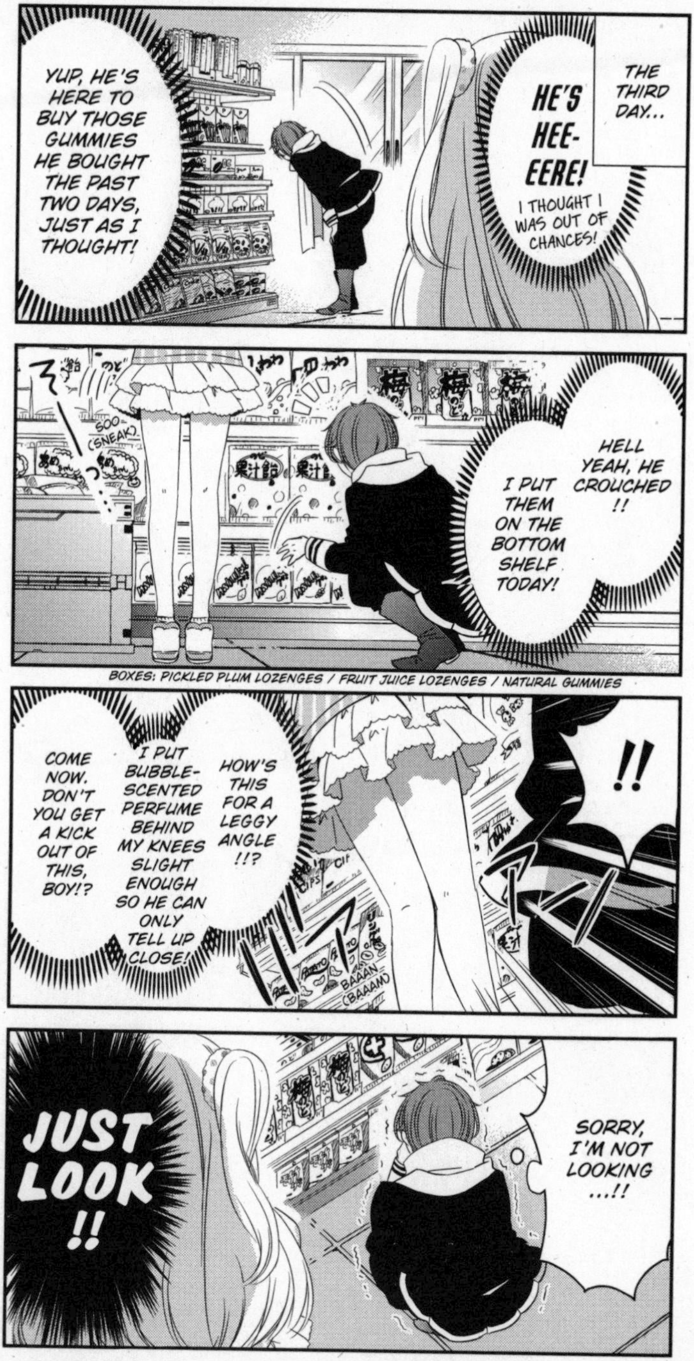

THE THIRD DAY...
HE'S HEE-EERE!
I THOUGHT I WAS OUT OF CHANCES!
YUP, HE'S HERE TO BUY THOSE GUMMIES HE BOUGHT THE PAST TWO DAYS, JUST AS I THOUGHT!
HELL YEAH, HE CROUCHED !!
I PUT THEM ON THE BOTTOM SHELF TODAY!
SOO- (SNEAK)
BOXES: PICKLED PLUM LOZENGES / FRUIT JUICE LOZENGES / NATURAL GUMMIES
!!
HOW'S THIS FOR A LEGGY ANGLE !!?
I PUT BUBBLE-SCENTED PERFUME BEHIND MY KNEES SLIGHT ENOUGH SO HE CAN ONLY TELL UP CLOSE!
COME NOW. DON'T YOU GET A KICK OUT OF THIS, BOY!?
BAAAN (BAAAM)
SORRY, I'M NOT LOOKING ...!!
JUST LOOK !!

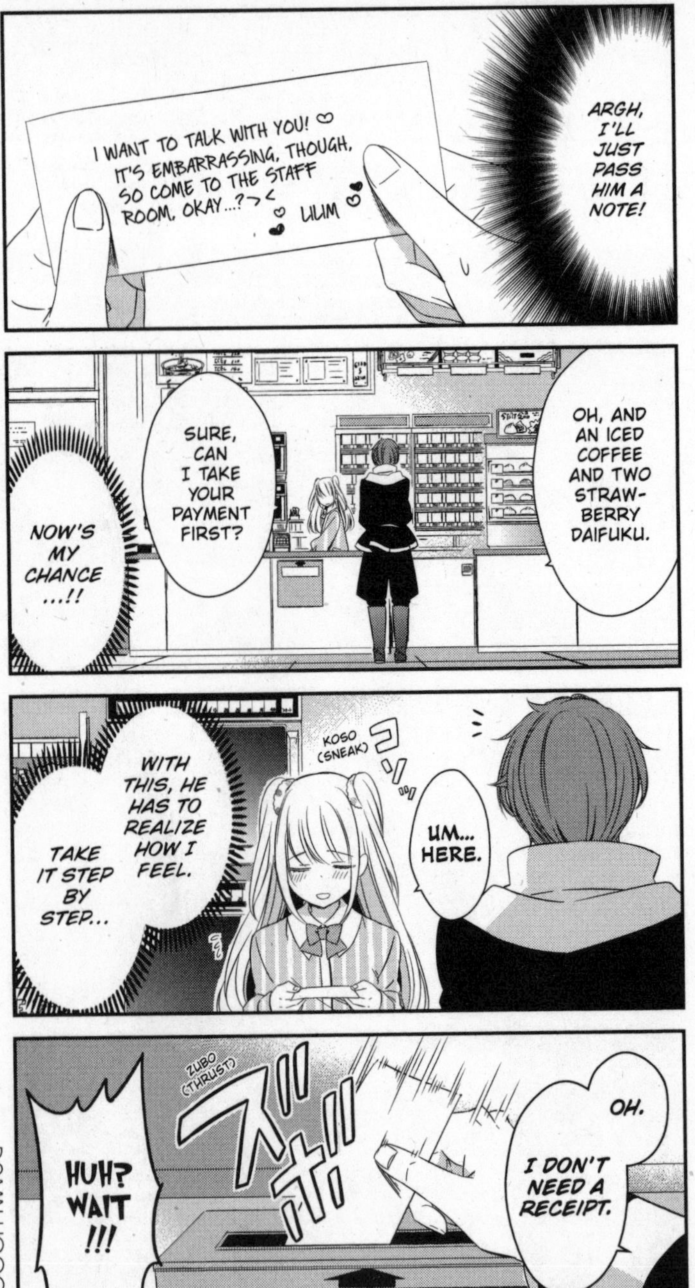
ARGH, I'LL JUST PASS HIM A NOTE!
I WANT TO TALK WITH YOU! IT'S EMBARRASSING, THOUGH, SO COME TO THE STAFF ROOM, OKAY...?>< LIUM
OH, AND AN ICED COFFEE AND TWO STRAW-BERRY DAIFUKU.
SURE, CAN I TAKE YOUR PAYMENT FIRST?
NOW'S MY CHANCE ...!!
UM... HERE.
KOSO (SNEAK)
WITH THIS, HE HAS TO REALIZE HOW I FEEL.
TAKE IT STEP BY STEP...
OH.
I DON'T NEED A RECEIPT.
ZUBO (THRUST)
HUH? WAIT !!!
PLEASE PLACE RECEIPTS HERE

DAMN YOOOUUU!!!

A COMPLICATED DEFEAT

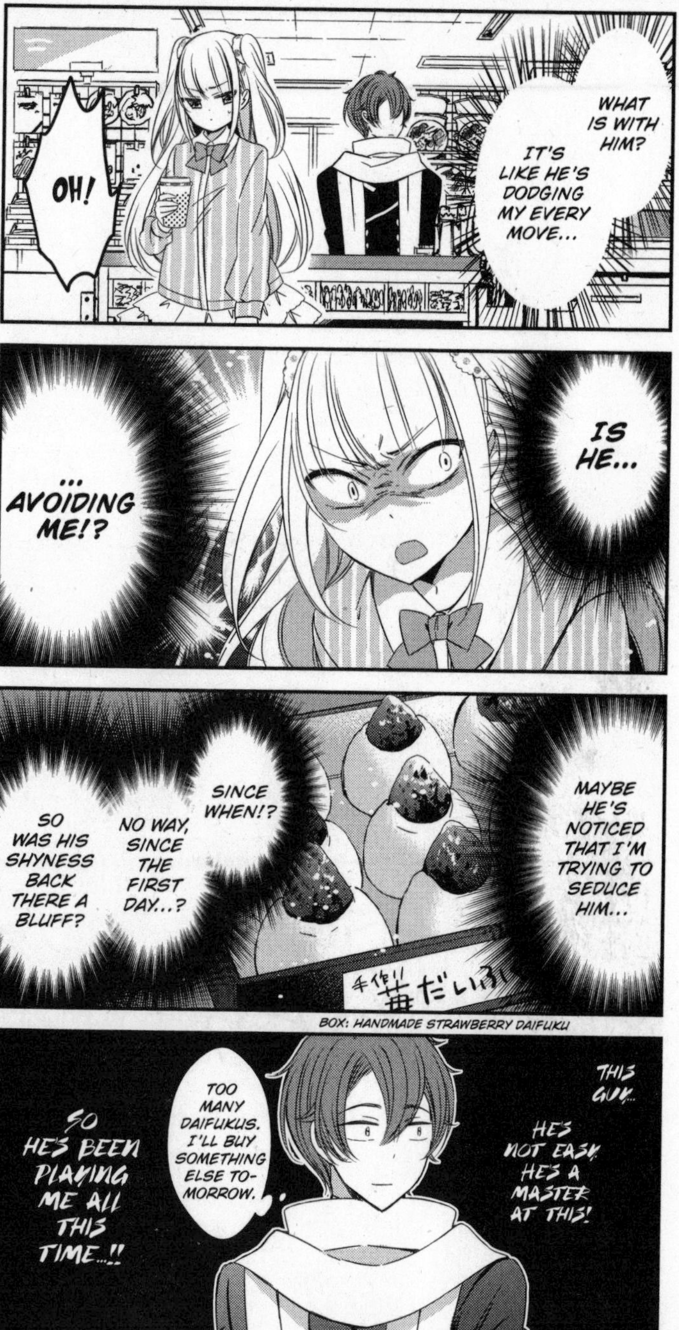
WHAT IS WITH HIM? IT'S LIKE HE'S DODGING MY EVERY MOVE...
OH!
IS HE...
... AVOIDING ME!?
MAYBE HE'S NOTICED THAT I'M TRYING TO SEDUCE HIM...
SINCE WHEN!?
NO WAY, SINCE THE FIRST DAY...?
SO WAS HIS SHYNESS BACK THERE A BLUFF?
手作り
苺だいふ
THIS GUY...
HE'S NOT EASY. HE'S A MASTER AT THIS!
TOO MANY DAIFUKUS. I'LL BUY SOMETHING ELSE TO-MORROW.
SO HE'S BEEN PLAYING ME ALL THIS TIME...!!

BOX: HANDMADE STRAWBERRY DAIFUKU

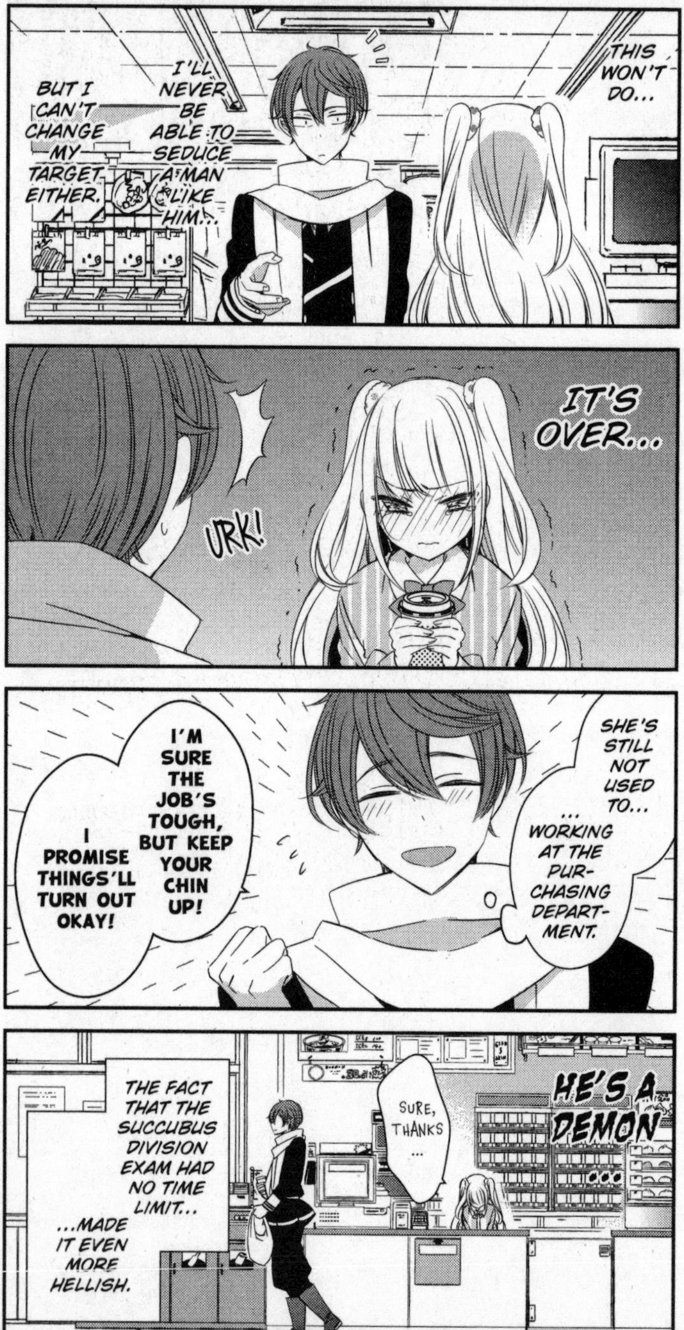
THIS WON'T DO...
I'LL NEVER BE ABLE TO SEDUCE A MAN LIKE HIM...
BUT I CAN'T CHANGE MY TARGET EITHER.
IT'S OVER...
URK!
SHE'S STILL NOT USED TO...
...WORKING AT THE PUR-CHASING DEPART-MENT.
I'M SURE THE JOB'S TOUGH, BUT KEEP YOUR CHIN UP!
I PROMISE THINGS'LL TURN OUT OKAY!
HE'S A DEMON
SURE, THANKS ...
THE FACT THAT THE SUCCUBUS DIVISION EXAM HAD NO TIME LIMIT...
...MADE IT EVEN MORE HELLISH.

As Miss Beelzebub Likes

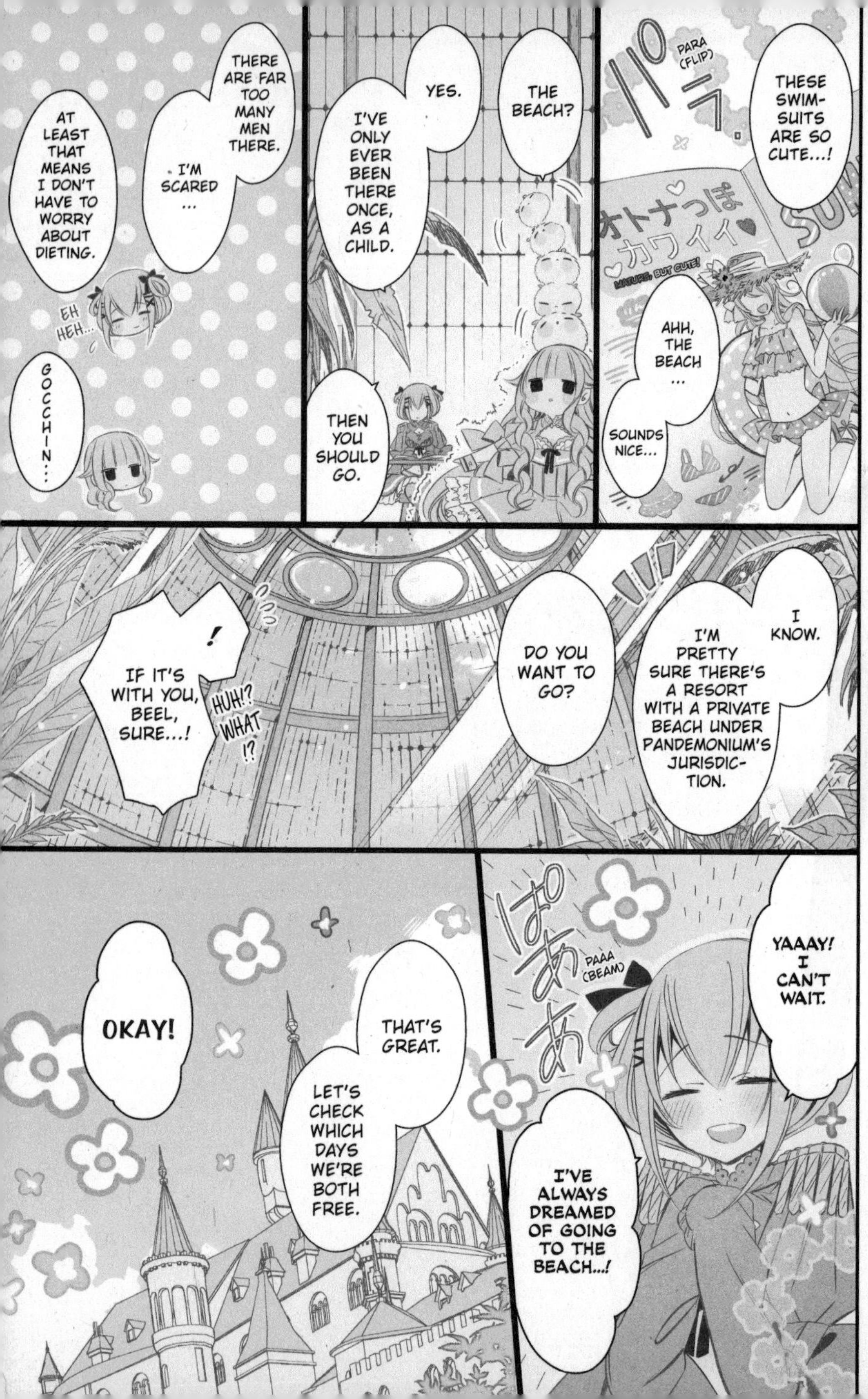
PARA (FLIP)
THESE SWIM-SUITS ARE SO CUTE...!
オトナっぽ カワイイ
MATURE, BUT CUTE!
AHH, THE BEACH...
SOUNDS NICE...
THE BEACH?
YES.
I'VE ONLY EVER BEEN THERE ONCE, AS A CHILD.
THEN YOU SHOULD GO.
THERE ARE FAR TOO MANY MEN THERE.
I'M SCARED...
AT LEAST THAT MEANS I DON'T HAVE TO WORRY ABOUT DIETING.
EH HEH...
GOCCHIN...
I KNOW.
I'M PRETTY SURE THERE'S A RESORT WITH A PRIVATE BEACH UNDER PANDEMONIUM'S JURISDICTION.
DO YOU WANT TO GO?
!
IF IT'S WITH YOU, BEEL, SURE...!
HUH!? WHAT!?
PAAA (BEAM)
YAAAY! I CAN'T WAIT.
I'VE ALWAYS DREAMED OF GOING TO THE BEACH...!
THAT'S GREAT.
LET'S CHECK WHICH DAYS WE'RE BOTH FREE.
OKAY!

CHAPTER 18

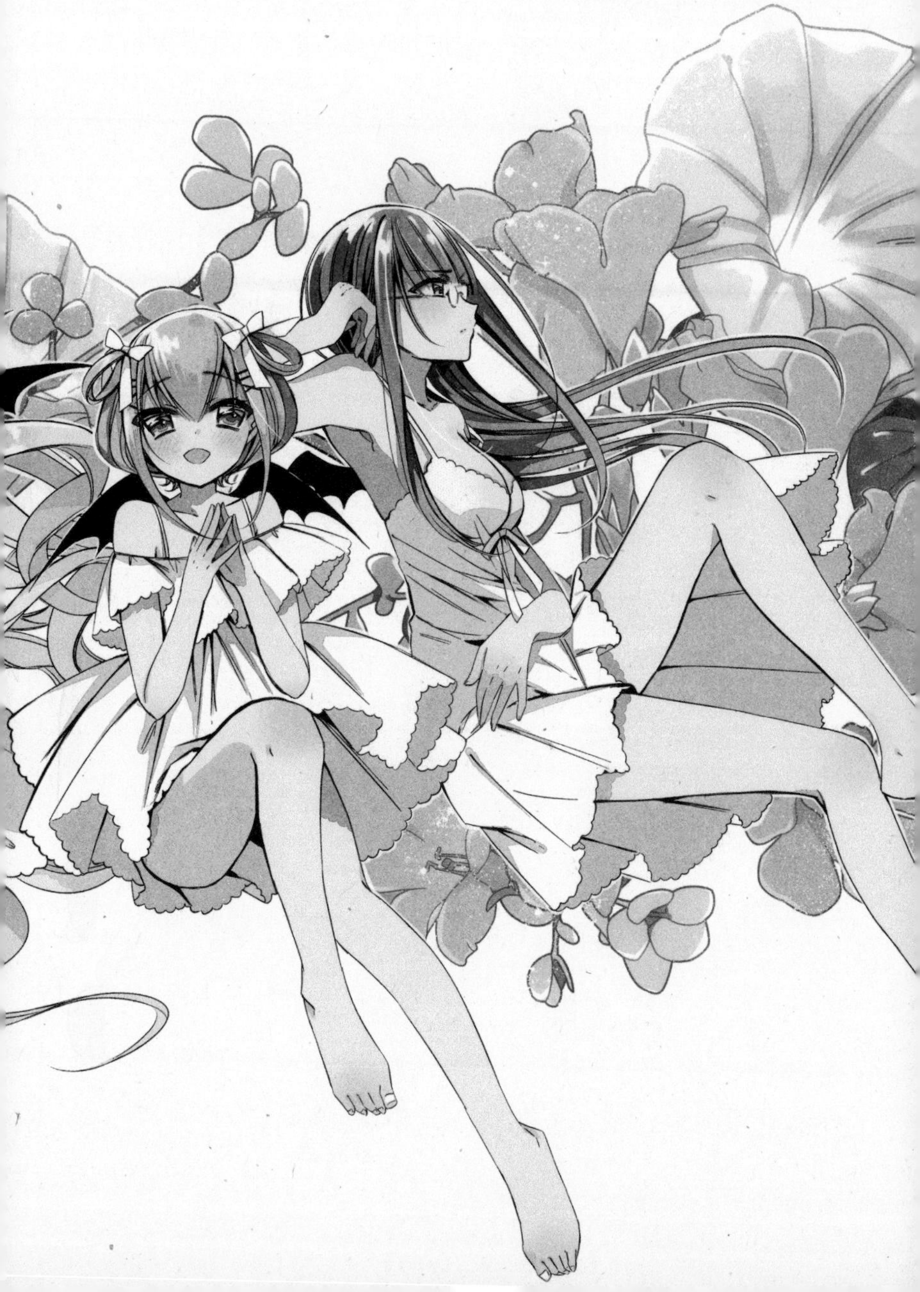

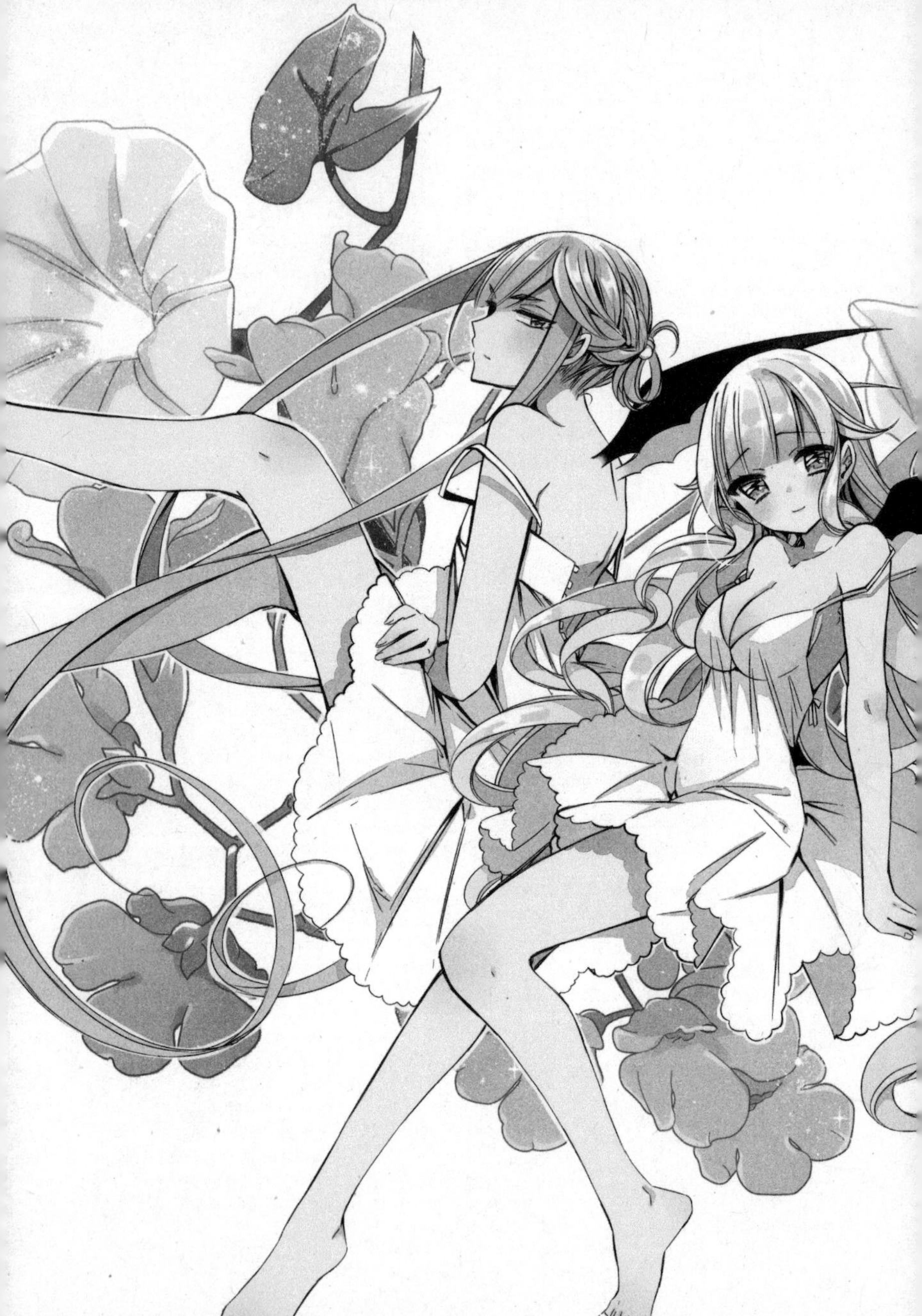

As Miss Beelzebub Likes

HELP ME, BRO!

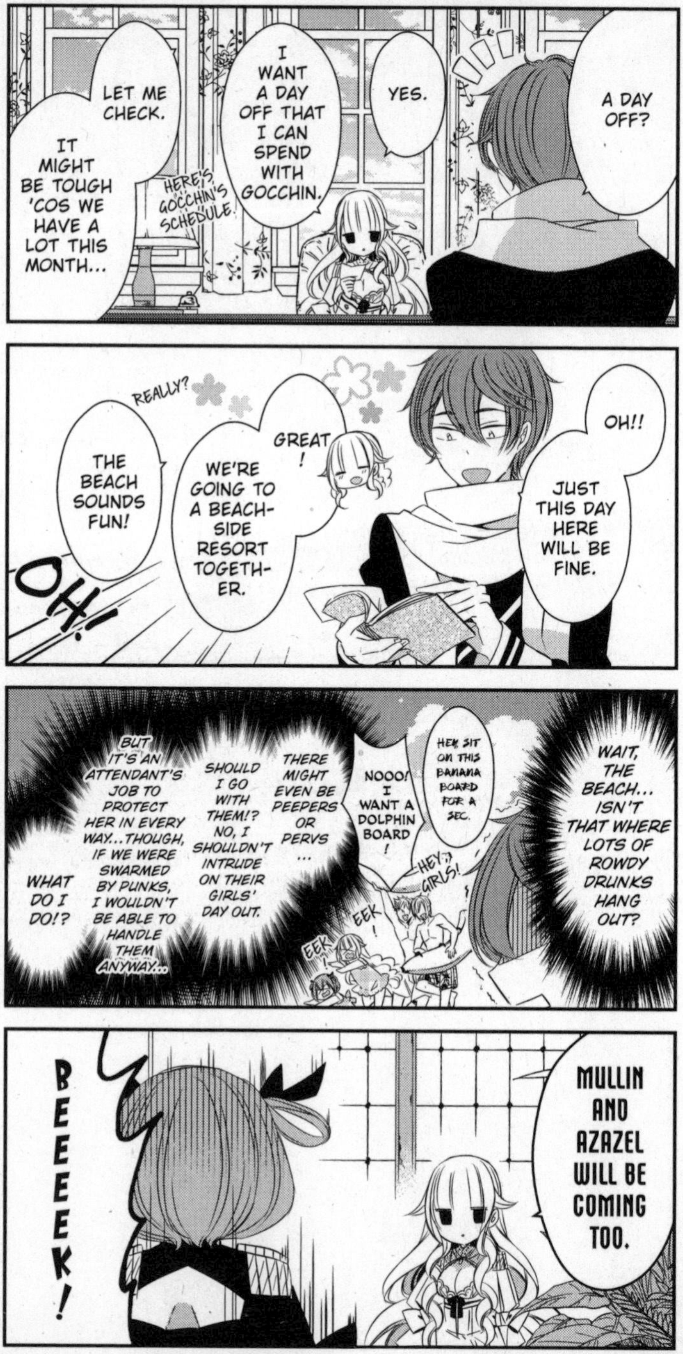
A DAY OFF?
YES.
I WANT A DAY OFF THAT I CAN SPEND WITH GOCCHIN.
HERE'S GOCCHIN'S SCHEDULE.
LET ME CHECK.
IT MIGHT BE TOUGH 'COS WE HAVE A LOT THIS MONTH...
OH!!
JUST THIS DAY HERE WILL BE FINE.
GREAT!
WE'RE GOING TO A BEACH-SIDE RESORT TOGETH-ER.
REALLY?
THE BEACH SOUNDS FUN!
OH!
WAIT, THE BEACH... ISN'T THAT WHERE LOTS OF ROWDY DRUNKS HANG OUT?
HEY, SIT ON THIS BANANA BOARD FOR A SEC.
HEY, GIRLS!
NOOO! I WANT A DOLPHIN BOARD!
EEK!
EEK!
THERE MIGHT EVEN BE PEEPERS OR PERVS...
SHOULD I GO WITH THEM!? NO, I SHOULDN'T INTRUDE ON THEIR GIRLS' DAY OUT.
BUT IT'S AN ATTENDANT'S JOB TO PROTECT HER IN EVERY WAY...THOUGH, IF WE WERE SWARMED BY PUNKS, I WOULDN'T BE ABLE TO HANDLE THEM ANYWAY...
WHAT DO I DO!?
MULLIN AND AZAZEL WILL BE COMING TOO.
BEEEEEK!

I'M HAPPY, BUT...

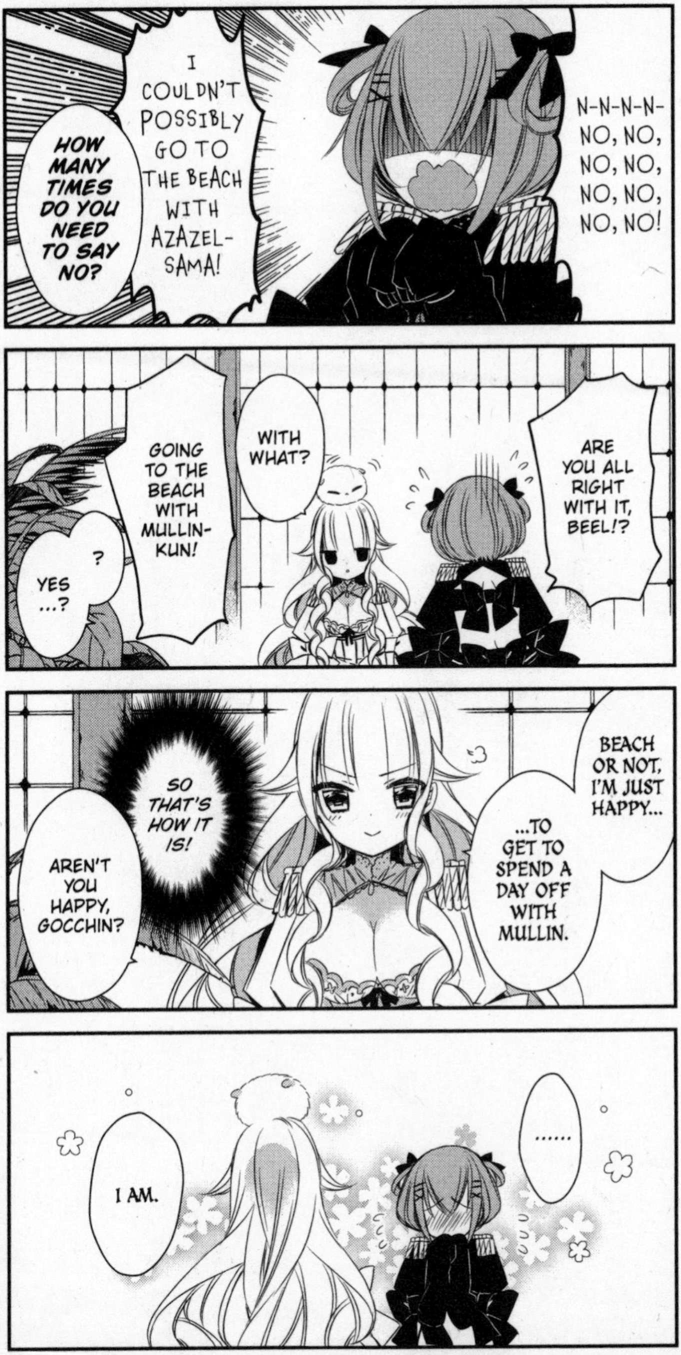
N-N-N-N-NO, NO, NO, NO, NO, NO, NO, NO!
I COULDN'T POSSIBLY GO TO THE BEACH WITH AZAZEL-SAMA!
HOW MANY TIMES DO YOU NEED TO SAY NO?
ARE YOU ALL RIGHT WITH IT, BEEL!?
WITH WHAT?
GOING TO THE BEACH WITH MULLIN-KUN!
? YES ...?
BEACH OR NOT, I'M JUST HAPPY...
...TO GET TO SPEND A DAY OFF WITH MULLIN.
SO THAT'S HOW IT IS!
AREN'T YOU HAPPY, GOCCHIN?
......
I AM.

NERVOUS ABOUT A SIX-PACK

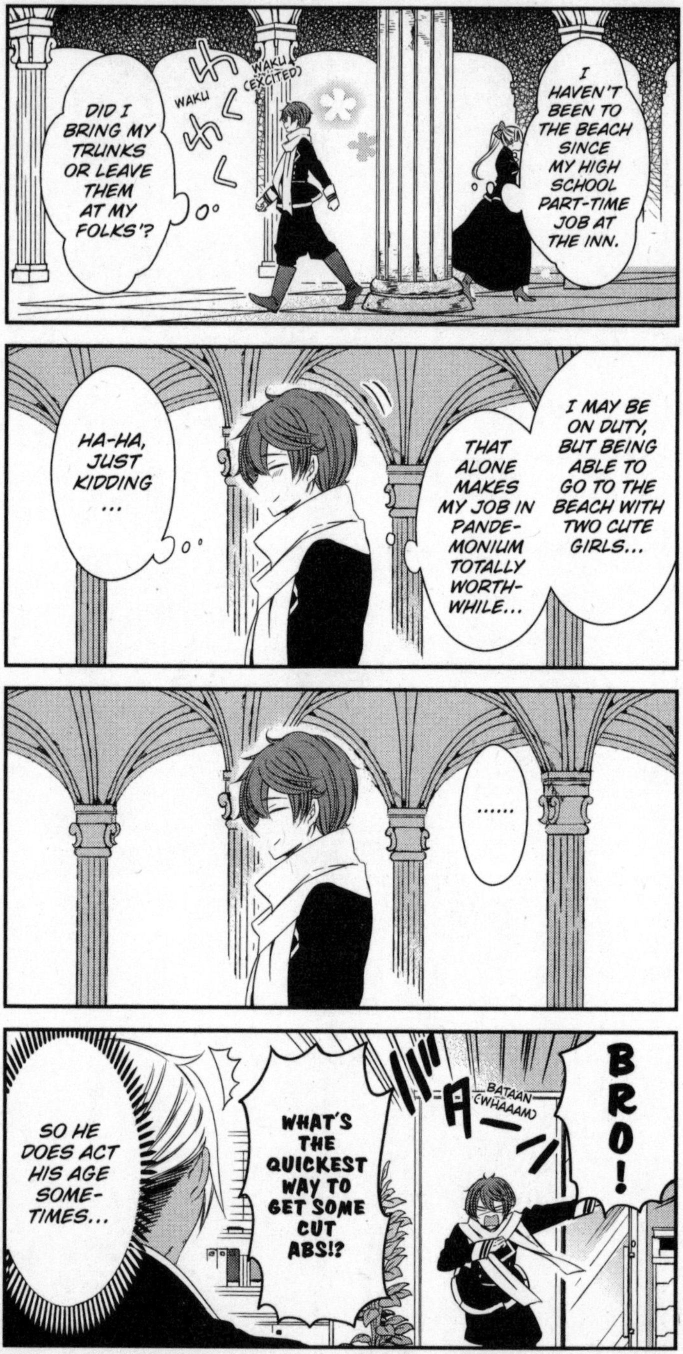
I HAVEN'T BEEN TO THE BEACH SINCE MY HIGH SCHOOL PART-TIME JOB AT THE INN.
WAKU WAKU (EXCITED)
DID I BRING MY TRUNKS OR LEAVE THEM AT MY FOLKS'?
I MAY BE ON DUTY, BUT BEING ABLE TO GO TO THE BEACH WITH TWO CUTE GIRLS...
THAT ALONE MAKES MY JOB IN PANDEMONIUM TOTALLY WORTHWHILE...
HA-HA, JUST KIDDING...
......
BRO!
BATAAN (WHAAAM)
WHAT'S THE QUICKEST WAY TO GET SOME CUT ABS!?
SO HE DOES ACT HIS AGE SOMETIMES...

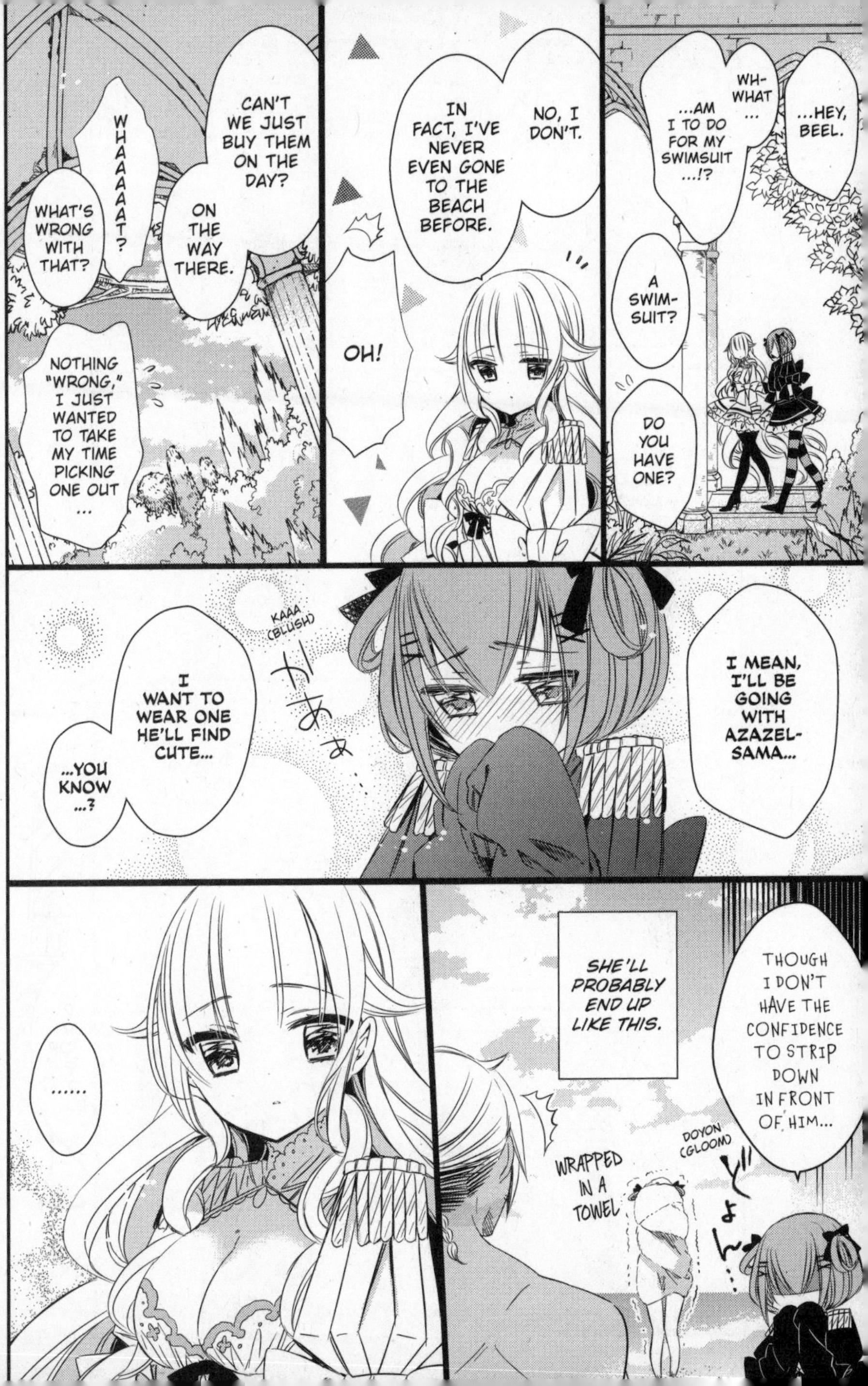
...HEY, BEEL.
WH-WHAT ... ...AM I TO DO FOR MY SWIMSUIT ...!?
A SWIM-SUIT?
DO YOU HAVE ONE?
NO, I DON'T.
IN FACT, I'VE NEVER EVEN GONE TO THE BEACH BEFORE.
OH!
CAN'T WE JUST BUY THEM ON THE DAY?
ON THE WAY THERE.
WHAAAAAAT?
WHAT'S WRONG WITH THAT?
NOTHING "WRONG," I JUST WANTED TO TAKE MY TIME PICKING ONE OUT ...
I MEAN, I'LL BE GOING WITH AZAZEL-SAMA...
KAAA (BLUSH)
I WANT TO WEAR ONE HE'LL FIND CUTE...
...YOU KNOW ...?
THOUGH I DON'T HAVE THE CONFIDENCE TO STRIP DOWN IN FRONT OF HIM...
SHE'LL PROBABLY END UP LIKE THIS.
DOYON (GLOOM)
WRAPPED IN A TOWEL
......

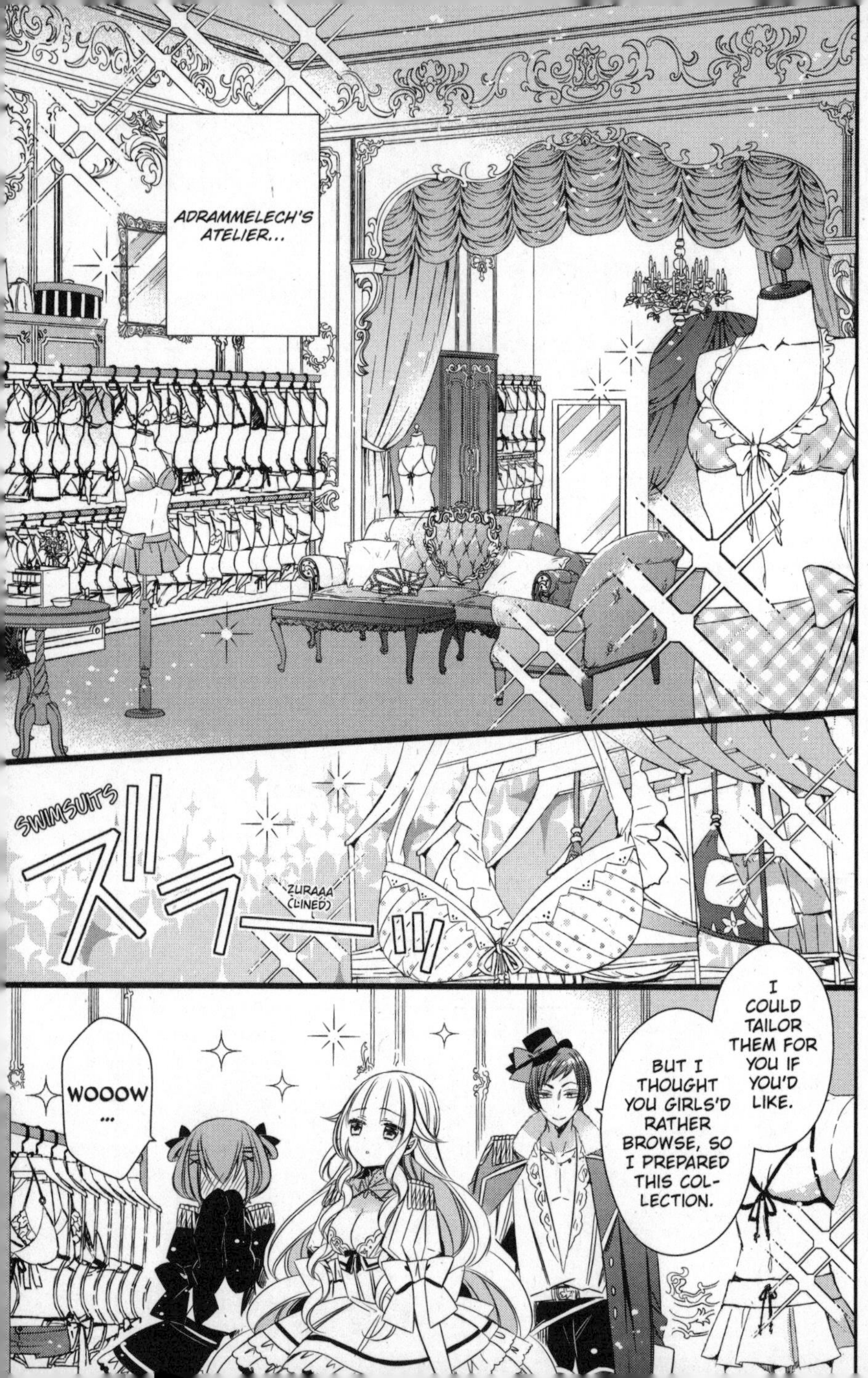
ADRAMMELECH'S ATELIER...
SWIMSUITS
ズラー
ZURAAA (LINED)
I COULD TAILOR THEM FOR YOU IF YOU'D LIKE.
BUT I THOUGHT YOU GIRLS'D RATHER BROWSE, SO I PREPARED THIS COLLECTION.
WOOOW ...

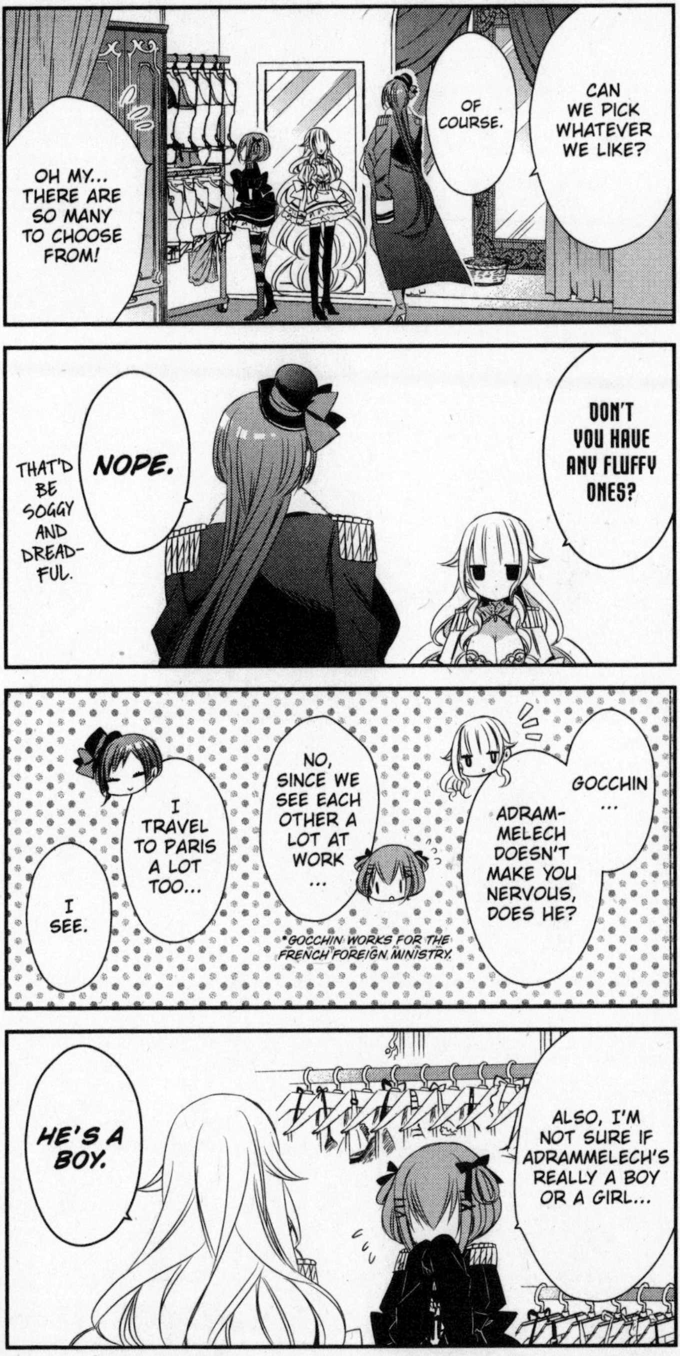
CAN WE PICK WHATEVER WE LIKE?
OF COURSE.
OH MY... THERE ARE SO MANY TO CHOOSE FROM!
DON'T YOU HAVE ANY FLUFFY ONES?
NOPE.
THAT'D BE SOGGY AND DREAD-FUL.
GOCCHIN... ADRAMMELECH DOESN'T MAKE YOU NERVOUS, DOES HE?
NO, SINCE WE SEE EACH OTHER A LOT AT WORK...
*GOCCHIN WORKS FOR THE FRENCH FOREIGN MINISTRY.
I TRAVEL TO PARIS A LOT TOO...
I SEE.
ALSO, I'M NOT SURE IF ADRAMMELECH'S REALLY A BOY OR A GIRL...
HE'S A BOY.

WHAT HEN___KAMEN WEARS

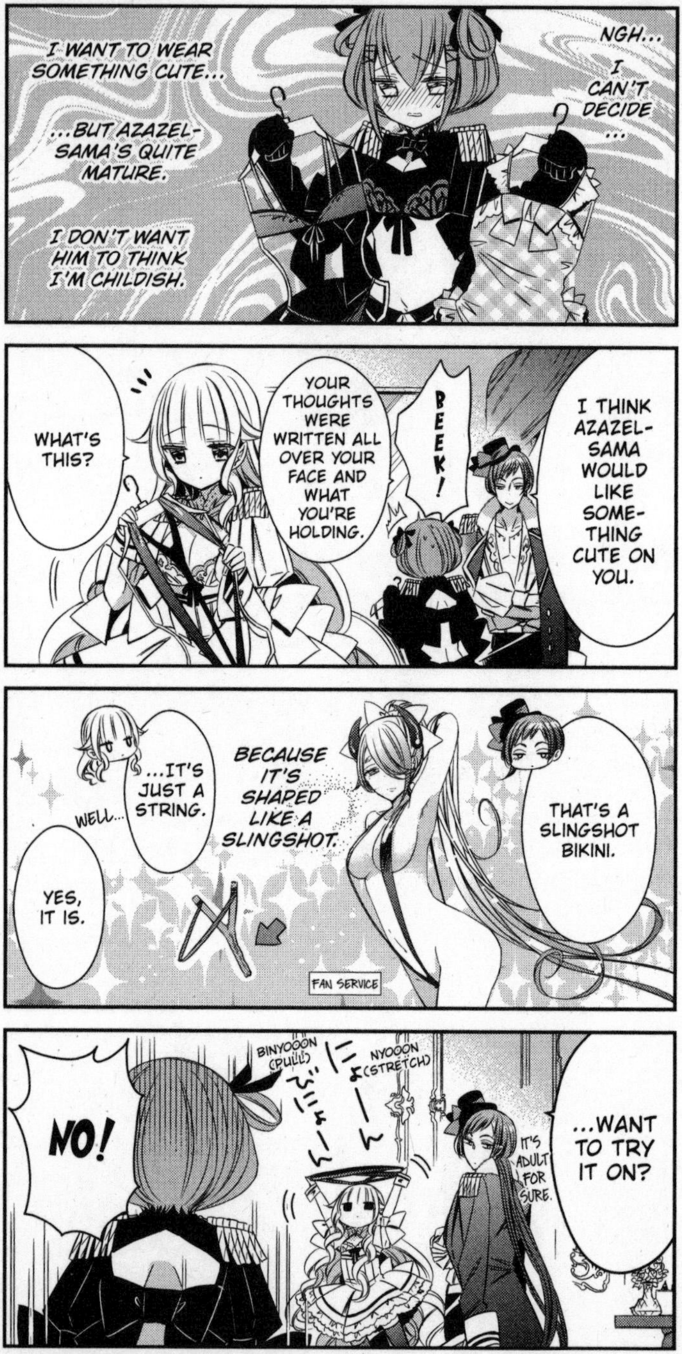
NGH... I CAN'T DECIDE...
I WANT TO WEAR SOMETHING CUTE...
...BUT AZAZEL-SAMA'S QUITE MATURE.
I DON'T WANT HIM TO THINK I'M CHILDISH.
I THINK AZAZEL-SAMA WOULD LIKE SOMETHING CUTE ON YOU.
BEEK!
YOUR THOUGHTS WERE WRITTEN ALL OVER YOUR FACE AND WHAT YOU'RE HOLDING.
WHAT'S THIS?
THAT'S A SLINGSHOT BIKINI.
BECAUSE IT'S SHAPED LIKE A SLINGSHOT.
...IT'S JUST A STRING.
WELL...
YES, IT IS.
FAN SERVICE
...WANT TO TRY IT ON?
IT'S ADULT FOR SURE.
NYOOON (STRETCH)
にょーん
BINYOOON (PULL!)
びにょーん
NO!

SOMETIMES SHE MISSES THE POINT OF EMBARRASSMENT

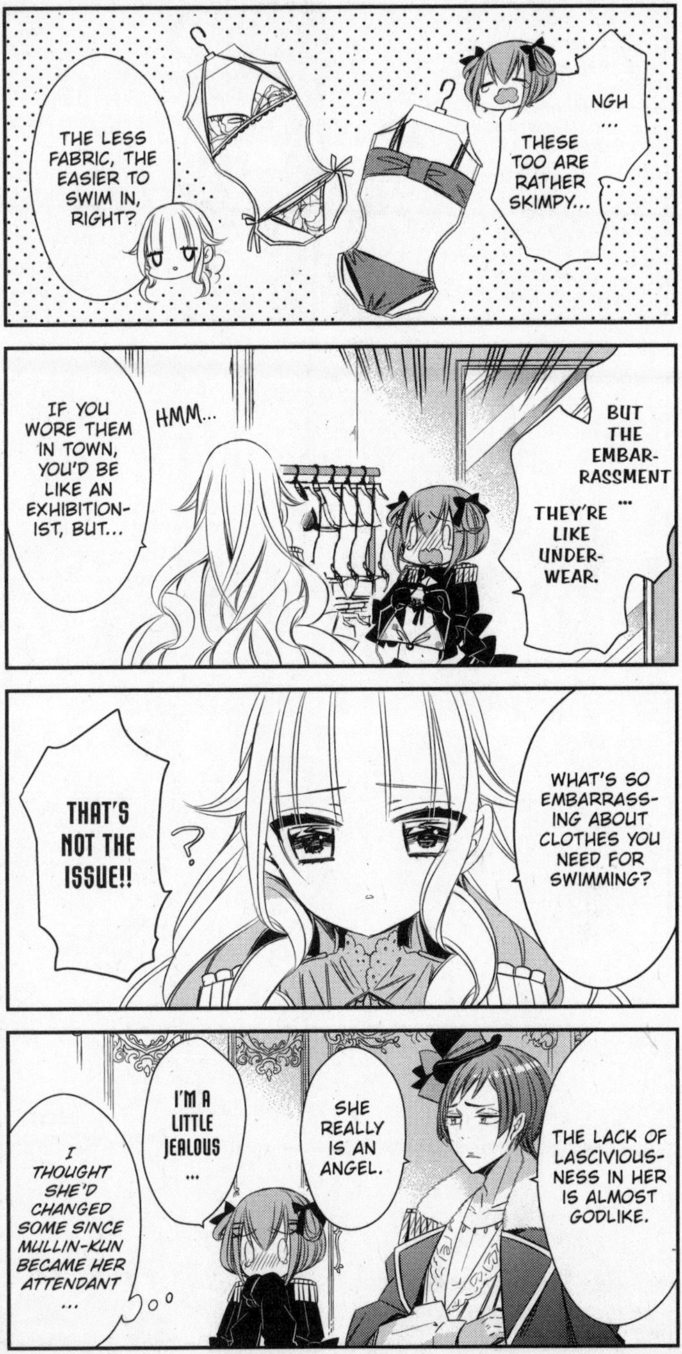

NGH...
THESE TOO ARE RATHER SKIMPY...
THE LESS FABRIC, THE EASIER TO SWIM IN, RIGHT?
BUT THE EMBARRASSMENT...
THEY'RE LIKE UNDERWEAR.
HMM...
IF YOU WORE THEM IN TOWN, YOU'D BE LIKE AN EXHIBITIONIST, BUT...
WHAT'S SO EMBARRASSING ABOUT CLOTHES YOU NEED FOR SWIMMING?
?
THAT'S NOT THE ISSUE!!
THE LACK OF LASCIVIOUSNESS IN HER IS ALMOST GODLIKE.
SHE REALLY IS AN ANGEL.
I'M A LITTLE JEALOUS...
I THOUGHT SHE'D CHANGED SOME SINCE MULLIN-KUN BECAME HER ATTENDANT...

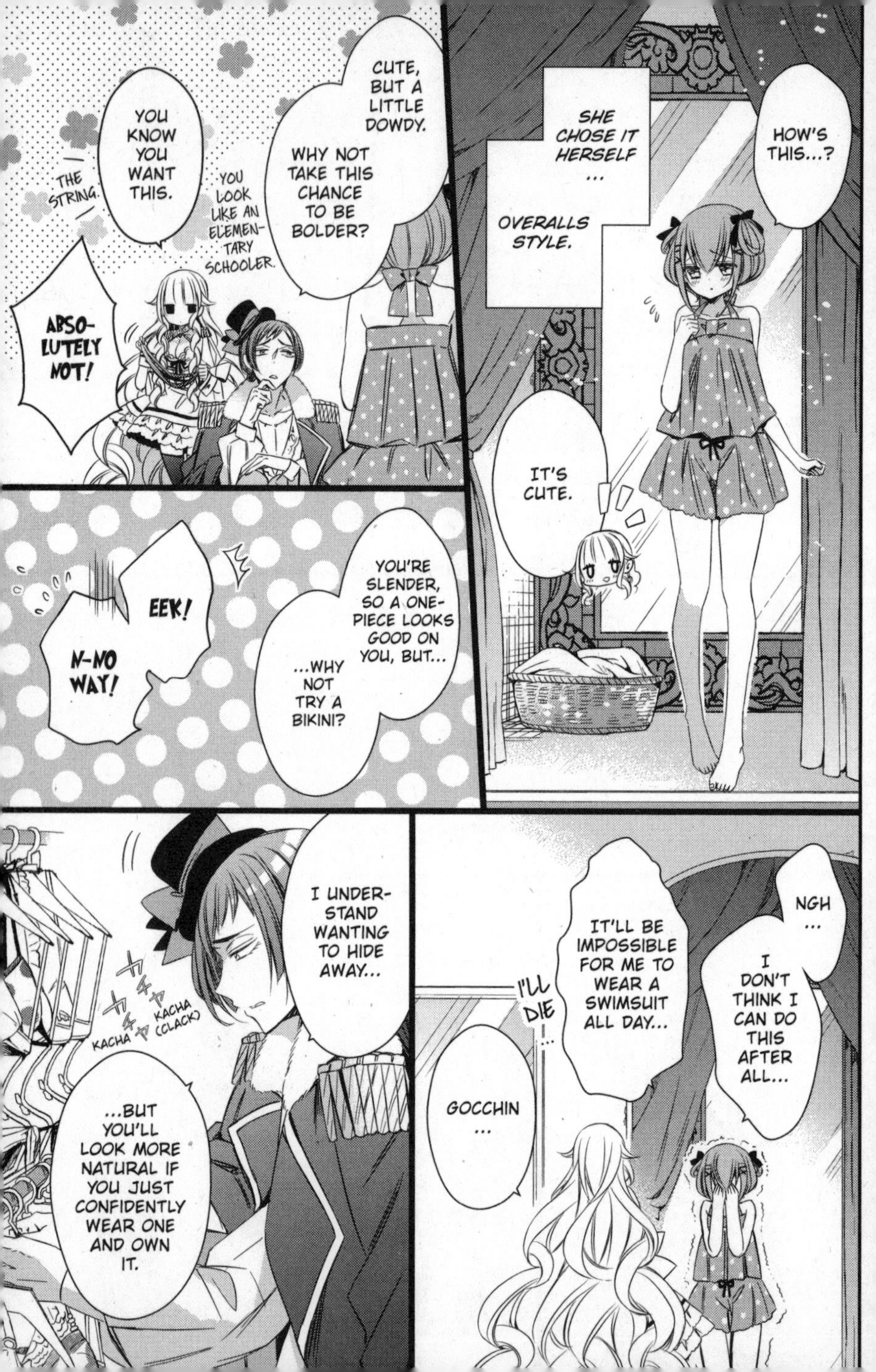
HOW'S THIS...?
SHE CHOSE IT HERSELF...
OVERALLS STYLE.
IT'S CUTE.
CUTE, BUT A LITTLE DOWDY.
WHY NOT TAKE THIS CHANCE TO BE BOLDER?
YOU LOOK LIKE AN ELEMEN-TARY SCHOOLER.
YOU KNOW YOU WANT THIS.
THE STRING.
ABSO-LUTELY NOT!
YOU'RE SLENDER, SO A ONE-PIECE LOOKS GOOD ON YOU, BUT...
...WHY NOT TRY A BIKINI?
EEK!
N-NO WAY!
NGH...
I DON'T THINK I CAN DO THIS AFTER ALL...
IT'LL BE IMPOSSIBLE FOR ME TO WEAR A SWIMSUIT ALL DAY...
I'LL DIE...
GOCCHIN...
I UNDER-STAND WANTING TO HIDE AWAY...
KACHA KACHA (CLACK)
...BUT YOU'LL LOOK MORE NATURAL IF YOU JUST CONFIDENTLY WEAR ONE AND OWN IT.

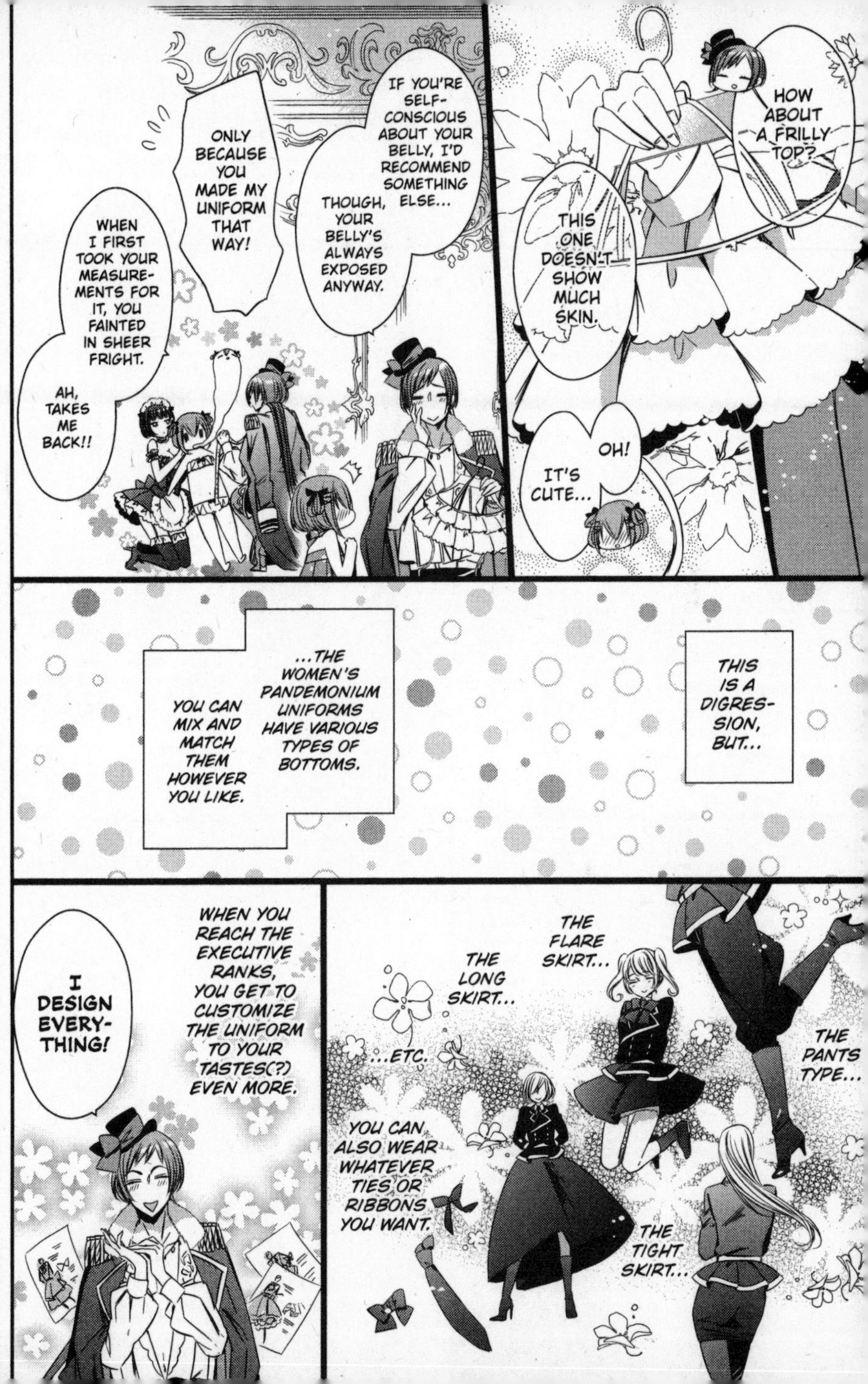
HOW ABOUT A FRILLY TOP?
THIS ONE DOESN'T SHOW MUCH SKIN.
OH!
IT'S CUTE...
IF YOU'RE SELF-CONSCIOUS ABOUT YOUR BELLY, I'D RECOMMEND SOMETHING ELSE...
THOUGH, YOUR BELLY'S ALWAYS EXPOSED ANYWAY.
ONLY BECAUSE YOU MADE MY UNIFORM THAT WAY!
WHEN I FIRST TOOK YOUR MEASUREMENTS FOR IT, YOU FAINTED IN SHEER FRIGHT.
AH, TAKES ME BACK!!
THIS IS A DIGRESSION, BUT...
...THE WOMEN'S PANDEMONIUM UNIFORMS HAVE VARIOUS TYPES OF BOTTOMS.
YOU CAN MIX AND MATCH THEM HOWEVER YOU LIKE.
THE PANTS TYPE...
THE FLARE SKIRT...
THE LONG SKIRT...
...ETC.
YOU CAN ALSO WEAR WHATEVER TIES OR RIBBONS YOU WANT.
THE TIGHT SKIRT...
WHEN YOU REACH THE EXECUTIVE RANKS, YOU GET TO CUSTOMIZE THE UNIFORM TO YOUR TASTES(?) EVEN MORE.
I DESIGN EVERYTHING!

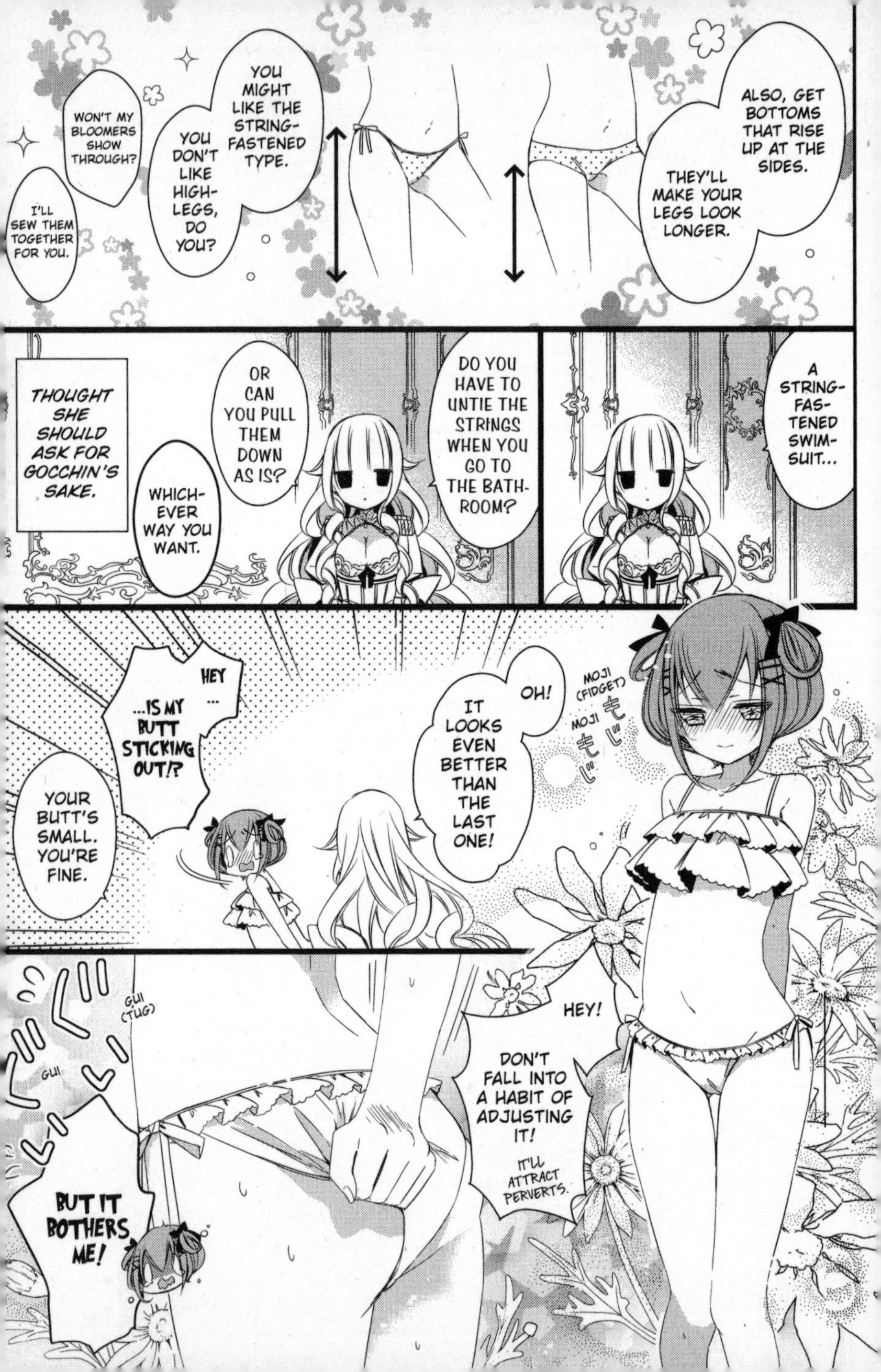
ALSO, GET BOTTOMS THAT RISE UP AT THE SIDES.
THEY'LL MAKE YOUR LEGS LOOK LONGER.
YOU MIGHT LIKE THE STRING-FASTENED TYPE.
YOU DON'T LIKE HIGH-LEGS, DO YOU?
WON'T MY BLOOMERS SHOW THROUGH?
I'LL SEW THEM TOGETHER FOR YOU.
A STRING-FASTENED SWIMSUIT...
DO YOU HAVE TO UNTIE THE STRINGS WHEN YOU GO TO THE BATHROOM?
OR CAN YOU PULL THEM DOWN AS IS?
WHICHEVER WAY YOU WANT.
THOUGHT SHE SHOULD ASK FOR GOCCHIN'S SAKE.
MOJI (FIDGET) MOJI
もじもじ
OH!
IT LOOKS EVEN BETTER THAN THE LAST ONE!
HEY... ...IS MY BUTT STICKING OUT!?
YOUR BUTT'S SMALL. YOU'RE FINE.
HEY!
DON'T FALL INTO A HABIT OF ADJUSTING IT!
IT'LL ATTRACT PERVERTS.
GUI (TUG)
GUI
BUT IT BOTHERS ME!

THE STRING THING

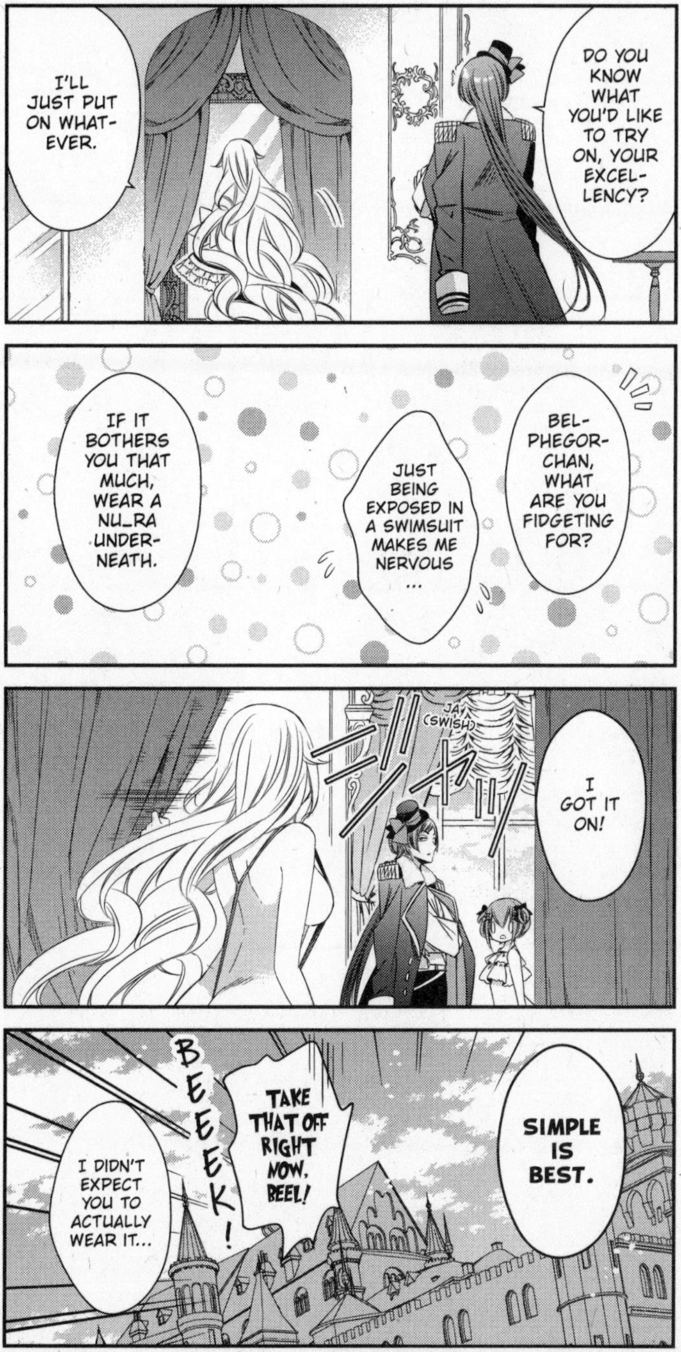
DO YOU KNOW WHAT YOU'D LIKE TO TRY ON, YOUR EXCELLENCY?
I'LL JUST PUT ON WHATEVER.
BELPHEGOR-CHAN, WHAT ARE YOU FIDGETING FOR?
JUST BEING EXPOSED IN A SWIMSUIT MAKES ME NERVOUS...
IF IT BOTHERS YOU THAT MUCH, WEAR A NU_RA UNDERNEATH.
JA (SWISH)
I GOT IT ON!
SIMPLE IS BEST.
TAKE THAT OFF RIGHT NOW, BEEL!
BEEEEK!
I DIDN'T EXPECT YOU TO ACTUALLY WEAR IT...

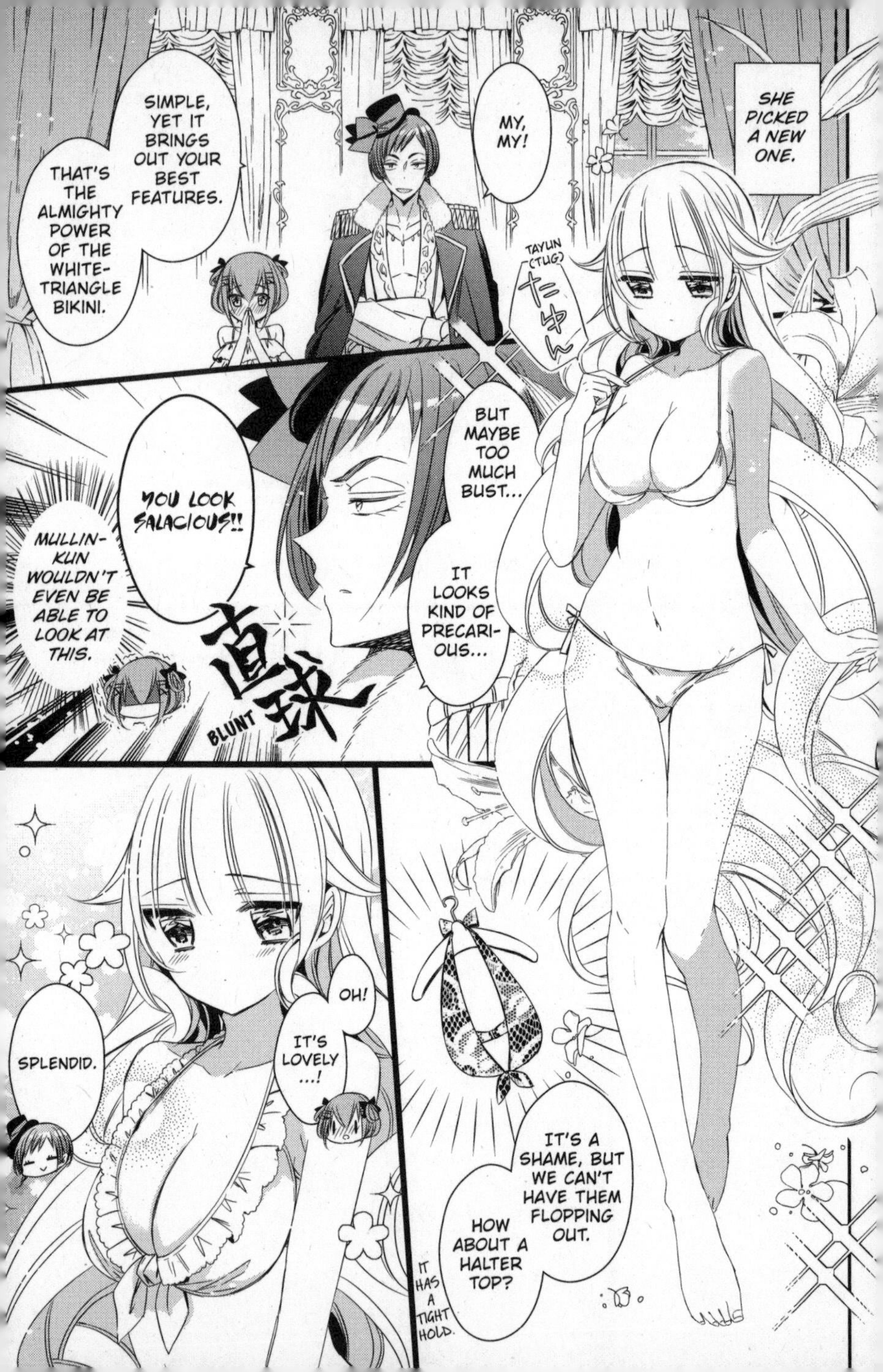
SHE PICKED A NEW ONE.
TAYUN (TUG)
たゆん
MY, MY!
SIMPLE, YET IT BRINGS OUT YOUR BEST FEATURES.
THAT'S THE ALMIGHTY POWER OF THE WHITE-TRIANGLE BIKINI.
BUT MAYBE TOO MUCH BUST...
IT LOOKS KIND OF PRECARIOUS...
YOU LOOK SALACIOUS!!
直球
BLUNT
MULLIN-KUN WOULDN'T EVEN BE ABLE TO LOOK AT THIS.
IT'S A SHAME, BUT WE CAN'T HAVE THEM FLOPPING OUT.
HOW ABOUT A HALTER TOP?
IT HAS A TIGHT HOLD.
OH!
IT'S LOVELY...!
SPLENDID.

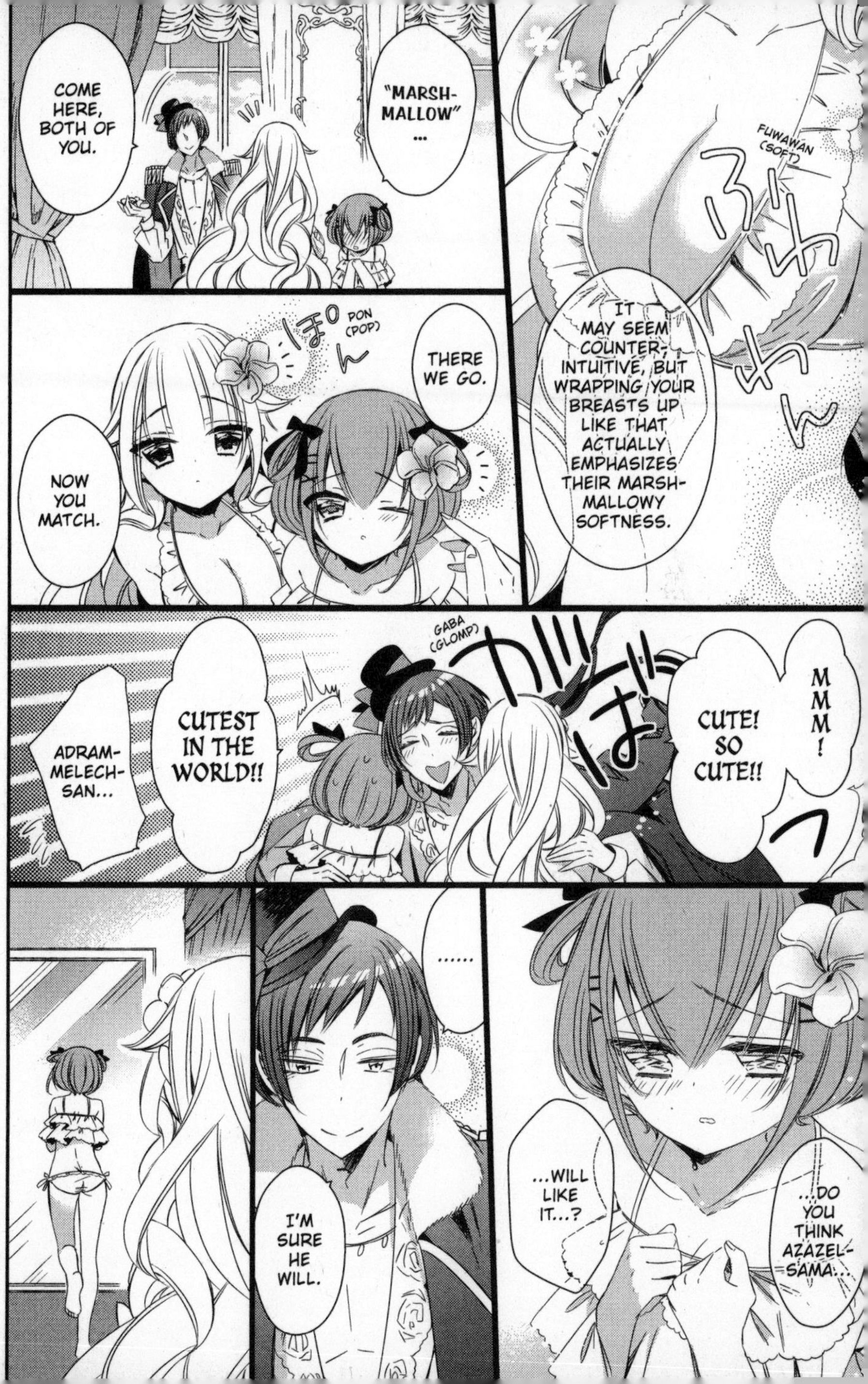
FUWAWAN (SOFT)
IT MAY SEEM COUNTER-INTUITIVE, BUT WRAPPING YOUR BREASTS UP LIKE THAT ACTUALLY EMPHASIZES THEIR MARSH-MALLOWY SOFTNESS.
"MARSH-MALLOW" ...
COME HERE, BOTH OF YOU.
PON (POP)
THERE WE GO.
NOW YOU MATCH.
MMM!
CUTE! SO CUTE!!
GABA (GLOMP)
CUTEST IN THE WORLD!!
ADRAM-MELECH-SAN...
...DO YOU THINK AZAZEL-SAMA...
...WILL LIKE IT...?
......
I'M SURE HE WILL.

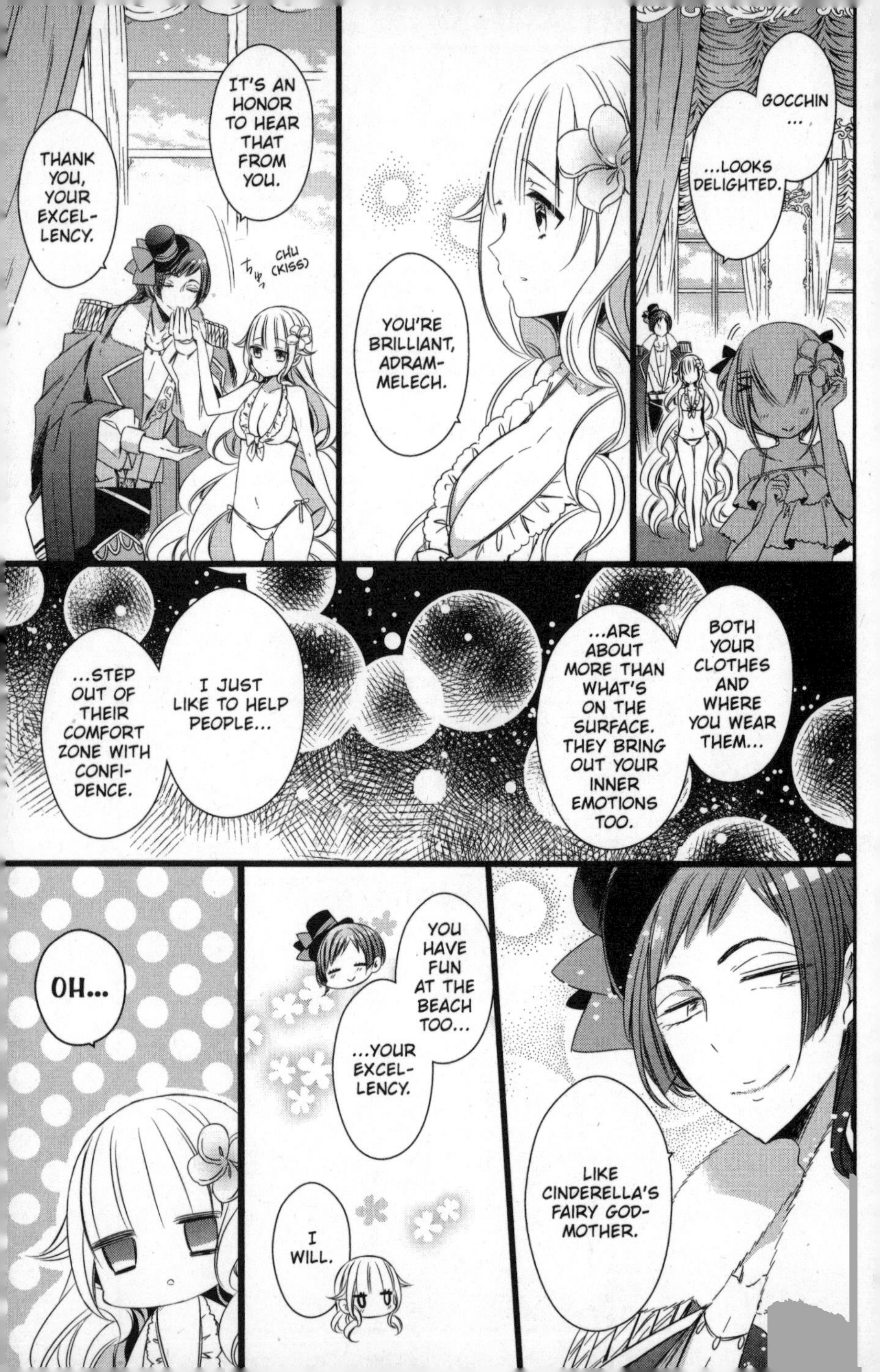
GOCCHIN...
...LOOKS DELIGHTED.
YOU'RE BRILLIANT, ADRAM-MELECH.
IT'S AN HONOR TO HEAR THAT FROM YOU.
THANK YOU, YOUR EXCEL-LENCY.
ちゅっ
CHU (KISS)
BOTH YOUR CLOTHES AND WHERE YOU WEAR THEM...
...ARE ABOUT MORE THAN WHAT'S ON THE SURFACE. THEY BRING OUT YOUR INNER EMOTIONS TOO.
I JUST LIKE TO HELP PEOPLE...
...STEP OUT OF THEIR COMFORT ZONE WITH CONFI-DENCE.
LIKE CINDERELLA'S FAIRY GOD-MOTHER.
YOU HAVE FUN AT THE BEACH TOO...
...YOUR EXCEL-LENCY.
I WILL.
OH...

SWIMSUITS LOOK MUCH MORE INDECENT INDOORS

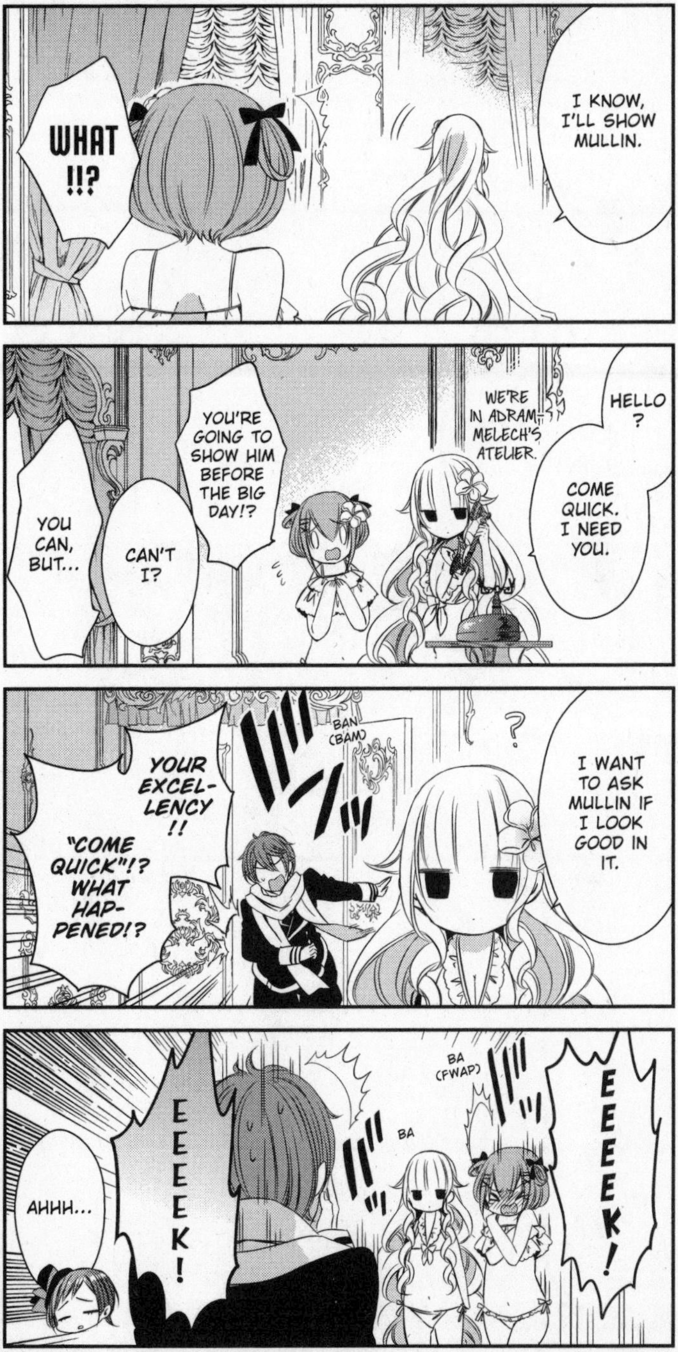
I KNOW, I'LL SHOW MULLIN.
WHAT!!?
HELLO?
COME QUICK. I NEED YOU.
WE'RE IN ADRAM-MELECH'S ATELIER.
YOU'RE GOING TO SHOW HIM BEFORE THE BIG DAY!?
CAN'T I?
YOU CAN, BUT...
I WANT TO ASK MULLIN IF I LOOK GOOD IN IT.
?
BAN (BAM)
YOUR EXCEL-LENCY!!
"COME QUICK"!? WHAT HAP-PENED!?
EEEEK!
BA (FWAP)
BA
EEEEK!
AHHH...

EYES ON ME

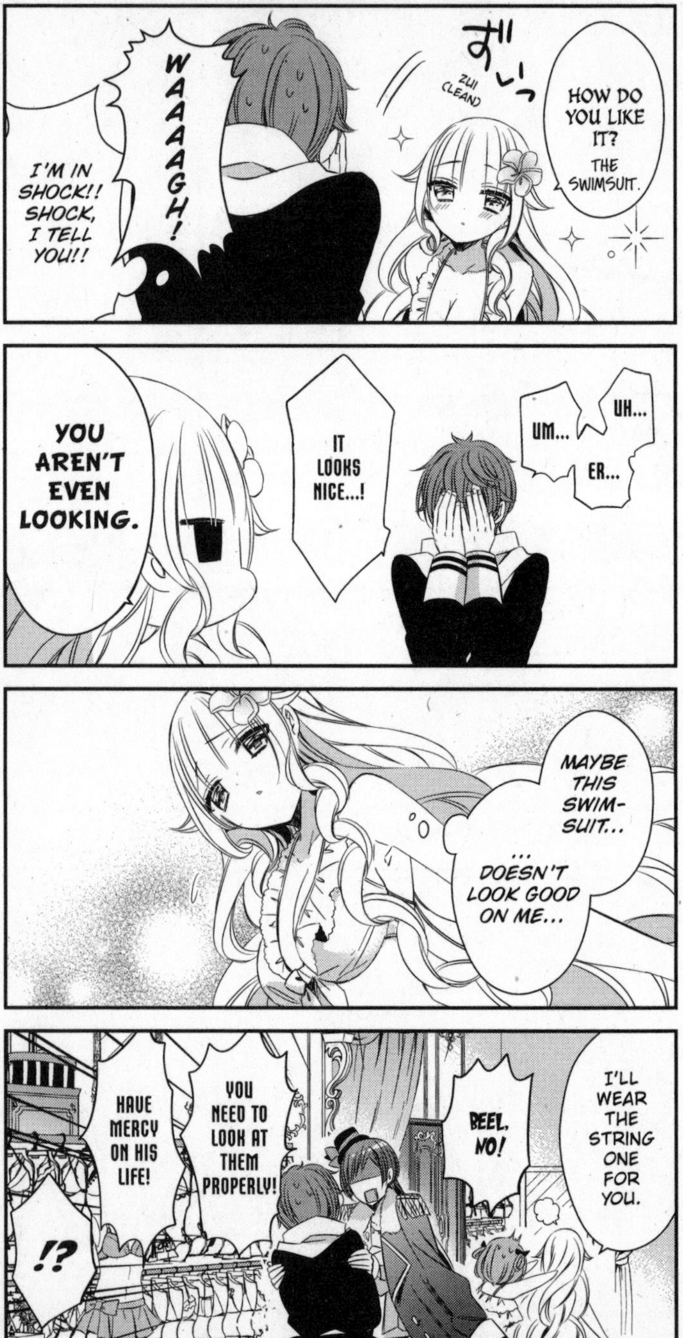
HOW DO YOU LIKE IT? THE SWIMSUIT.
ずいっ
ZUI (LEAN)
WAAAAAGH!
I'M IN SHOCK!! SHOCK, I TELL YOU!!
UH... UM... ER...
IT LOOKS NICE...!
YOU AREN'T EVEN LOOKING.
MAYBE THIS SWIM-SUIT...
...DOESN'T LOOK GOOD ON ME...
I'LL WEAR THE STRING ONE FOR YOU.
BEEL, NO!
YOU NEED TO LOOK AT THEM PROPERLY!
HAVE MERCY ON HIS LIFE!
!?

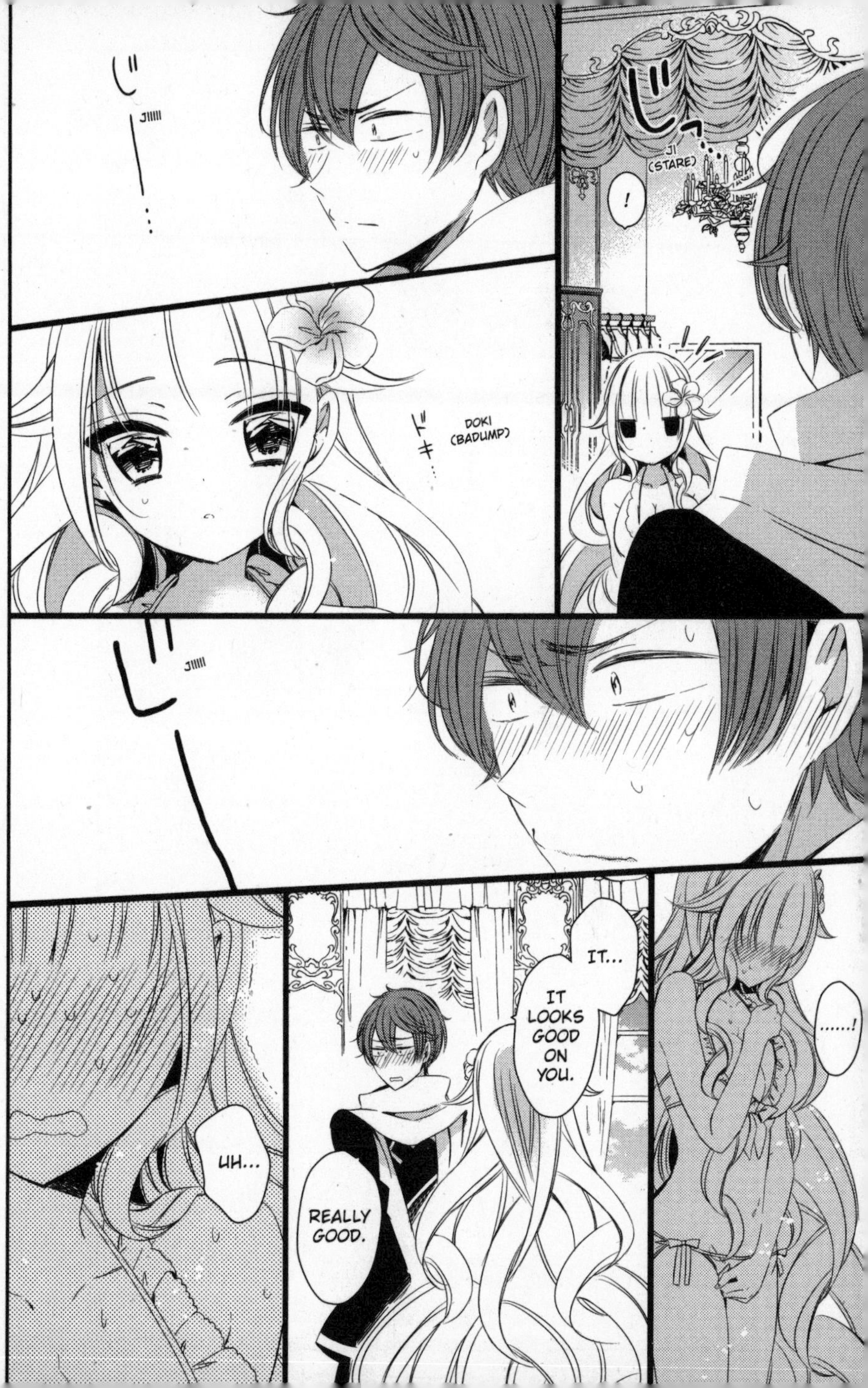
じっ…
JI (STARE)
!
じーー…
JIIIII
ドキ…
DOKI (BADUMP)
じーー
JIIIII
......!
IT...
IT LOOKS GOOD ON YOU.
REALLY GOOD.
UH...

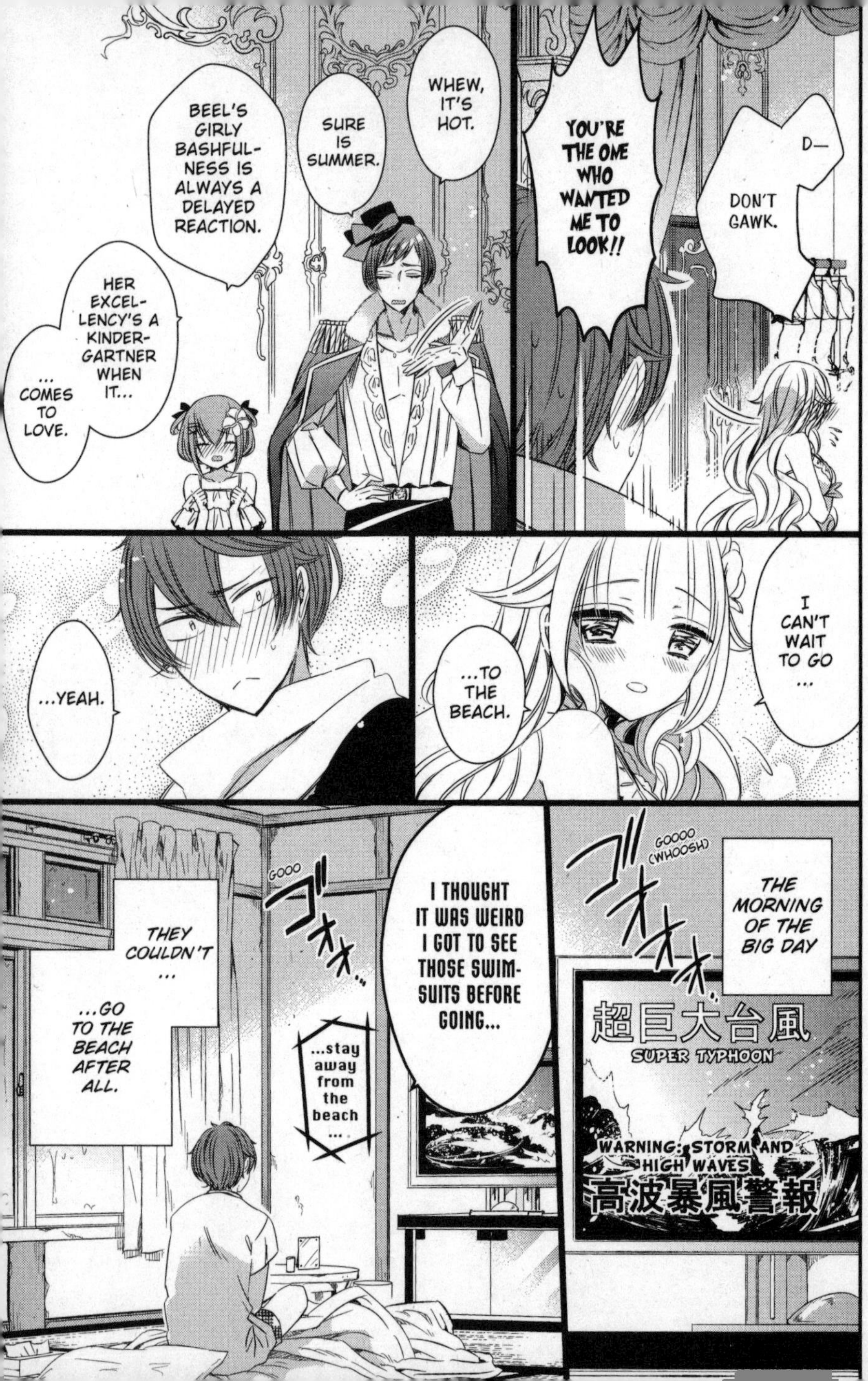
D— DON'T GAWK.
YOU'RE THE ONE WHO WANTED ME TO LOOK!!
WHEW, IT'S HOT.
SURE IS SUMMER.
BEEL'S GIRLY BASHFUL-NESS IS ALWAYS A DELAYED REACTION.
HER EXCEL-LENCY'S A KINDER-GARTNER WHEN IT...
...COMES TO LOVE.
I CAN'T WAIT TO GO...
...TO THE BEACH.
...YEAH.
THE MORNING OF THE BIG DAY
GOOOO (WHOOSH)
超巨大台風
SUPER TYPHOON
WARNING: STORM AND HIGH WAVES
高波暴風警報
I THOUGHT IT WAS WEIRD I GOT TO SEE THOSE SWIM-SUITS BEFORE GOING...
GOOO
...stay away from the beach...
THEY COULDN'T...
...GO TO THE BEACH AFTER ALL.

As Miss Beelzebub Likes

IMPACT

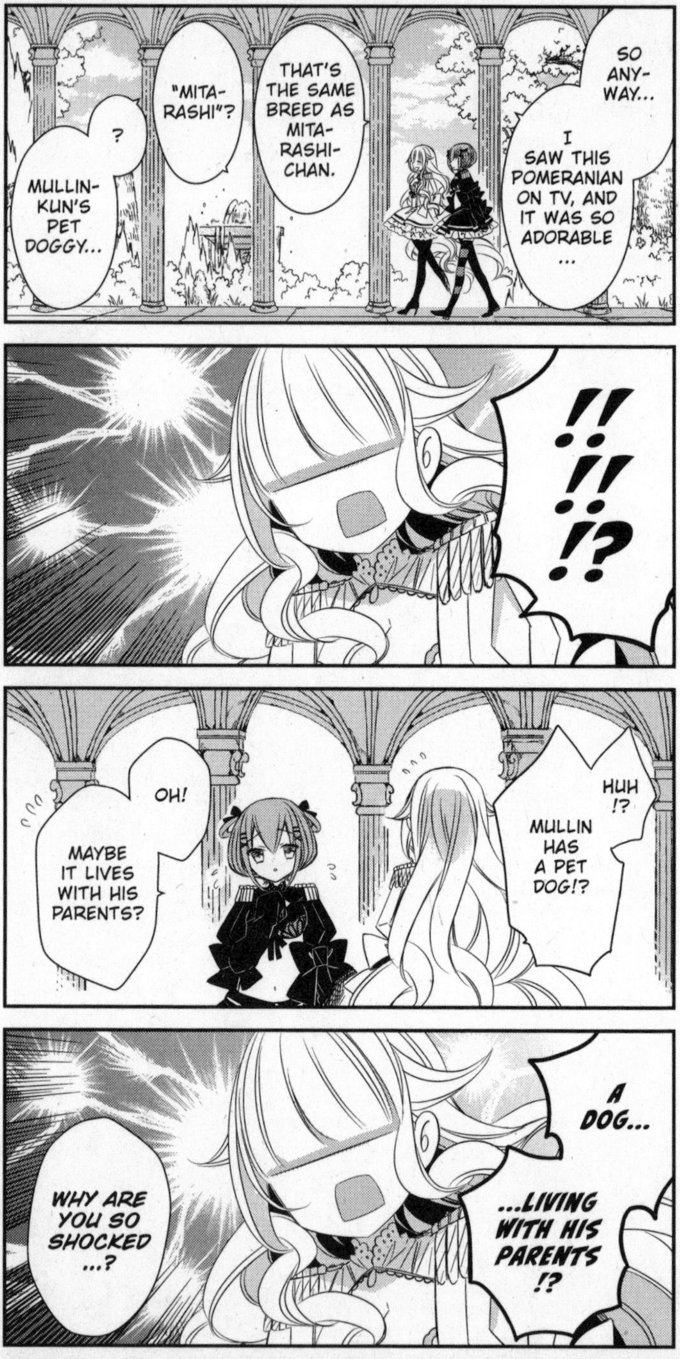
SO ANYWAY...
I SAW THIS POMERANIAN ON TV, AND IT WAS SO ADORABLE ...
THAT'S THE SAME BREED AS MITA-RASHI-CHAN.
"MITA-RASHI"?
?
MULLIN-KUN'S PET DOGGY...
!!!!!!?
HUH!?
MULLIN HAS A PET DOG!?
OH!
MAYBE IT LIVES WITH HIS PARENTS?
A DOG...
...LIVING WITH HIS PARENTS!?
WHY ARE YOU SO SHOCKED...?

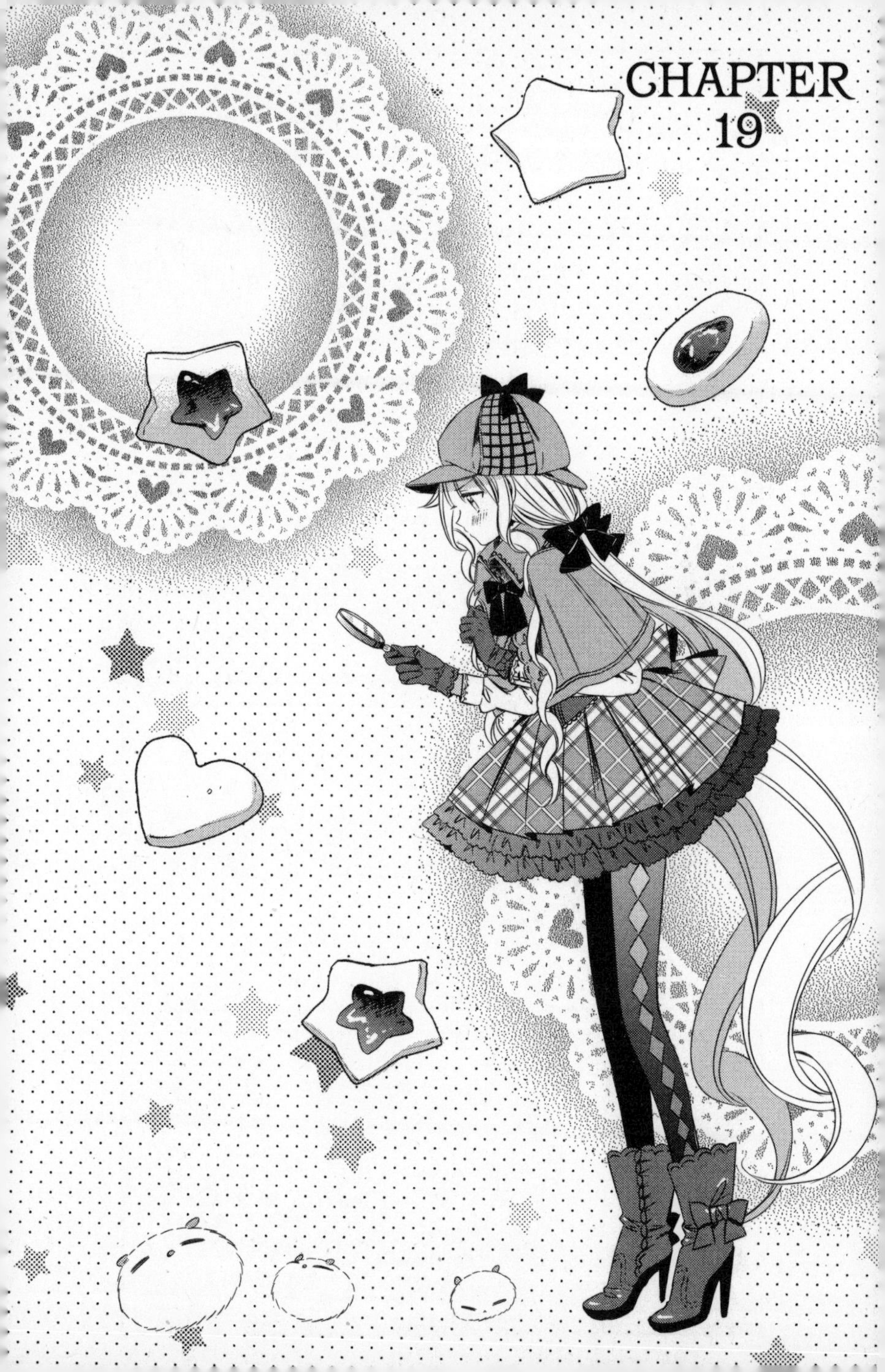
CHAPTER
19

THE TOO-CONSIDERATE BOSS

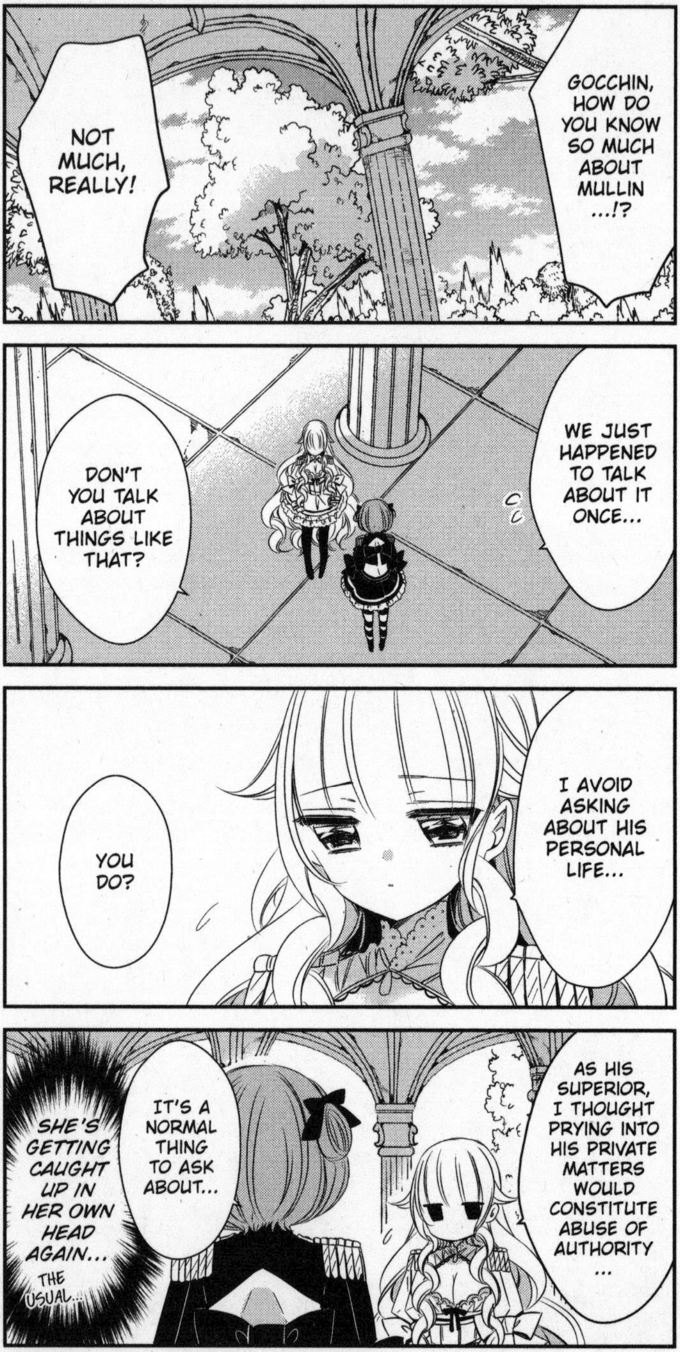
GOCCHIN, HOW DO YOU KNOW SO MUCH ABOUT MULLIN ...!?
NOT MUCH, REALLY!
WE JUST HAPPENED TO TALK ABOUT IT ONCE...
DON'T YOU TALK ABOUT THINGS LIKE THAT?
I AVOID ASKING ABOUT HIS PERSONAL LIFE...
YOU DO?
AS HIS SUPERIOR, I THOUGHT PRYING INTO HIS PRIVATE MATTERS WOULD CONSTITUTE ABUSE OF AUTHORITY ...
IT'S A NORMAL THING TO ASK ABOUT...
SHE'S GETTING CAUGHT UP IN HER OWN HEAD AGAIN...
THE USUAL...

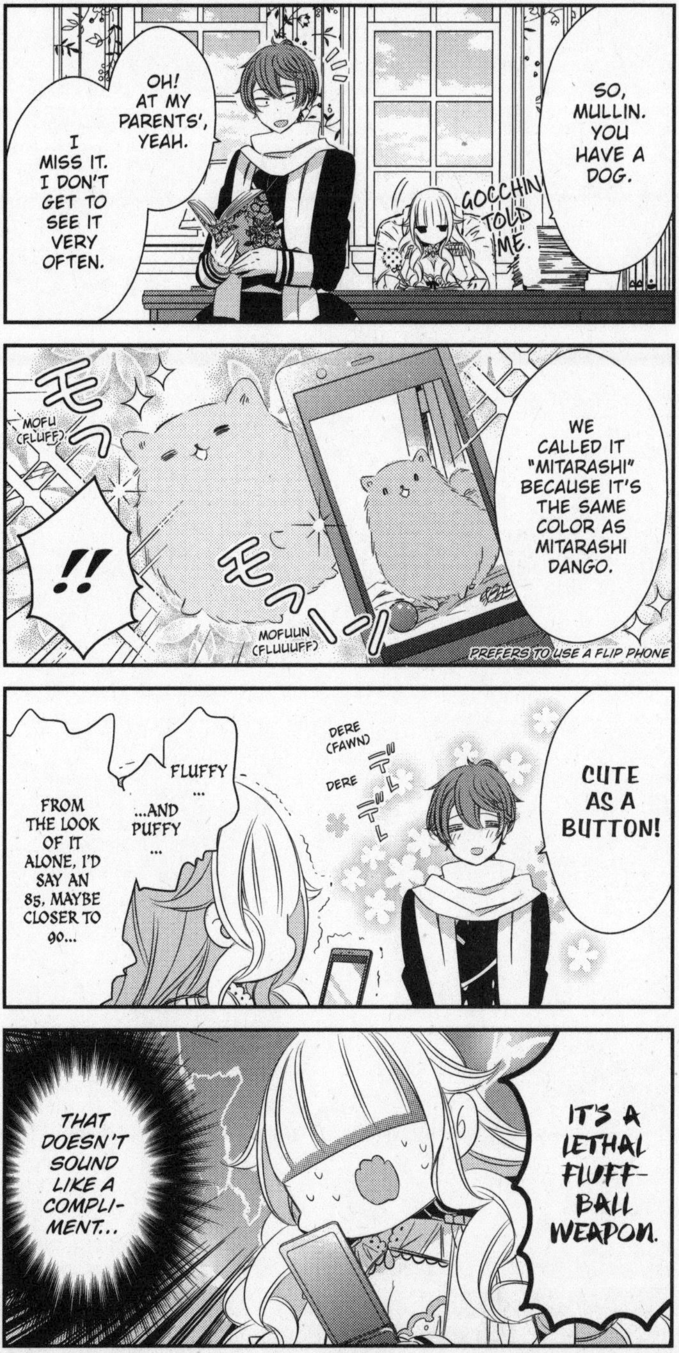
SO, MULLIN. YOU HAVE A DOG.
GOCCHIN TOLD ME.
OH! AT MY PARENTS', YEAH.
I MISS IT. I DON'T GET TO SEE IT VERY OFTEN.
WE CALLED IT "MITARASHI" BECAUSE IT'S THE SAME COLOR AS MITARASHI DANGO.
PREFERS TO USE A FLIP PHONE
MOFUUN (FLUUUFF)
!!
MOFU (FLUFF)
CUTE AS A BUTTON!
DERE (FAWN) DERE
FLUFFY ...
...AND PUFFY ...
FROM THE LOOK OF IT ALONE, I'D SAY AN 85, MAYBE CLOSER TO 90...
IT'S A LETHAL FLUFF-BALL WEAPON.
THAT DOESN'T SOUND LIKE A COMPLIMENT...

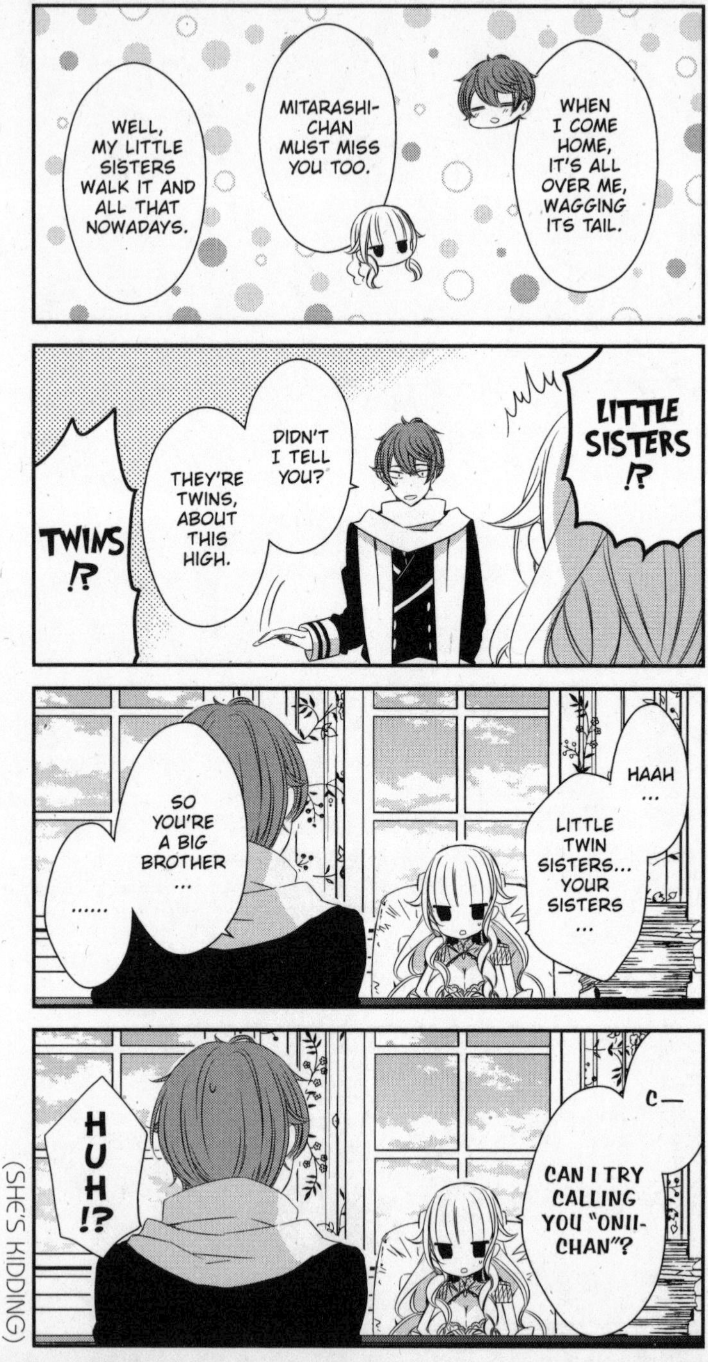
WHEN I COME HOME, IT'S ALL OVER ME, WAGGING ITS TAIL.
MITARASHI-CHAN MUST MISS YOU TOO.
WELL, MY LITTLE SISTERS WALK IT AND ALL THAT NOWADAYS.
LITTLE SISTERS!?
DIDN'T I TELL YOU?
THEY'RE TWINS, ABOUT THIS HIGH.
TWINS!?
HAAH... LITTLE TWIN SISTERS... YOUR SISTERS...
SO YOU'RE A BIG BROTHER...
......
C—
CAN I TRY CALLING YOU "ONII-CHAN"?
HUH!?
(SHE'S KIDDING)

A NATURAL PLACE TO LAY ONE'S HEAD

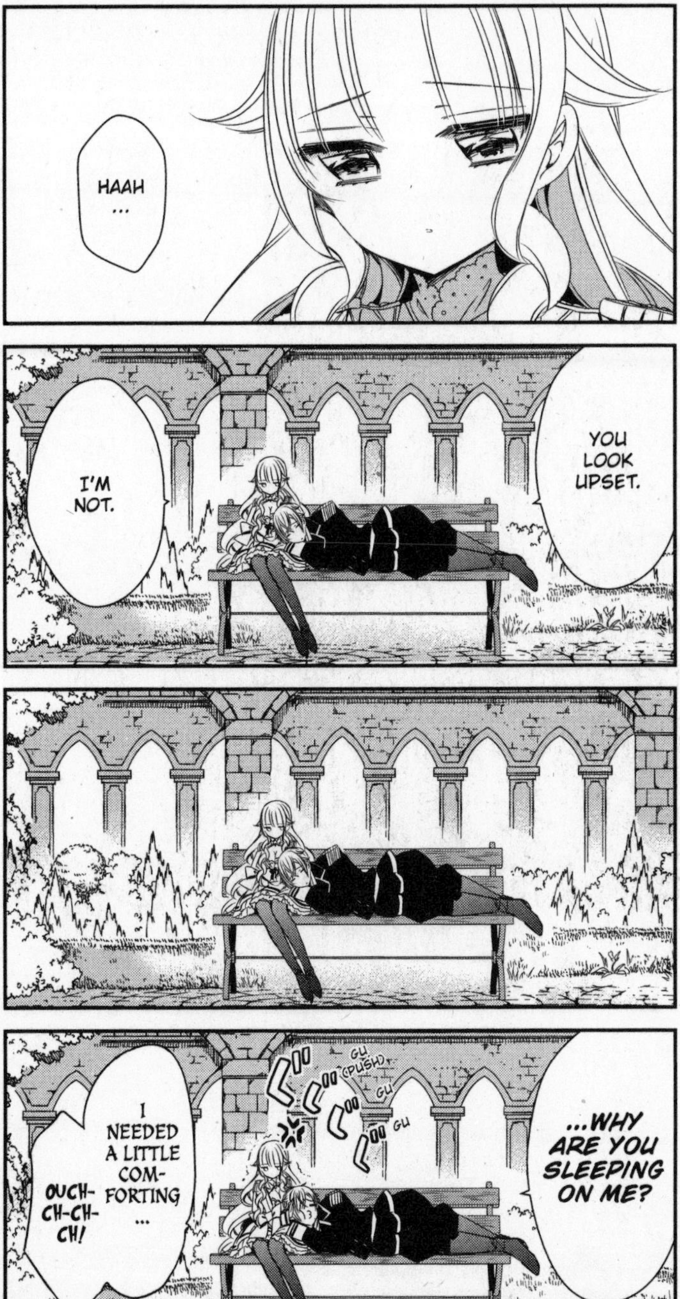
HAAH ...
YOU LOOK UPSET.
I'M NOT.
...WHY ARE YOU SLEEPING ON ME?
GU (PUSH)
GU
GU
I NEEDED A LITTLE COM-FORTING ...
OUCH-CH-CH-CH!

NO INTEREST AT ALL

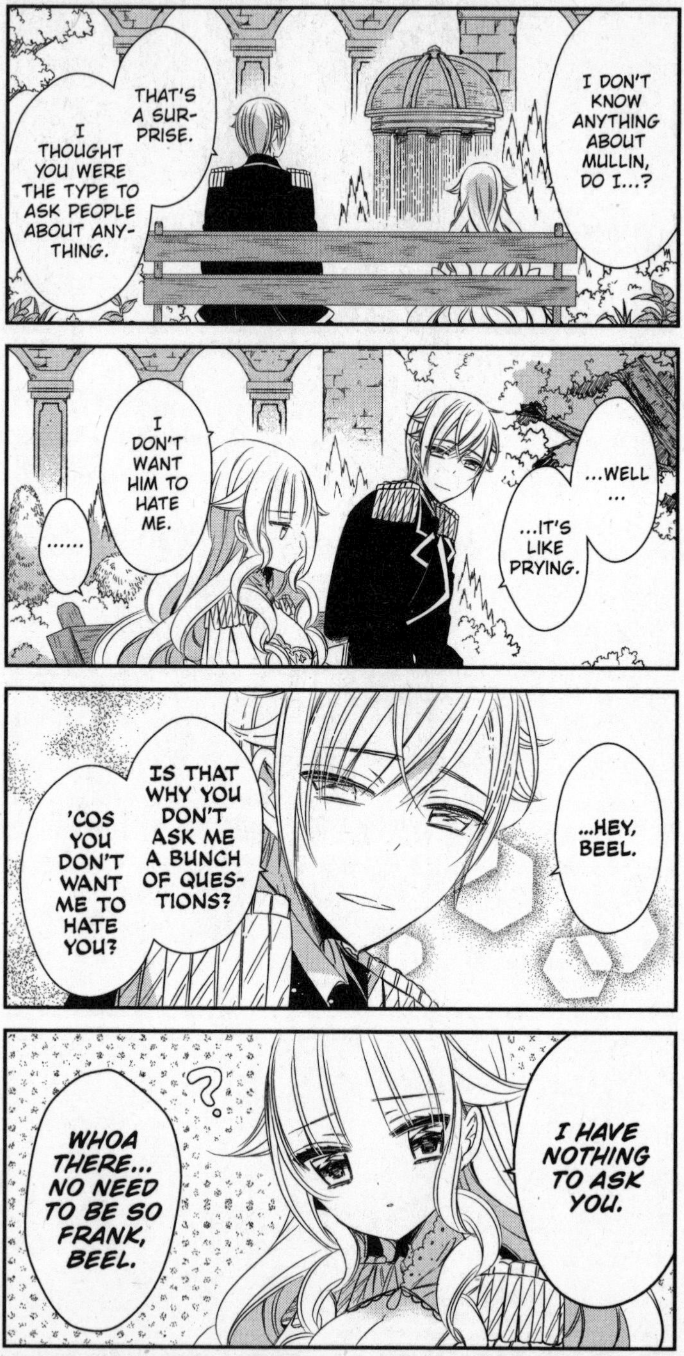

I DON'T KNOW ANYTHING ABOUT MULLIN, DO I...?
THAT'S A SURPRISE.
I THOUGHT YOU WERE THE TYPE TO ASK PEOPLE ABOUT ANYTHING.
...WELL ...
...IT'S LIKE PRYING.
I DON'T WANT HIM TO HATE ME.
......
...HEY, BEEL.
IS THAT WHY YOU DON'T ASK ME A BUNCH OF QUESTIONS?
'COS YOU DON'T WANT ME TO HATE YOU?
I HAVE NOTHING TO ASK YOU.
?
WHOA THERE... NO NEED TO BE SO FRANK, BEEL.

GIRLS DON'T BREAK IT TO YOU GENTLY

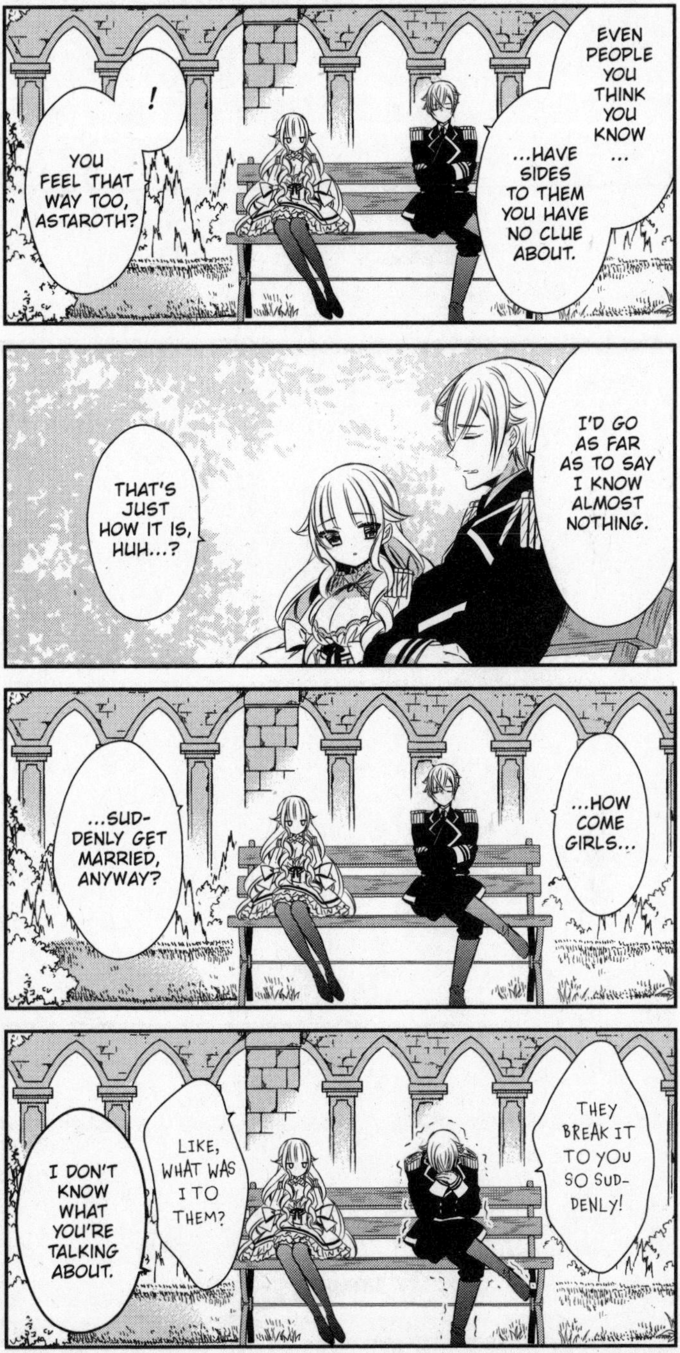
EVEN PEOPLE YOU THINK YOU KNOW...
...HAVE SIDES TO THEM YOU HAVE NO CLUE ABOUT.
!
YOU FEEL THAT WAY TOO, ASTAROTH?
I'D GO AS FAR AS TO SAY I KNOW ALMOST NOTHING.
THAT'S JUST HOW IT IS, HUH...?
...HOW COME GIRLS...
...SUD-DENLY GET MARRIED, ANYWAY?
THEY BREAK IT TO YOU SO SUD-DENLY!
LIKE, WHAT WAS I TO THEM?
I DON'T KNOW WHAT YOU'RE TALKING ABOUT.

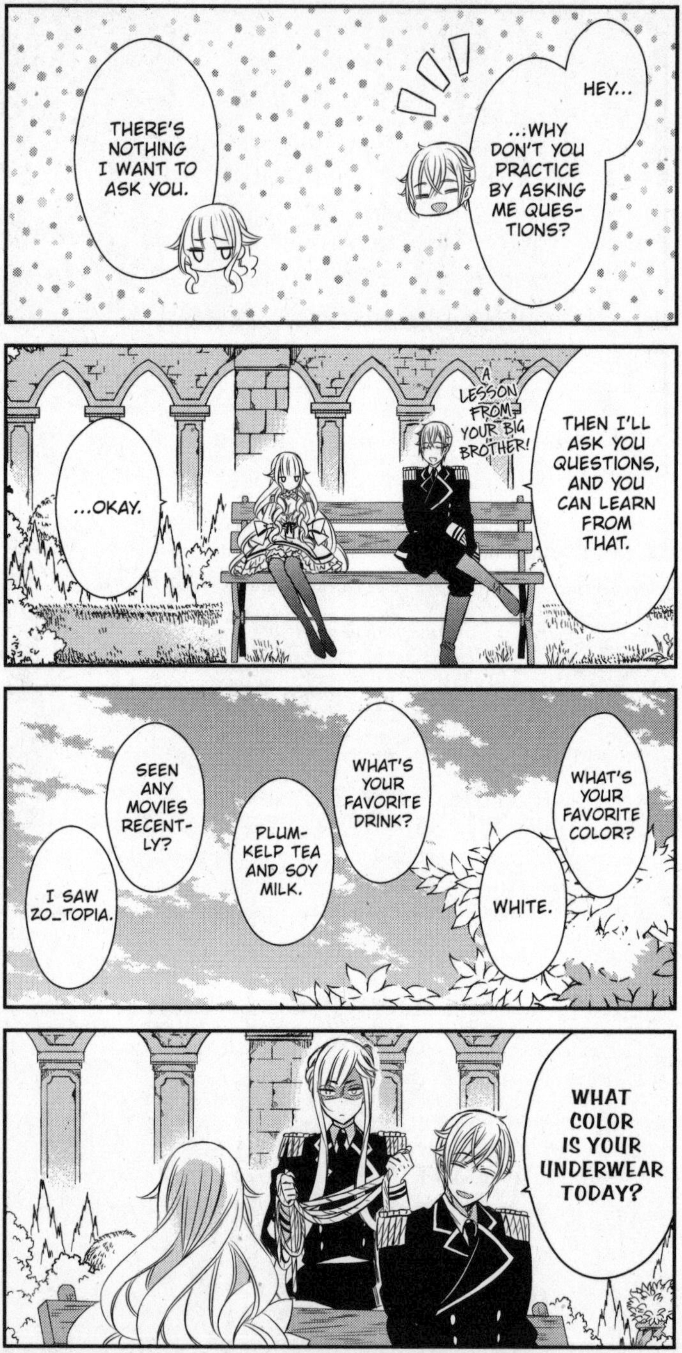
HEY... ...WHY DON'T YOU PRACTICE BY ASKING ME QUES-TIONS?
THERE'S NOTHING I WANT TO ASK YOU.
THEN I'LL ASK YOU QUESTIONS, AND YOU CAN LEARN FROM THAT.
A LESSON FROM YOUR BIG BROTHER!
...OKAY.
WHAT'S YOUR FAVORITE COLOR?
WHITE.
WHAT'S YOUR FAVORITE DRINK?
PLUM-KELP TEA AND SOY MILK.
SEEN ANY MOVIES RECENT-LY?
I SAW ZO_TOPIA.
WHAT COLOR IS YOUR UNDERWEAR TODAY?

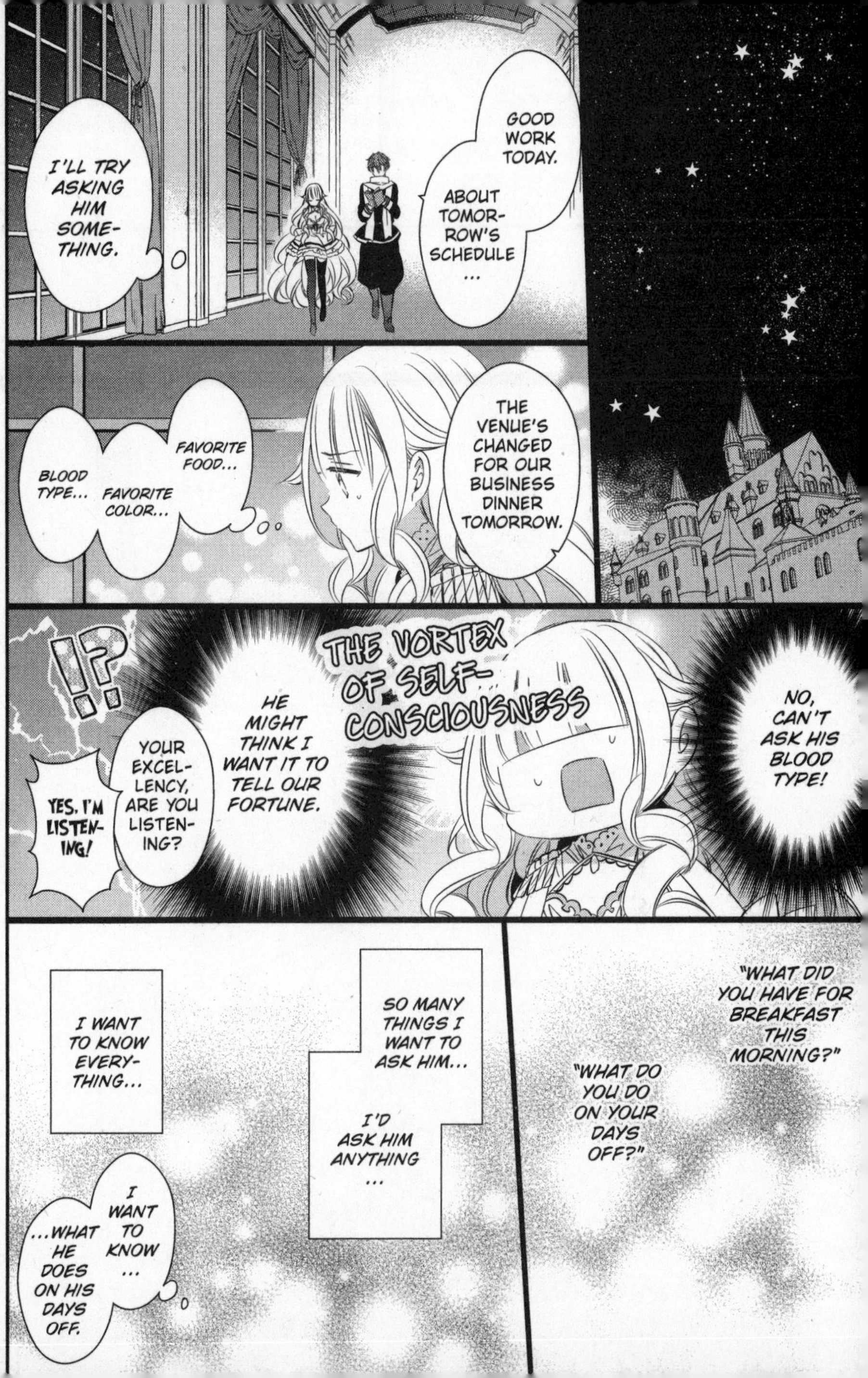
GOOD WORK TODAY.
ABOUT TOMORROW'S SCHEDULE...
I'LL TRY ASKING HIM SOMETHING.
THE VENUE'S CHANGED FOR OUR BUSINESS DINNER TOMORROW.
FAVORITE FOOD...
FAVORITE COLOR...
BLOOD TYPE...
NO, CAN'T ASK HIS BLOOD TYPE!
THE VORTEX OF SELF-CONSCIOUSNESS
HE MIGHT THINK I WANT IT TO TELL OUR FORTUNE.
YOUR EXCELLENCY, ARE YOU LISTENING?
!?
YES. I'M LISTENING!
"WHAT DID YOU HAVE FOR BREAKFAST THIS MORNING?"
"WHAT DO YOU DO ON YOUR DAYS OFF?"
SO MANY THINGS I WANT TO ASK HIM...
I WANT TO KNOW EVERYTHING...
I'D ASK HIM ANYTHING...
I WANT TO KNOW...
...WHAT HE DOES ON HIS DAYS OFF.

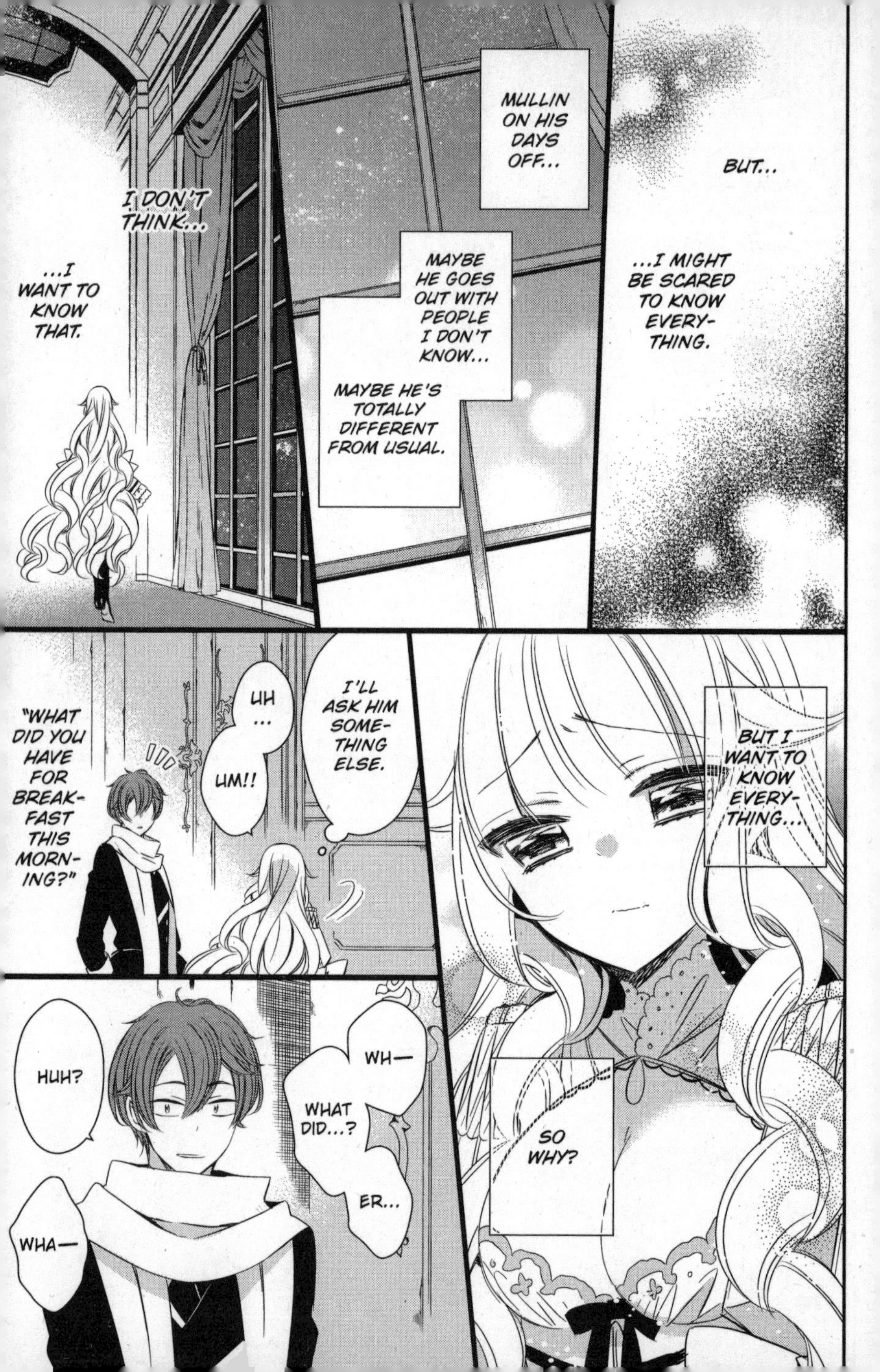
BUT...
...I MIGHT BE SCARED TO KNOW EVERY-THING.
MULLIN ON HIS DAYS OFF...
MAYBE HE GOES OUT WITH PEOPLE I DON'T KNOW...
MAYBE HE'S TOTALLY DIFFERENT FROM USUAL.
I DON'T THINK...
...I WANT TO KNOW THAT.
BUT I WANT TO KNOW EVERY-THING...
SO WHY?
I'LL ASK HIM SOME-THING ELSE.
UH ...
UM!!
"WHAT DID YOU HAVE FOR BREAK-FAST THIS MORN-ING?"
WH—
WHAT DID...?
ER...
HUH?
WHA—

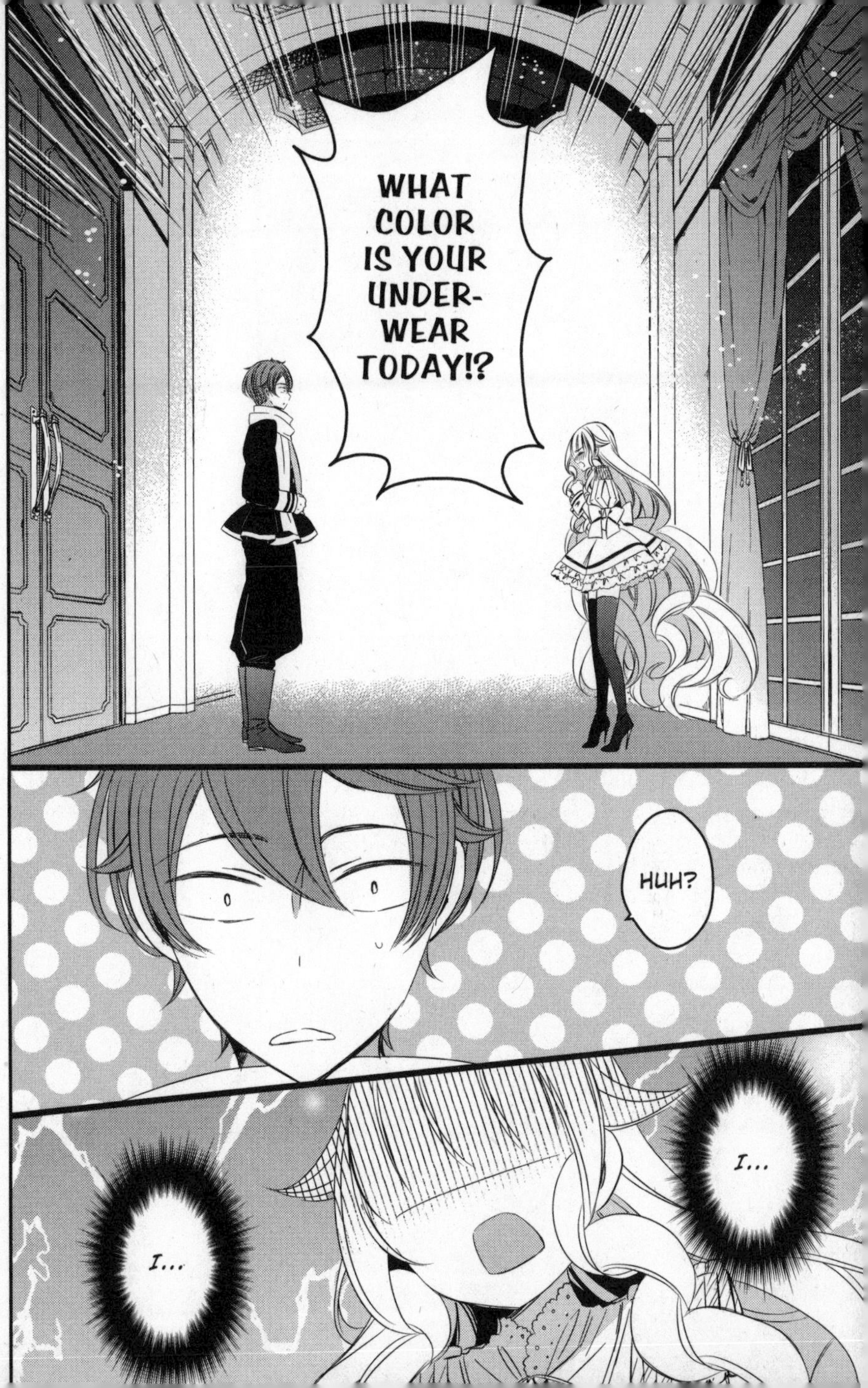
WHAT COLOR IS YOUR UNDER-WEAR TODAY!?
HUH?
I...
I...

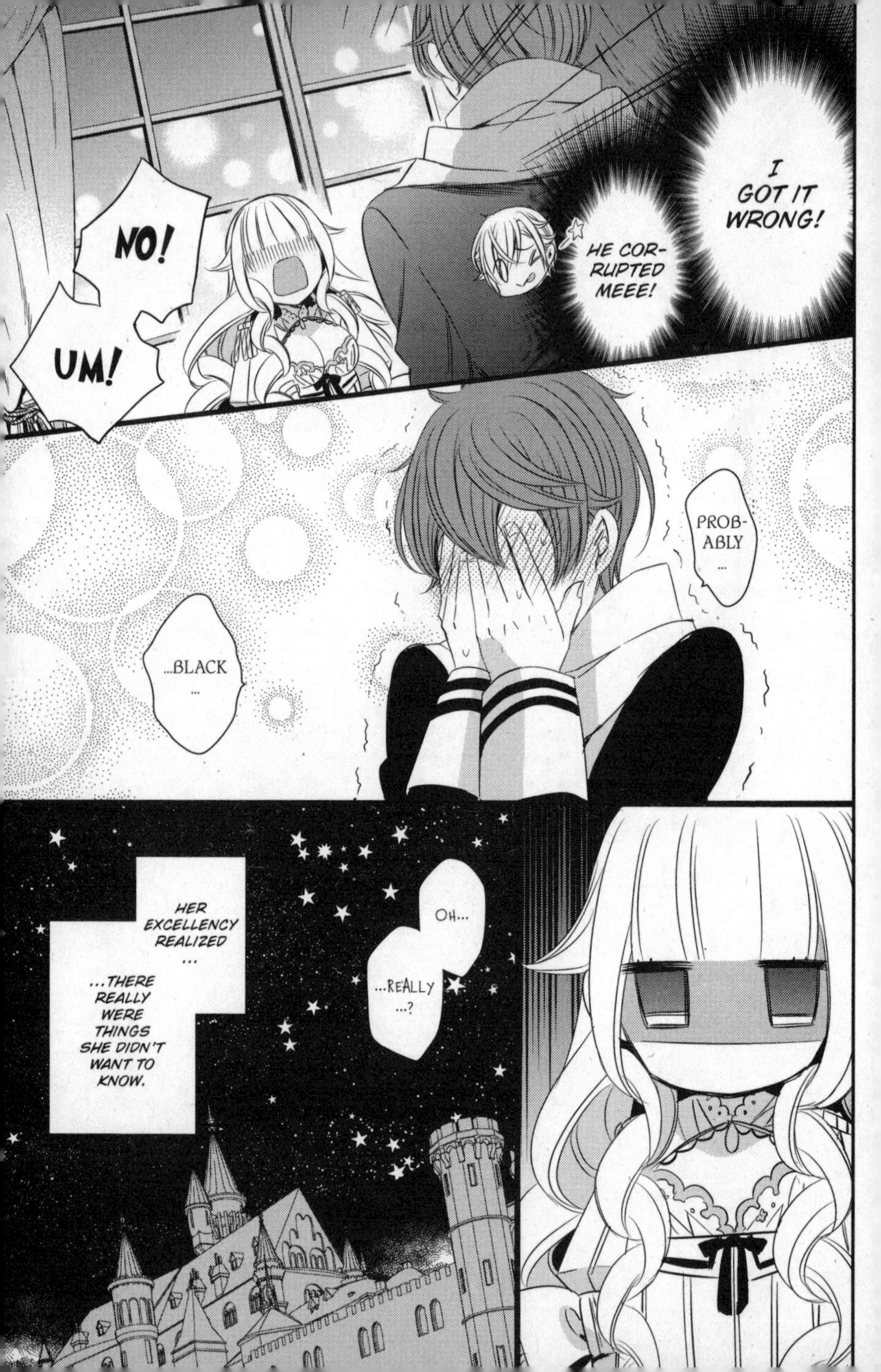
I GOT IT WRONG!
HE COR-RUPTED MEEE!
NO!
UM!
PROB-ABLY ...
...BLACK ...
OH...
...REALLY ...?
HER EXCELLENCY REALIZED ...
...THERE REALLY WERE THINGS SHE DIDN'T WANT TO KNOW.

As Miss Beelzebub Likes

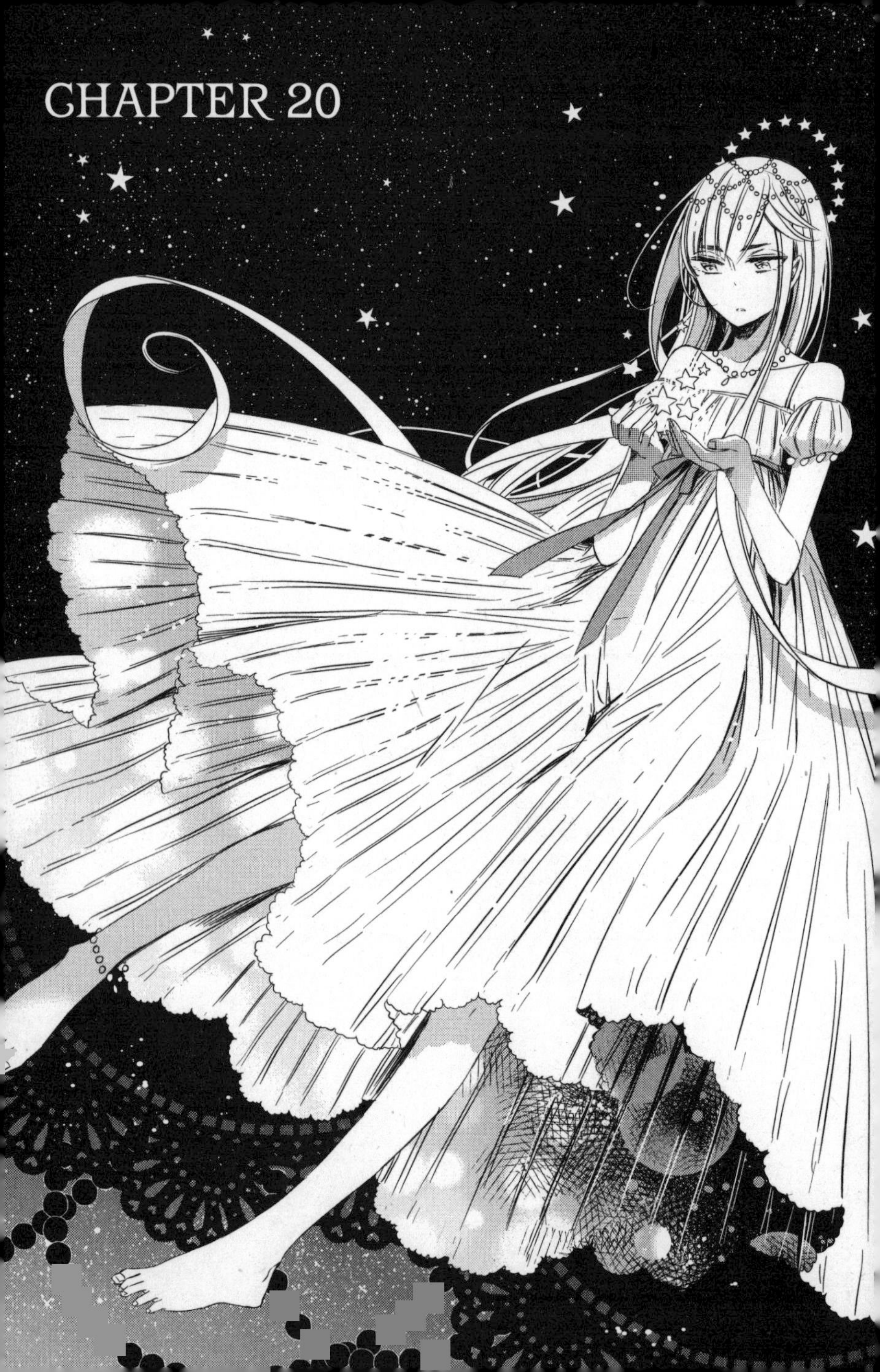
CHAPTER 20

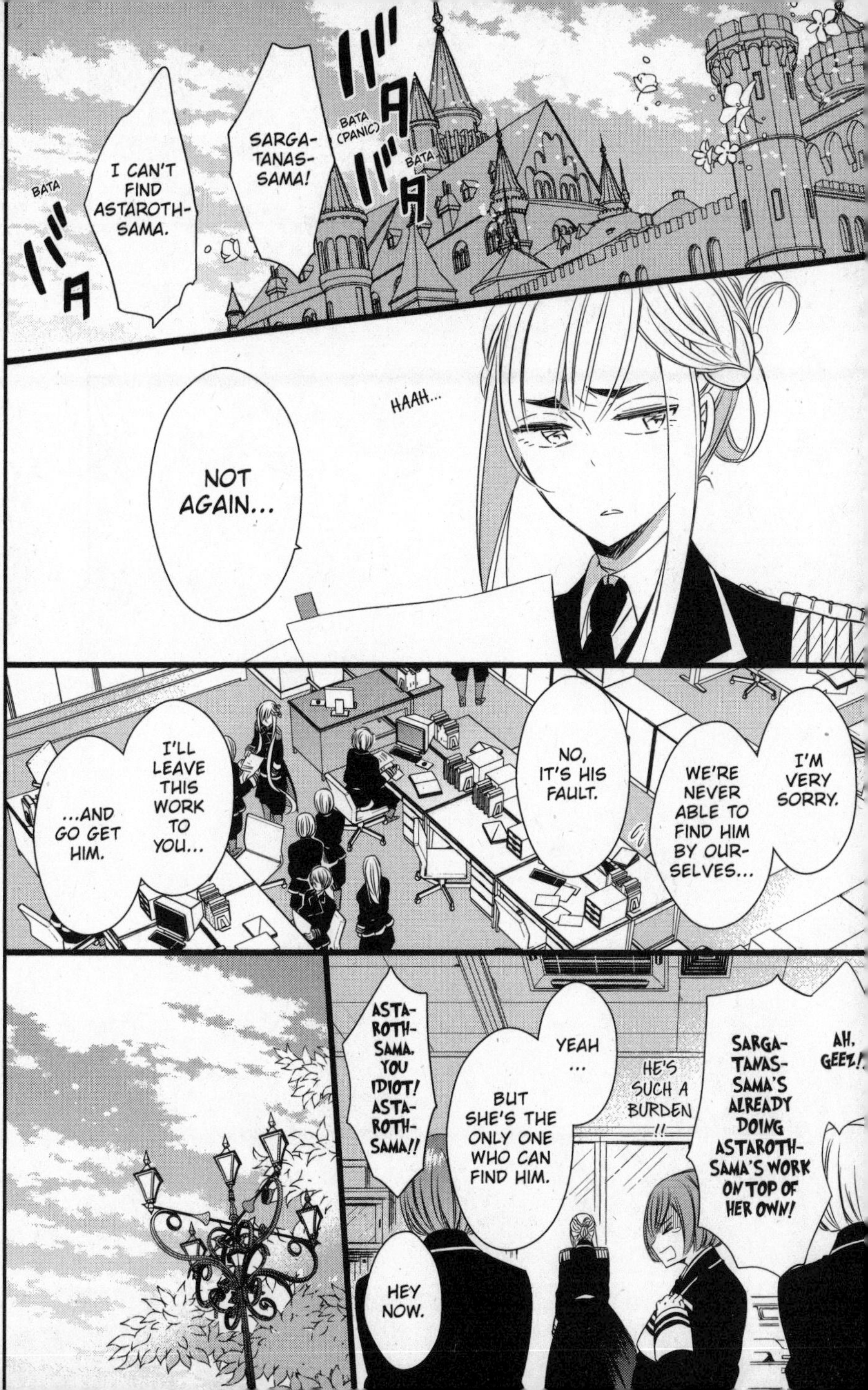
BATA (PANIC)
BATA
SARGA-TANAS-SAMA!
I CAN'T FIND ASTAROTH-SAMA.
BATA
HAAH...
NOT AGAIN...
I'M VERY SORRY.
WE'RE NEVER ABLE TO FIND HIM BY OUR-SELVES...
NO, IT'S HIS FAULT.
I'LL LEAVE THIS WORK TO YOU...
...AND GO GET HIM.
AH, GEEZ!
SARGA-TANAS-SAMA'S ALREADY DOING ASTAROTH-SAMA'S WORK ON TOP OF HER OWN!
HE'S SUCH A BURDEN!!
YEAH...
BUT SHE'S THE ONLY ONE WHO CAN FIND HIM.
ASTA-ROTH-SAMA. YOU IDIOT! ASTA-ROTH-SAMA!!
HEY NOW.

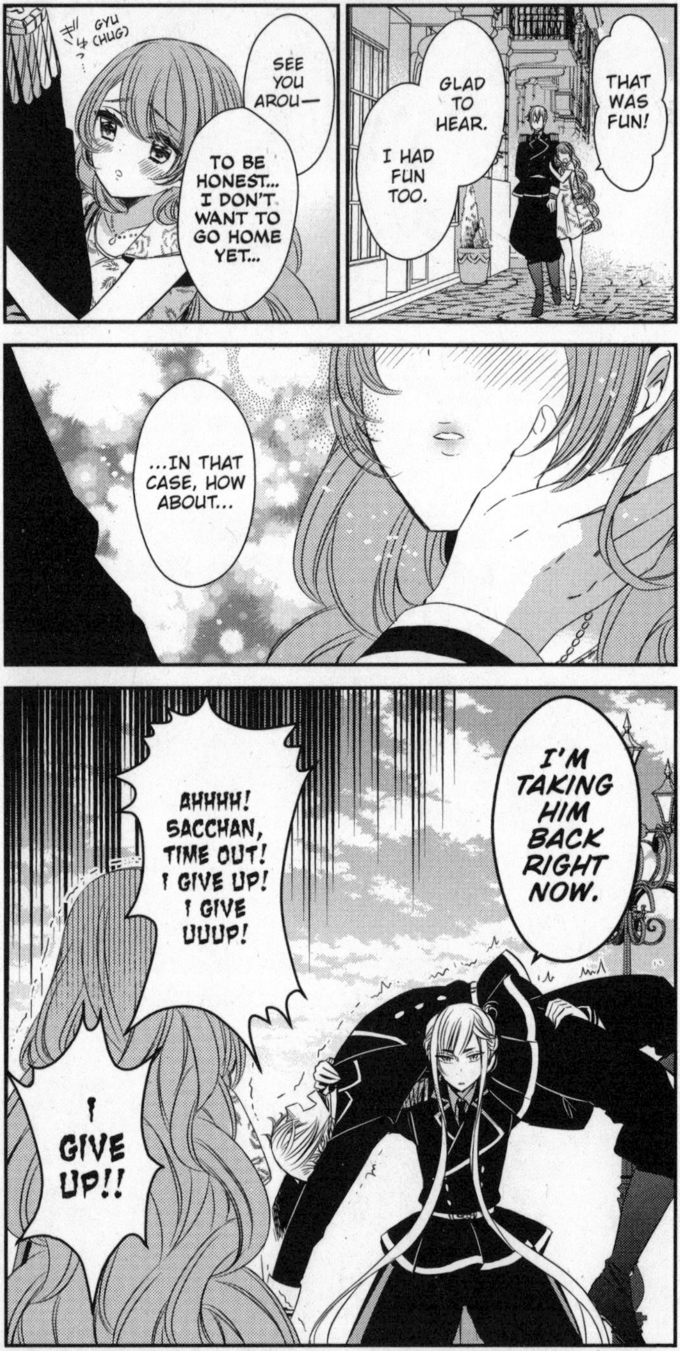
THAT WAS FUN!
GLAD TO HEAR.
I HAD FUN TOO.
SEE YOU AROU—
TO BE HONEST... I DON'T WANT TO GO HOME YET...
GYU (HUG)
...IN THAT CASE, HOW ABOUT...
I'M TAKING HIM BACK RIGHT NOW.
AHHHH! SACCHAN, TIME OUT! I GIVE UP! I GIVE UUUP!
I GIVE UP!!

BACKBREAKER SACCHAN

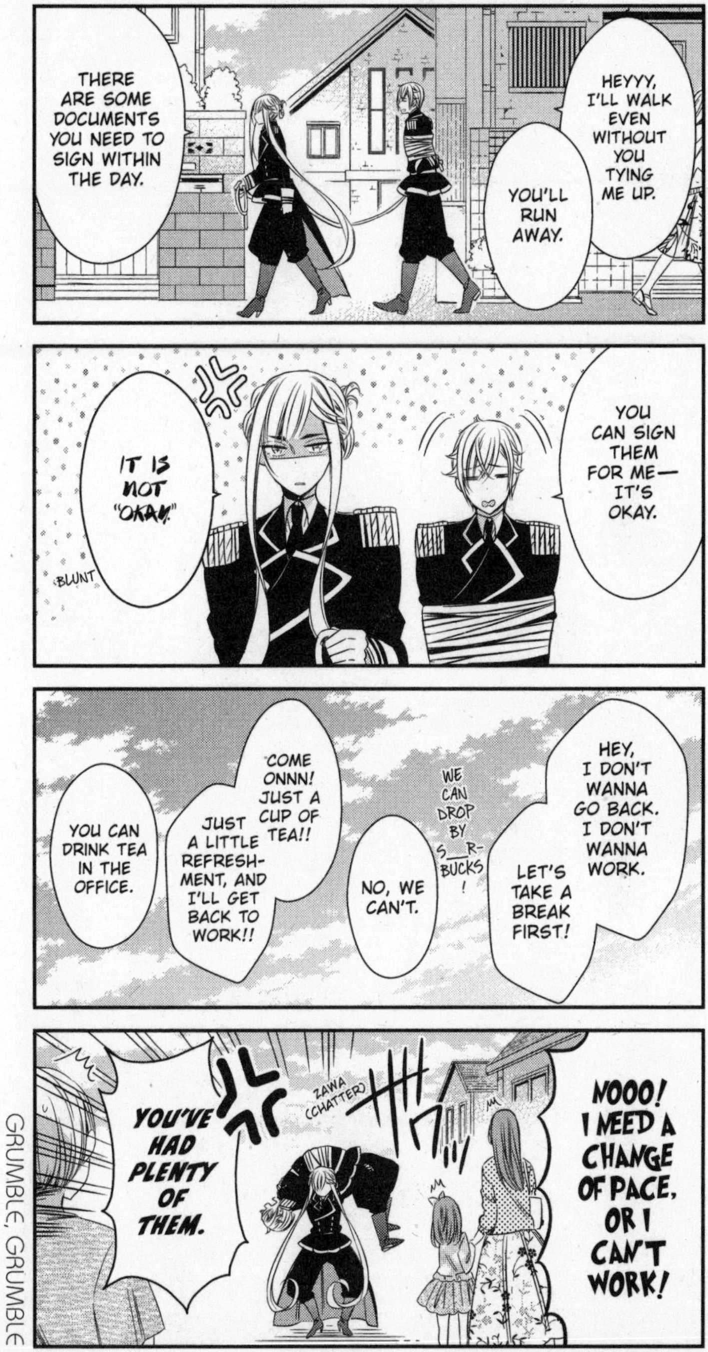
HEYYY, I'LL WALK EVEN WITHOUT YOU TYING ME UP.
YOU'LL RUN AWAY.
THERE ARE SOME DOCUMENTS YOU NEED TO SIGN WITHIN THE DAY.
YOU CAN SIGN THEM FOR ME— IT'S OKAY.
IT IS NOT "OKAY."
BLUNT
HEY, I DON'T WANNA GO BACK. I DON'T WANNA WORK.
LET'S TAKE A BREAK FIRST!
WE CAN DROP BY S__R-BUCKS!
NO, WE CAN'T.
COME ONNN! JUST A CUP OF TEA!!
JUST A LITTLE REFRESHMENT, AND I'LL GET BACK TO WORK!!
YOU CAN DRINK TEA IN THE OFFICE.
NOOO! I NEED A CHANGE OF PACE, OR I CAN'T WORK!
ZAWA (CHATTER)
YOU'VE HAD PLENTY OF THEM.
GRUMBLE, GRUMBLE

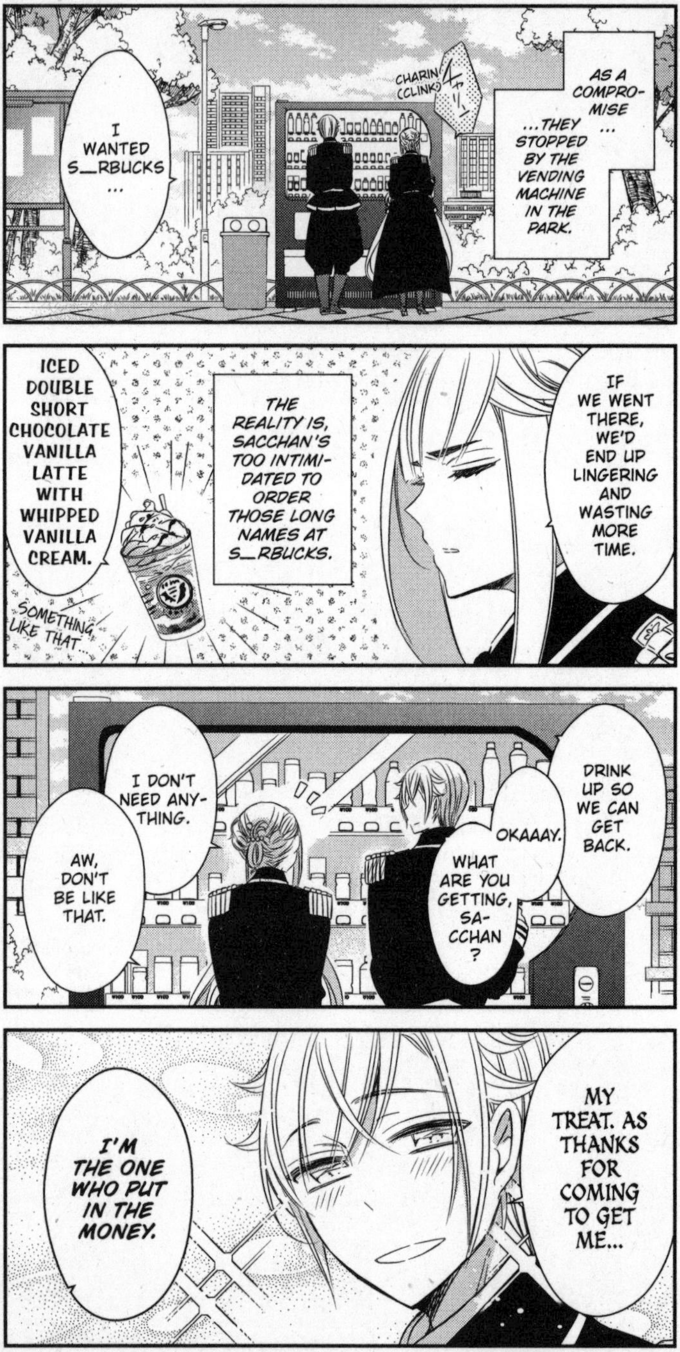
AS A COMPROMISE ... ...THEY STOPPED BY THE VENDING MACHINE IN THE PARK.
CHARIN (CLINK)
I WANTED S_RBUCKS ...
IF WE WENT THERE, WE'D END UP LINGERING AND WASTING MORE TIME.
THE REALITY IS, SACCHAN'S TOO INTIMIDATED TO ORDER THOSE LONG NAMES AT S_RBUCKS.
ICED DOUBLE SHORT CHOCOLATE VANILLA LATTE WITH WHIPPED VANILLA CREAM.
SOMETHING LIKE THAT...
DRINK UP SO WE CAN GET BACK.
OKAAAY.
WHAT ARE YOU GETTING, SACCHAN?
I DON'T NEED ANYTHING.
AW, DON'T BE LIKE THAT.
MY TREAT. AS THANKS FOR COMING TO GET ME...
I'M THE ONE WHO PUT IN THE MONEY.

HEY, THEY'RE HAPPY

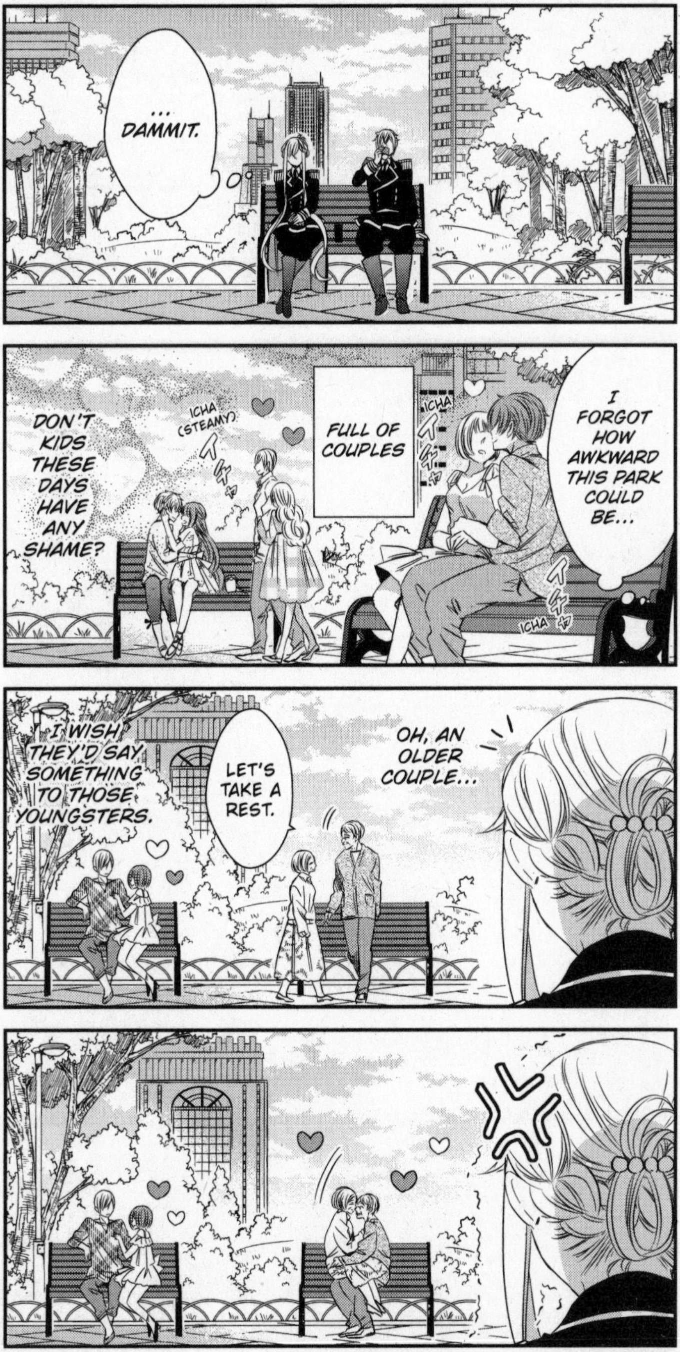
...DAMMIT.
I FORGOT HOW AWKWARD THIS PARK COULD BE...
ICHA
ICHA
FULL OF COUPLES
ICHA (STEAMY)
DON'T KIDS THESE DAYS HAVE ANY SHAME?
OH, AN OLDER COUPLE...
LET'S TAKE A REST.
I WISH THEY'D SAY SOMETHING TO THOSE YOUNGSTERS.

SELF-ANALYSIS

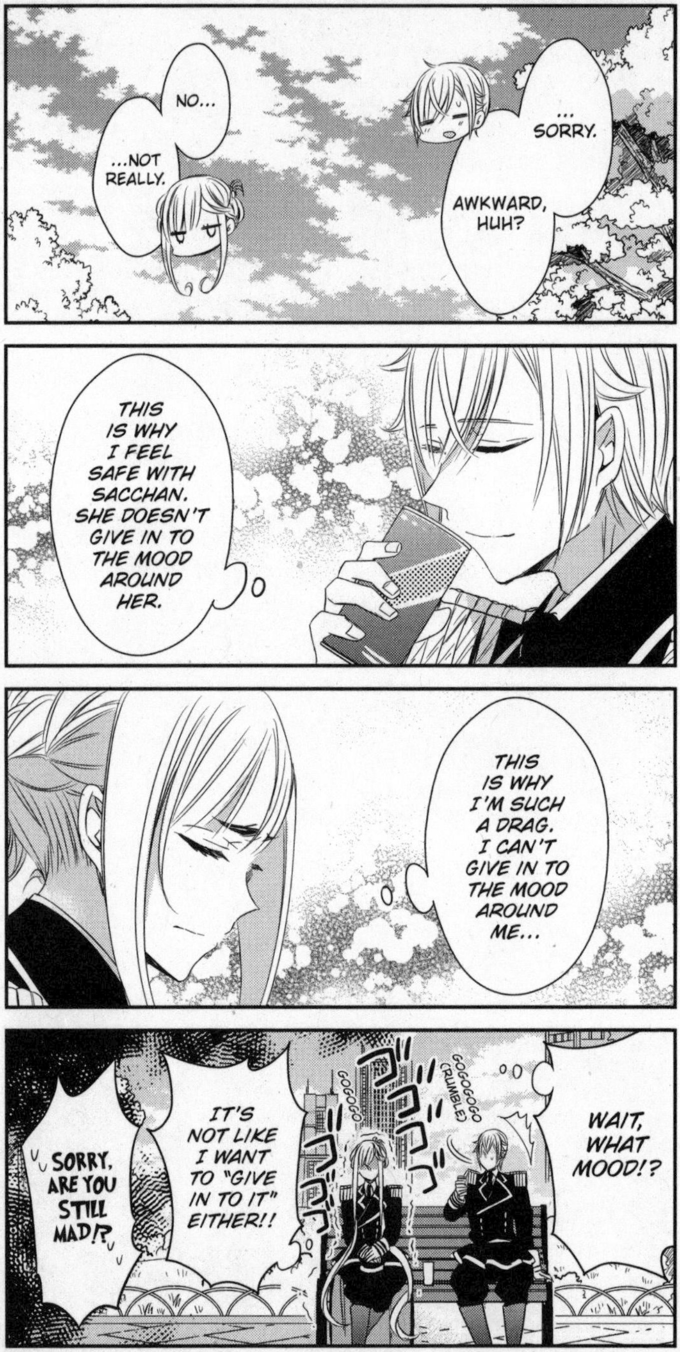
... SORRY.
AWKWARD, HUH?
NO...
...NOT REALLY.
THIS IS WHY I FEEL SAFE WITH SACCHAN. SHE DOESN'T GIVE IN TO THE MOOD AROUND HER.
THIS IS WHY I'M SUCH A DRAG. I CAN'T GIVE IN TO THE MOOD AROUND ME...
WAIT, WHAT MOOD!?
GOGOGOGO (CRUMBLE)
GOGOGO
IT'S NOT LIKE I WANT TO "GIVE IN TO IT" EITHER!!
SORRY, ARE YOU STILL MAD!?

THIS DISTANCE...

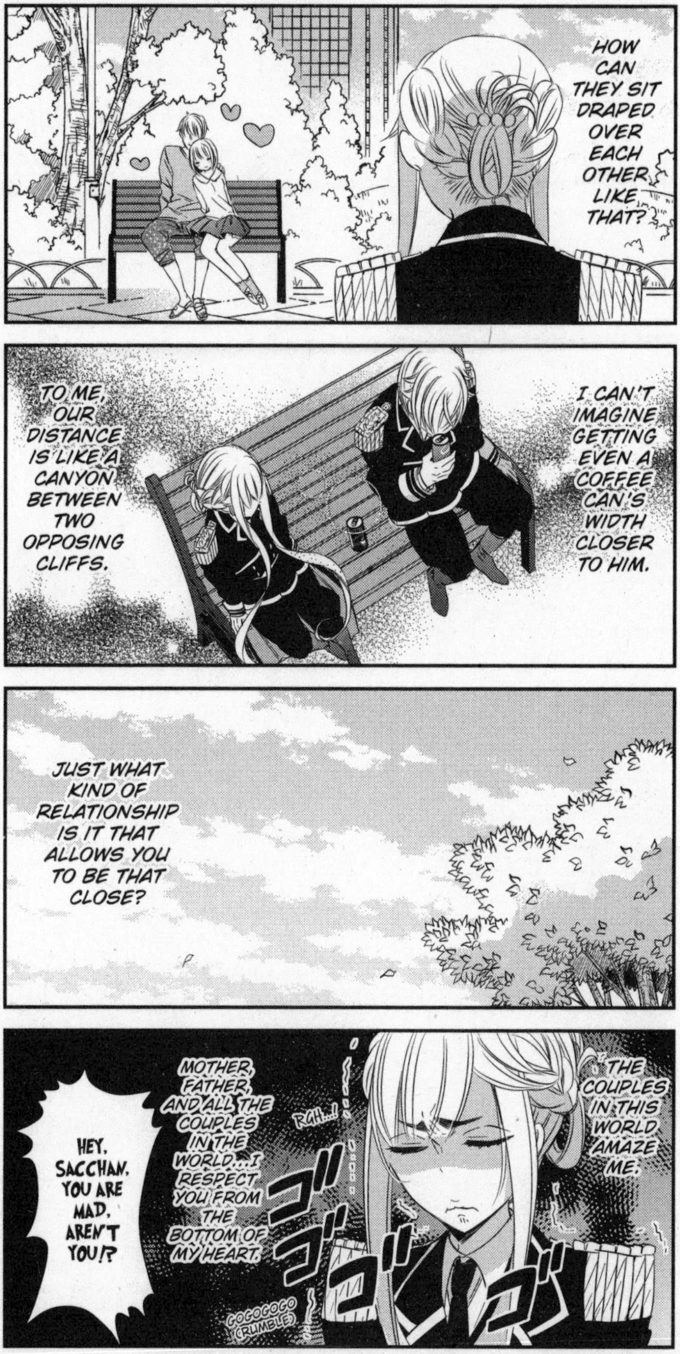
HOW CAN THEY SIT DRAPED OVER EACH OTHER LIKE THAT?
I CAN'T IMAGINE GETTING EVEN A COFFEE CAN'S WIDTH CLOSER TO HIM.
TO ME, OUR DISTANCE IS LIKE A CANYON BETWEEN TWO OPPOSING CLIFFS.
JUST WHAT KIND OF RELATIONSHIP IS IT THAT ALLOWS YOU TO BE THAT CLOSE?
THE COUPLES IN THIS WORLD AMAZE ME.
RGH...!
MOTHER, FATHER, AND ALL THE COUPLES IN THE WORLD...I RESPECT YOU FROM THE BOTTOM OF MY HEART.
GOGOGOGO (RUMBLE)
HEY, SACCHAN, YOU ARE MAD, AREN'T YOU!?

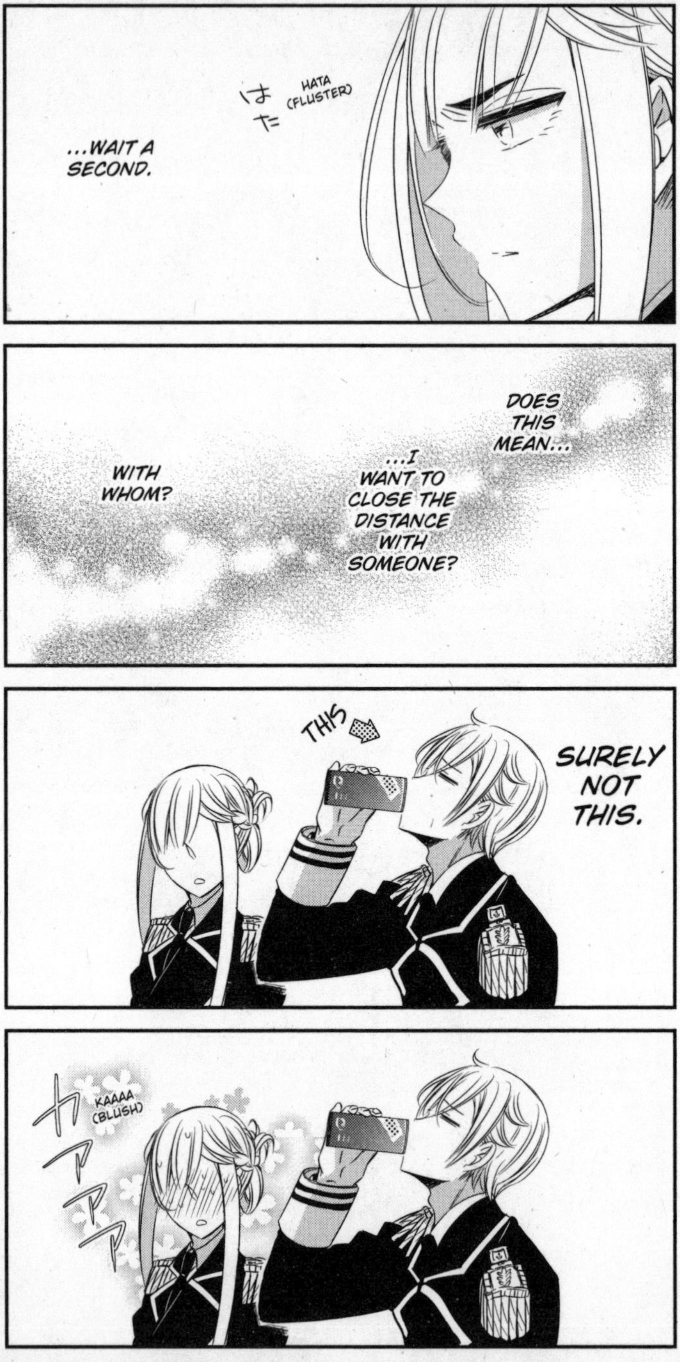
はた
HATA (FLUSTER)
...WAIT A SECOND.
DOES THIS MEAN...
...I WANT TO CLOSE THE DISTANCE WITH SOMEONE?
WITH WHOM?
SURELY NOT THIS.
THIS
KAAAA (BLUSH)
カァァァ

BUWA (BLUSH)
NO. NO, NO. NO WAY!
NO CHANCE.
IMPOS-SIBLE!
INCON-CEIVABLE!
I'M ONLY TAKING CARE OF HIM BECAUSE IT'S MY JOB AS HIS ATTENDANT.
I DID MAKE THAT PRESSED-FLOWER BOOKMARK, BUT ONLY BECAUSE THEY WERE PRETTY...
SO, UH...
...IT'S NOT LIKE I LIKE HIM OR ANY-THING...
UH...
"LIKE"...?
AGONIZED THAT SHE THOUGHT THE WORD "LIKE"

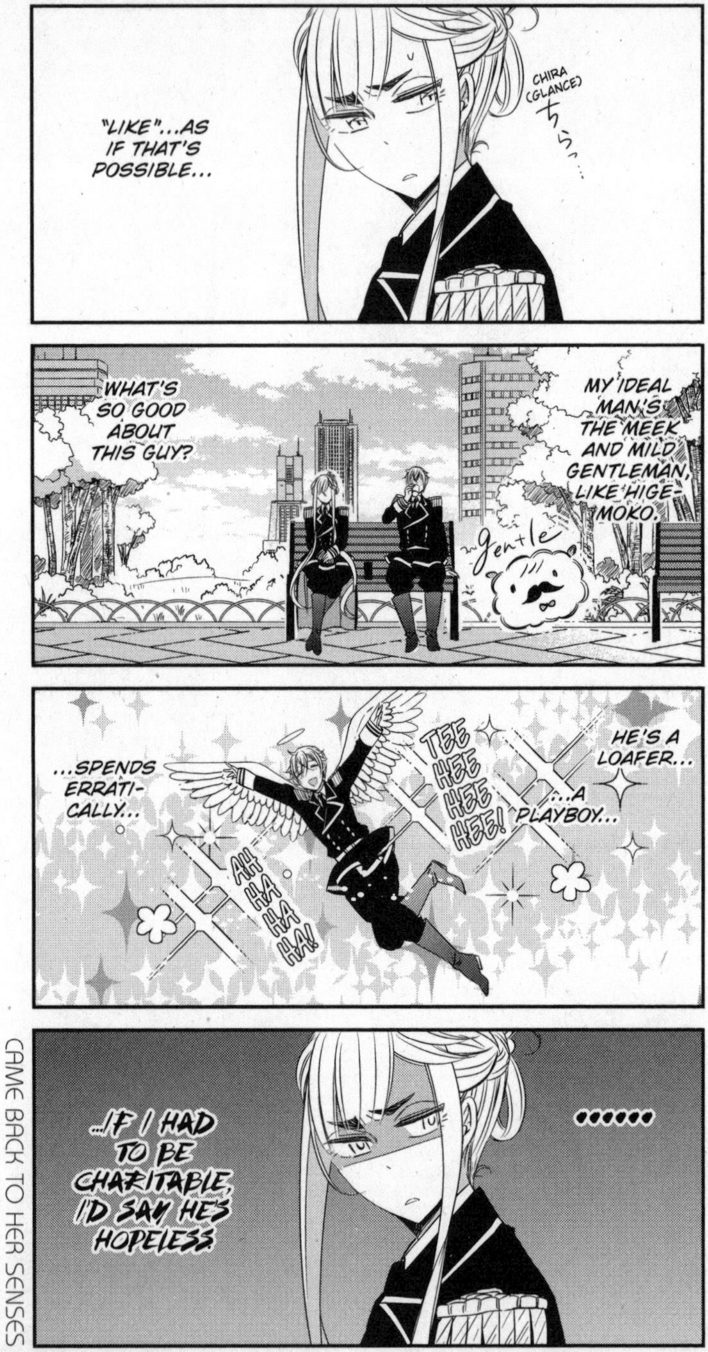
CAME BACK TO HER SENSES
CHIRA (GLANCE) ちらっ…
"LIKE"...AS IF THAT'S POSSIBLE...
MY IDEAL MAN'S THE MEEK AND MILD GENTLEMAN, LIKE HIGE-MOKO.
WHAT'S SO GOOD ABOUT THIS GUY?
Gentle
HE'S A LOAFER...
TEE HEE HEE HEE!
...A PLAYBOY...
...SPENDS ERRATI-CALLY...
AH HA HA HA HA!
......
...IF I HAD TO BE CHARITABLE, I'D SAY HE'S HOPELESS.

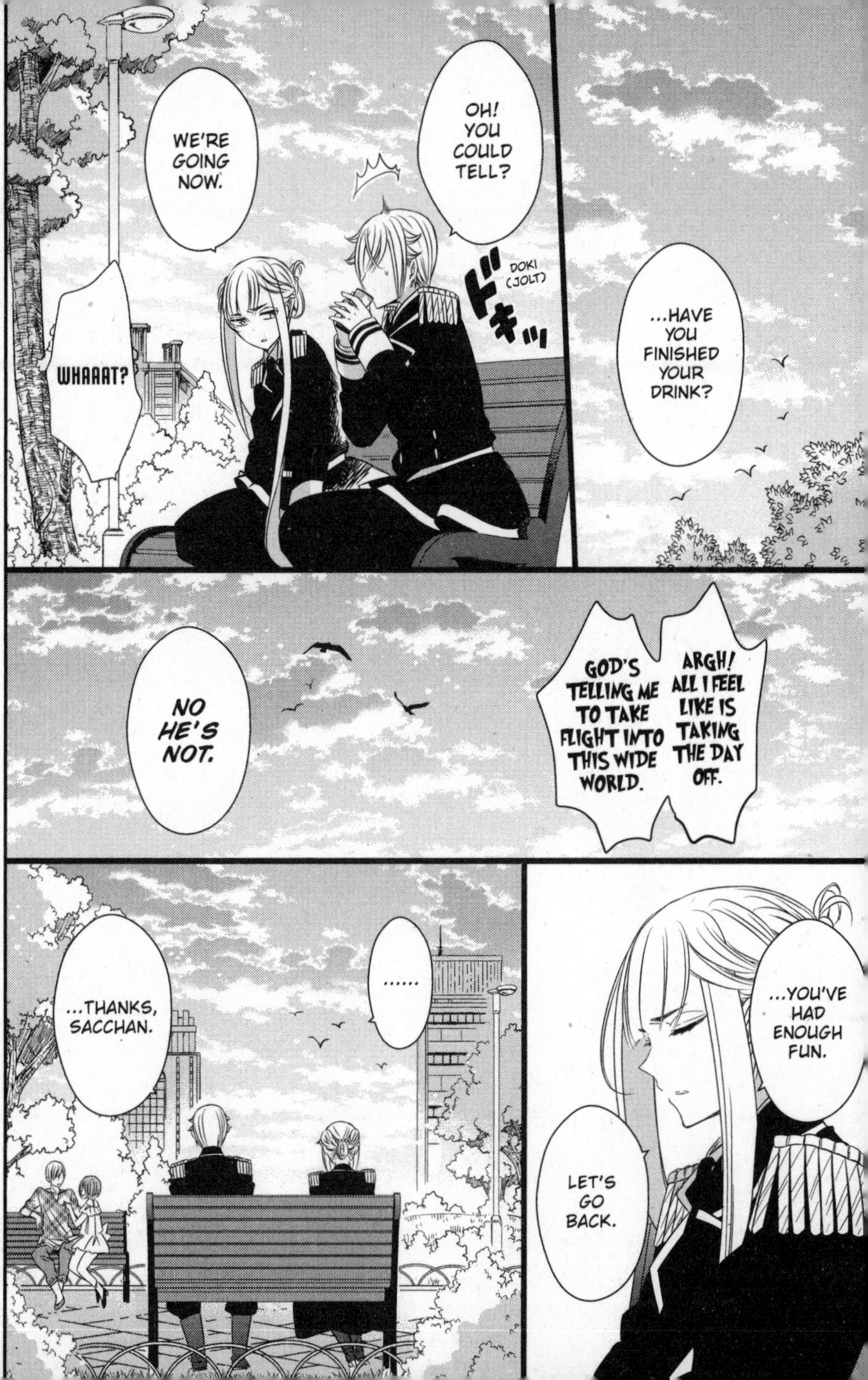
...HAVE YOU FINISHED YOUR DRINK?
OH! YOU COULD TELL?
DOKI (JOLT)
WE'RE GOING NOW.
WHAAAT?
ARGH! ALL I FEEL LIKE IS TAKING THE DAY OFF.
GOD'S TELLING ME TO TAKE FLIGHT INTO THIS WIDE WORLD.
NO HE'S NOT.
...YOU'VE HAD ENOUGH FUN.
LET'S GO BACK.
......
...THANKS, SACCHAN.

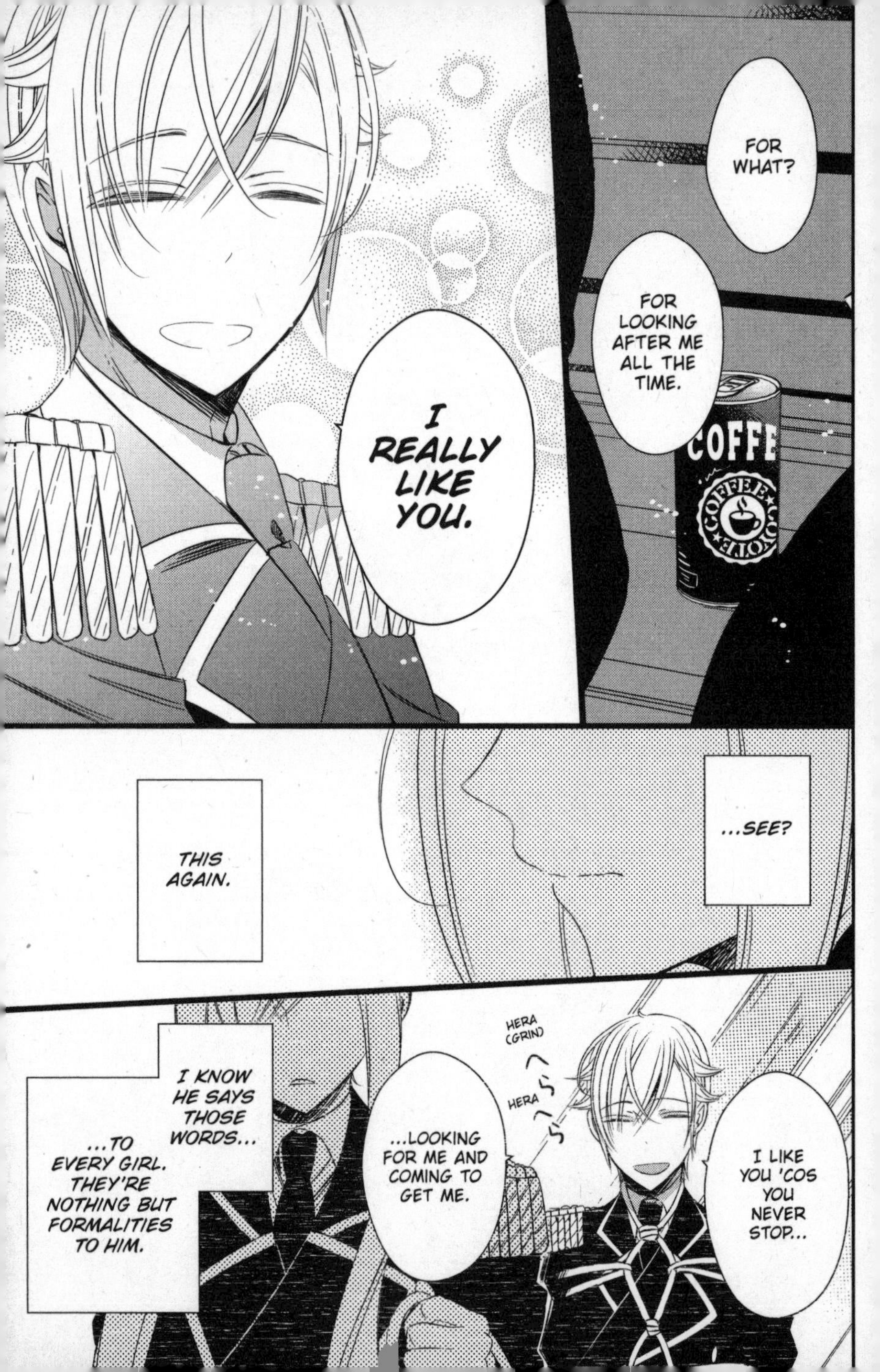
FOR WHAT?
FOR LOOKING AFTER ME ALL THE TIME.
COFFE
COFFEE COYOTE
I REALLY LIKE YOU.
...SEE?
THIS AGAIN.
I LIKE YOU 'COS YOU NEVER STOP...
HERA (GRIN)
HERA
...LOOKING FOR ME AND COMING TO GET ME.
I KNOW HE SAYS THOSE WORDS...
...TO EVERY GIRL. THEY'RE NOTHING BUT FORMALITIES TO HIM.

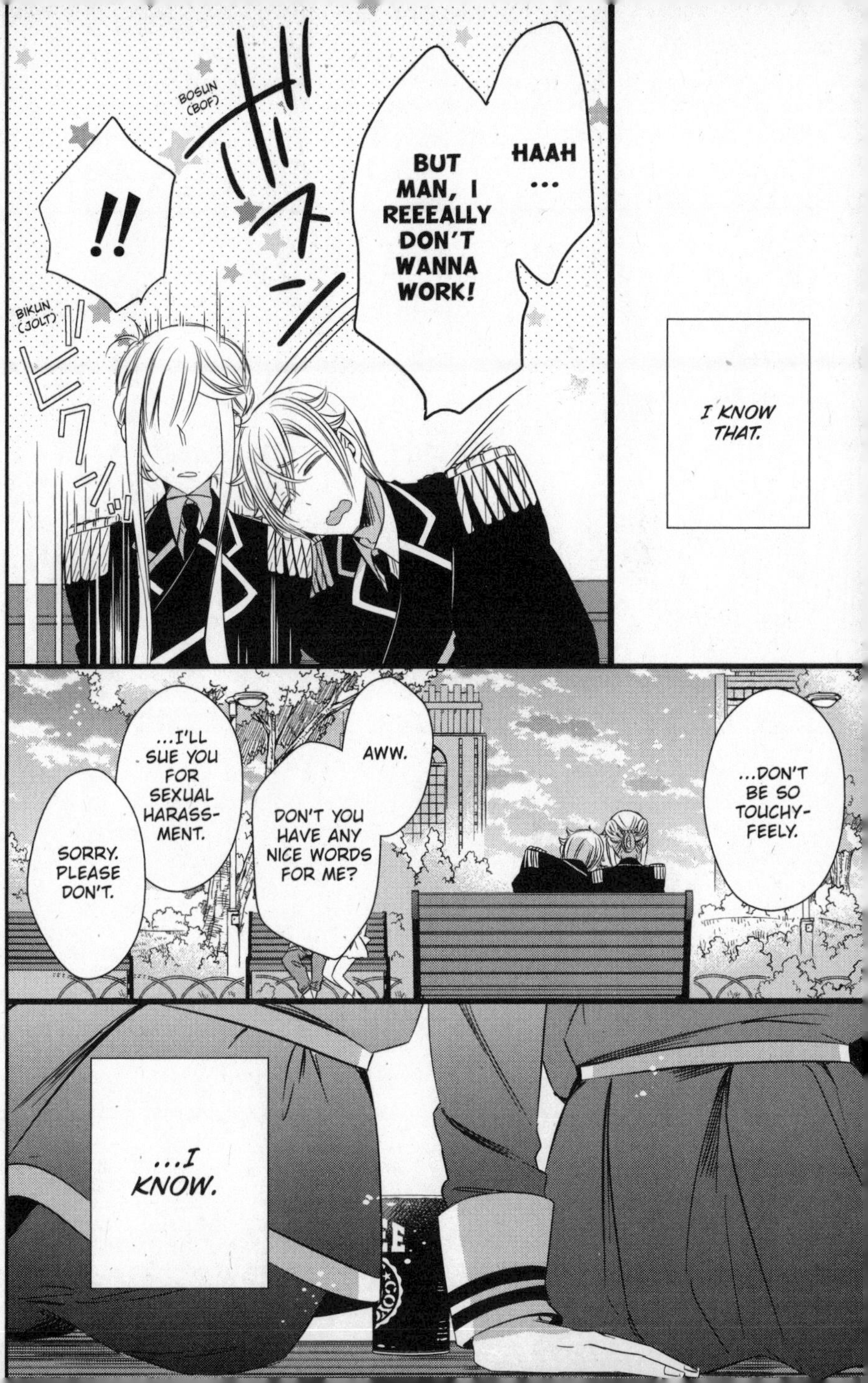
I KNOW THAT.
HAAH...
BUT MAN, I REEEALLY DON'T WANNA WORK!
BOSUN (BOF)
!!
BIKUN (JOLT)
...DON'T BE SO TOUCHY-FEELY.
AWW.
DON'T YOU HAVE ANY NICE WORDS FOR ME?
...I'LL SUE YOU FOR SEXUAL HARASS-MENT.
SORRY. PLEASE DON'T.
...I KNOW.

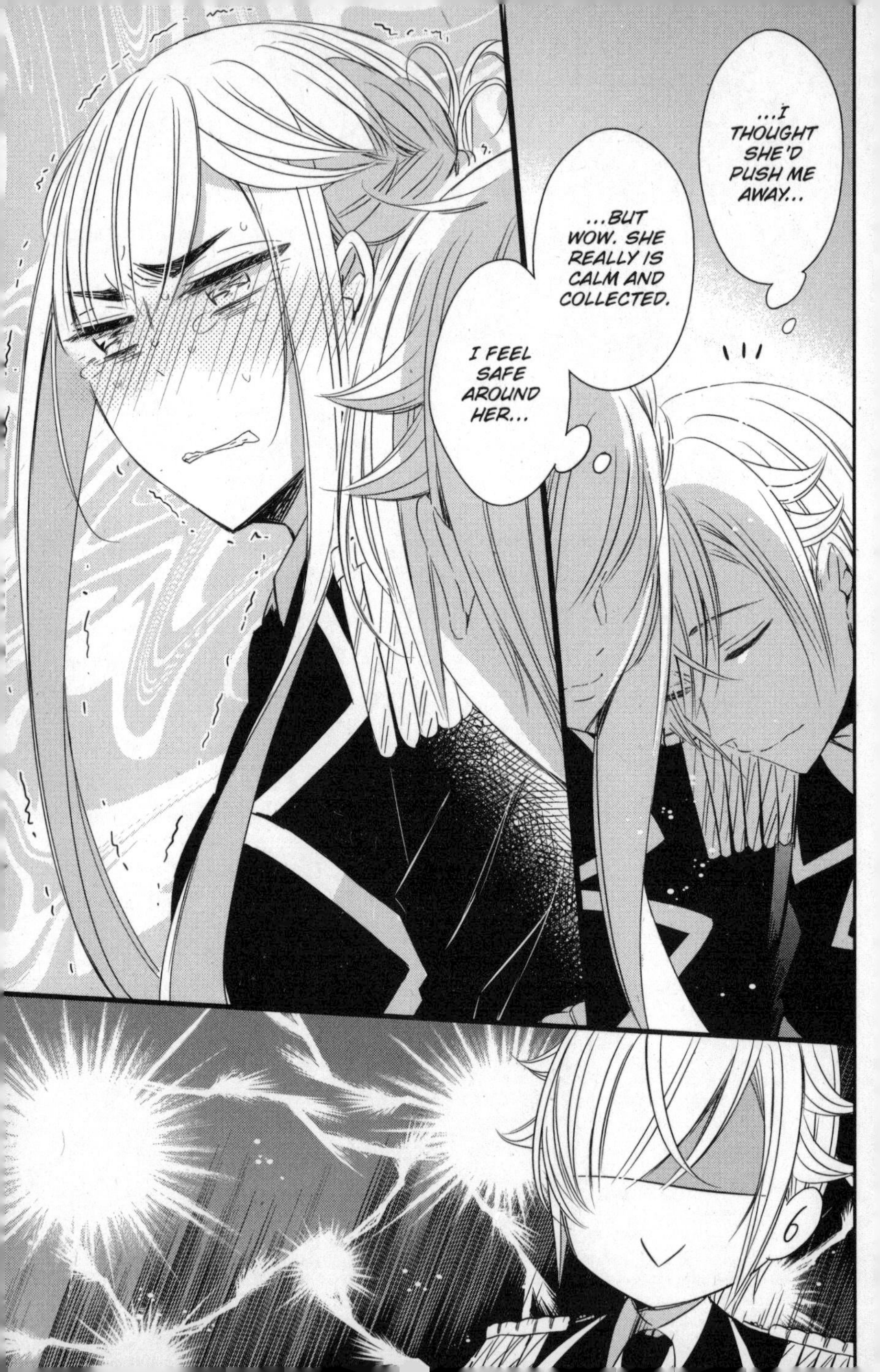
...I THOUGHT SHE'D PUSH ME AWAY...
...BUT WOW. SHE REALLY IS CALM AND COLLECTED.
I FEEL SAFE AROUND HER...

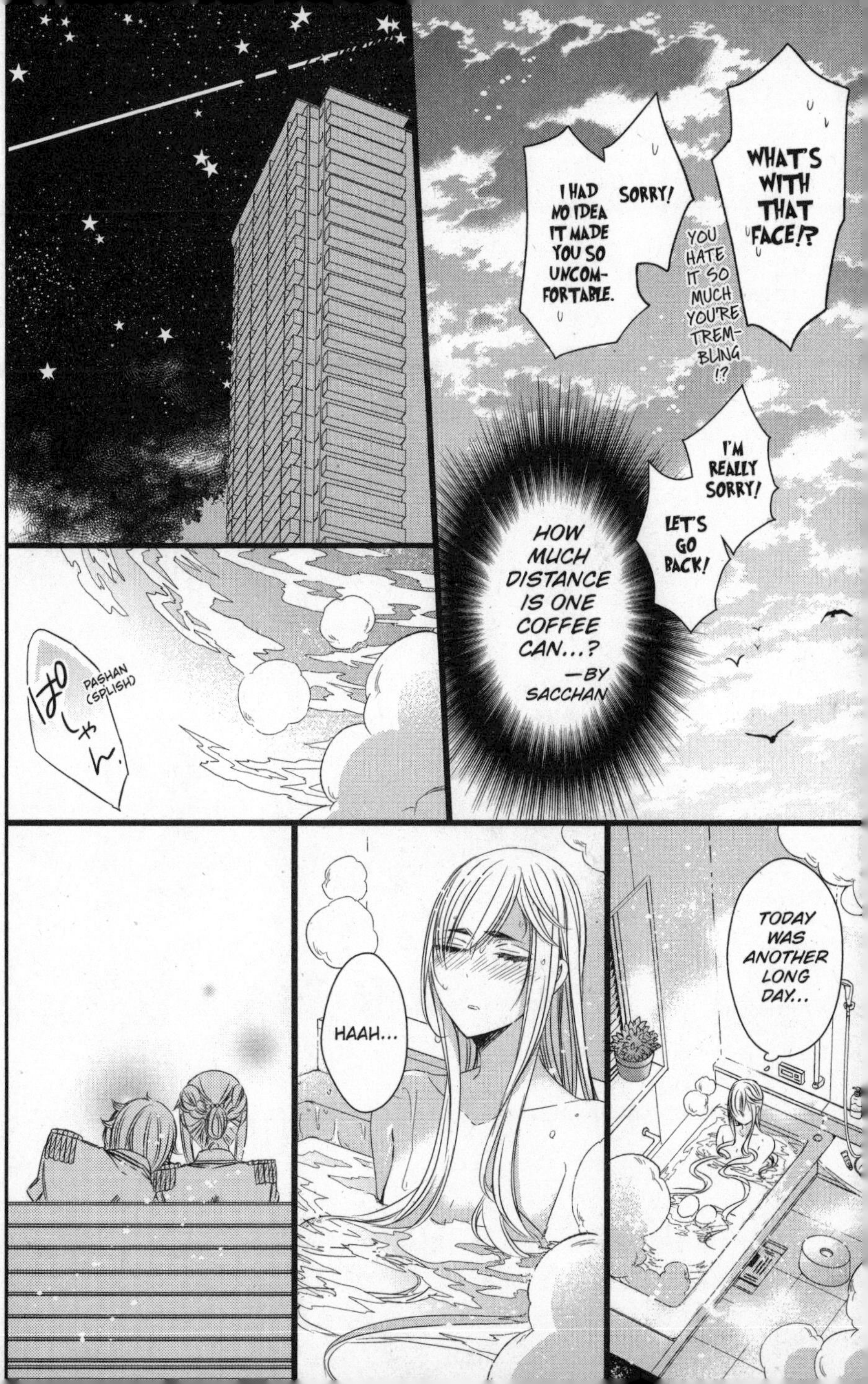
WHAT'S WITH THAT FACE!?
YOU HATE IT SO MUCH YOU'RE TREMBLING!?
SORRY!
I HAD NO IDEA IT MADE YOU SO UNCOMFORTABLE.
I'M REALLY SORRY!
LET'S GO BACK!
HOW MUCH DISTANCE IS ONE COFFEE CAN...? —BY SACCHAN
ぱしゃん
PASHAN (SPLISH)
TODAY WAS ANOTHER LONG DAY...
HAAH...

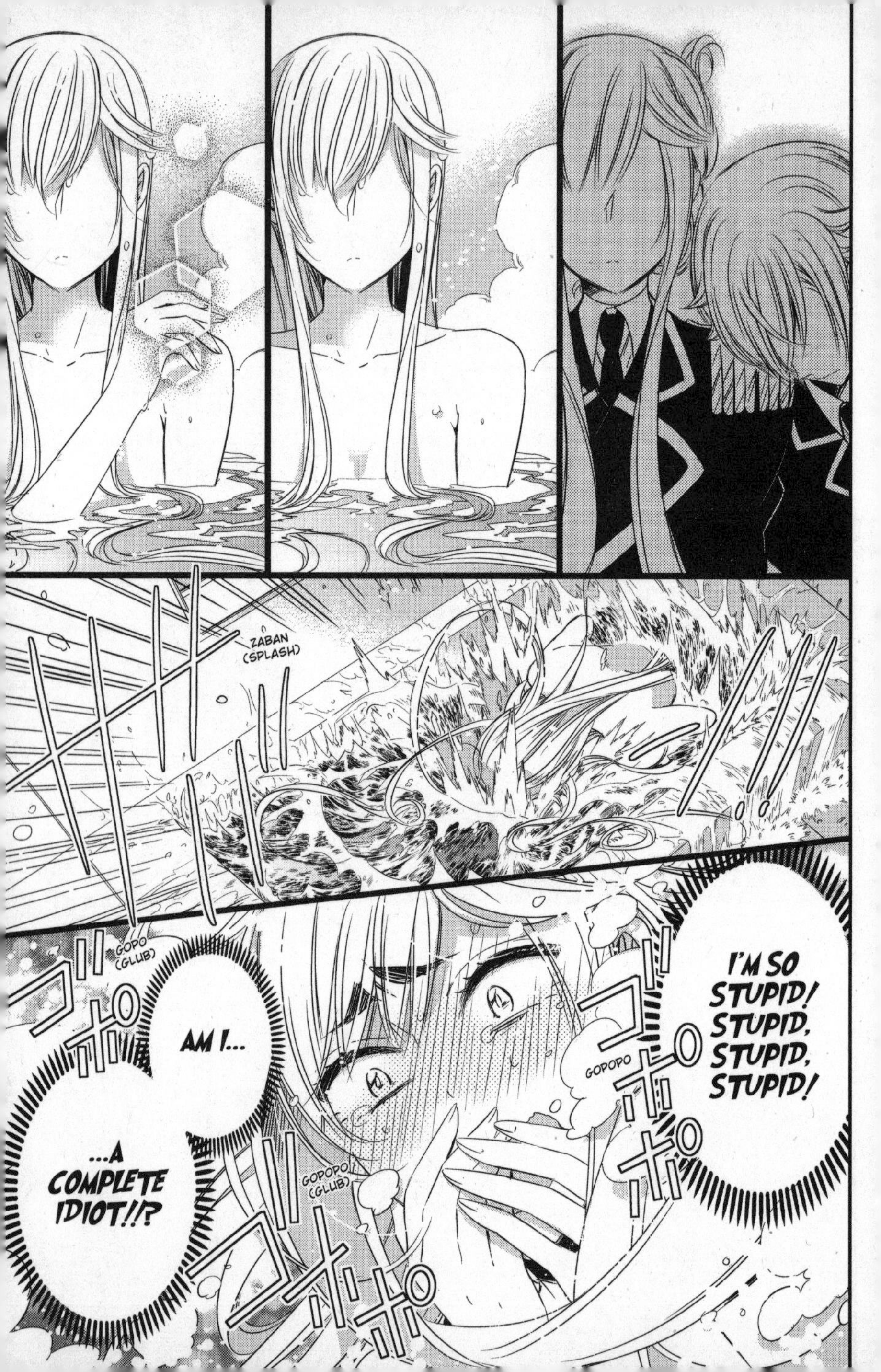
ZABAN (SPLASH)
I'M SO STUPID! STUPID, STUPID, STUPID!
GOPOPO
GOPO (GLUB)
AM I...
GOPOPO (GLUB)
...A COMPLETE IDIOT!!?

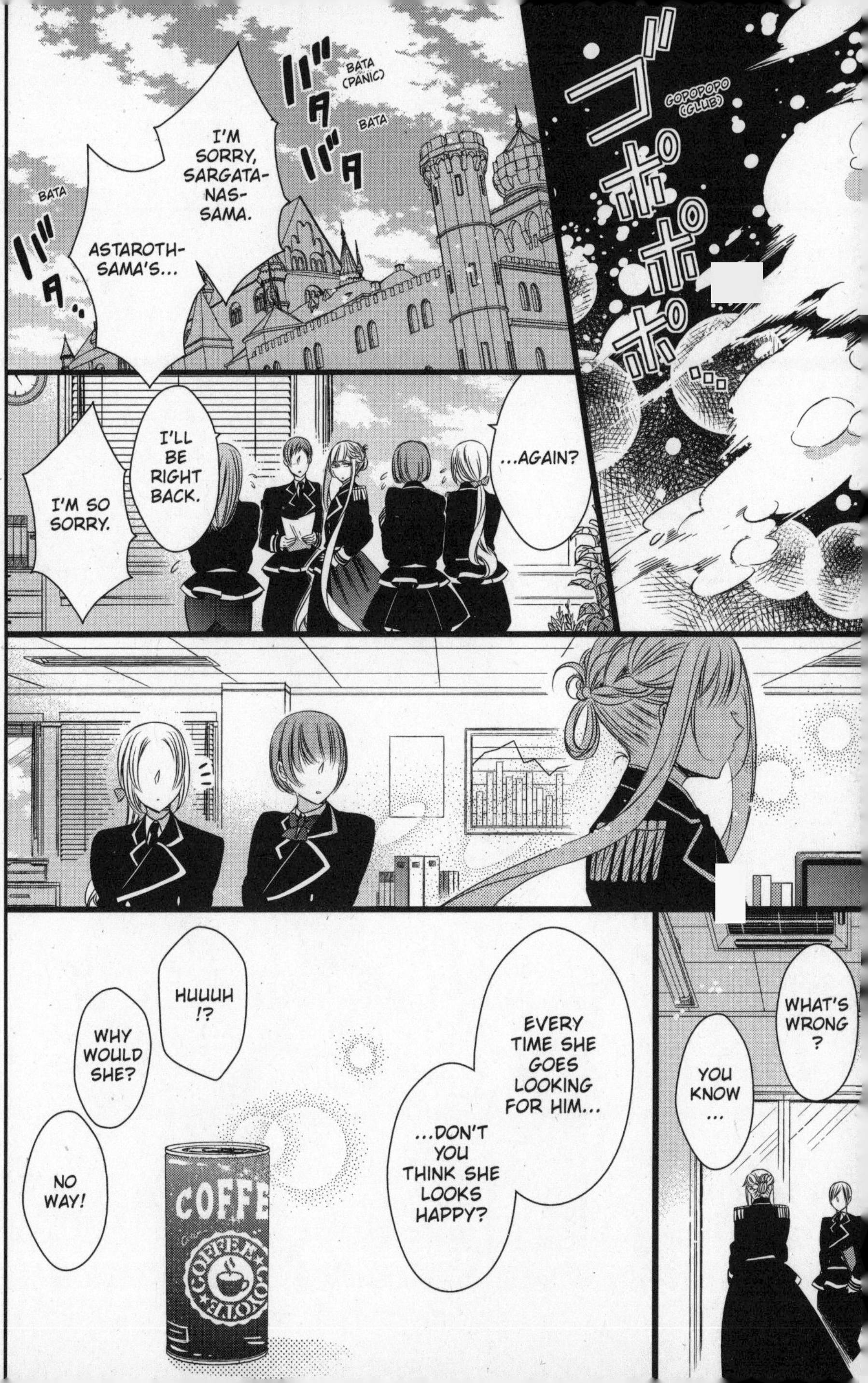
ゴポポポ…
GOPOPOPO (GLUB)
バタバタ
BATA (PANIC)
BATA
I'M SORRY, SARGATANAS-SAMA.
ASTAROTH-SAMA'S...
バタ…
BATA
...AGAIN?
I'LL BE RIGHT BACK.
I'M SO SORRY.
WHAT'S WRONG?
YOU KNOW...
EVERY TIME SHE GOES LOOKING FOR HIM...
...DON'T YOU THINK SHE LOOKS HAPPY?
HUUUH!?
WHY WOULD SHE?
NO WAY!
COFFE

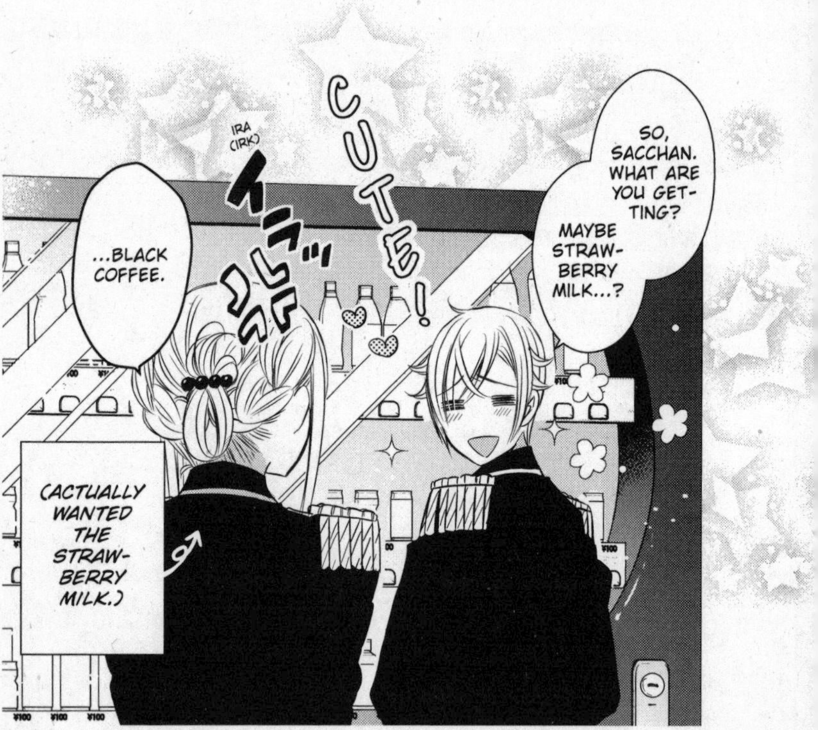
SO, SACCHAN. WHAT ARE YOU GET-TING?
MAYBE STRAW-BERRY MILK...?
CUTE!
IRA (IRK)
...BLACK COFFEE.
(ACTUALLY WANTED THE STRAW-BERRY MILK.)

As Miss Beelzebub Likes

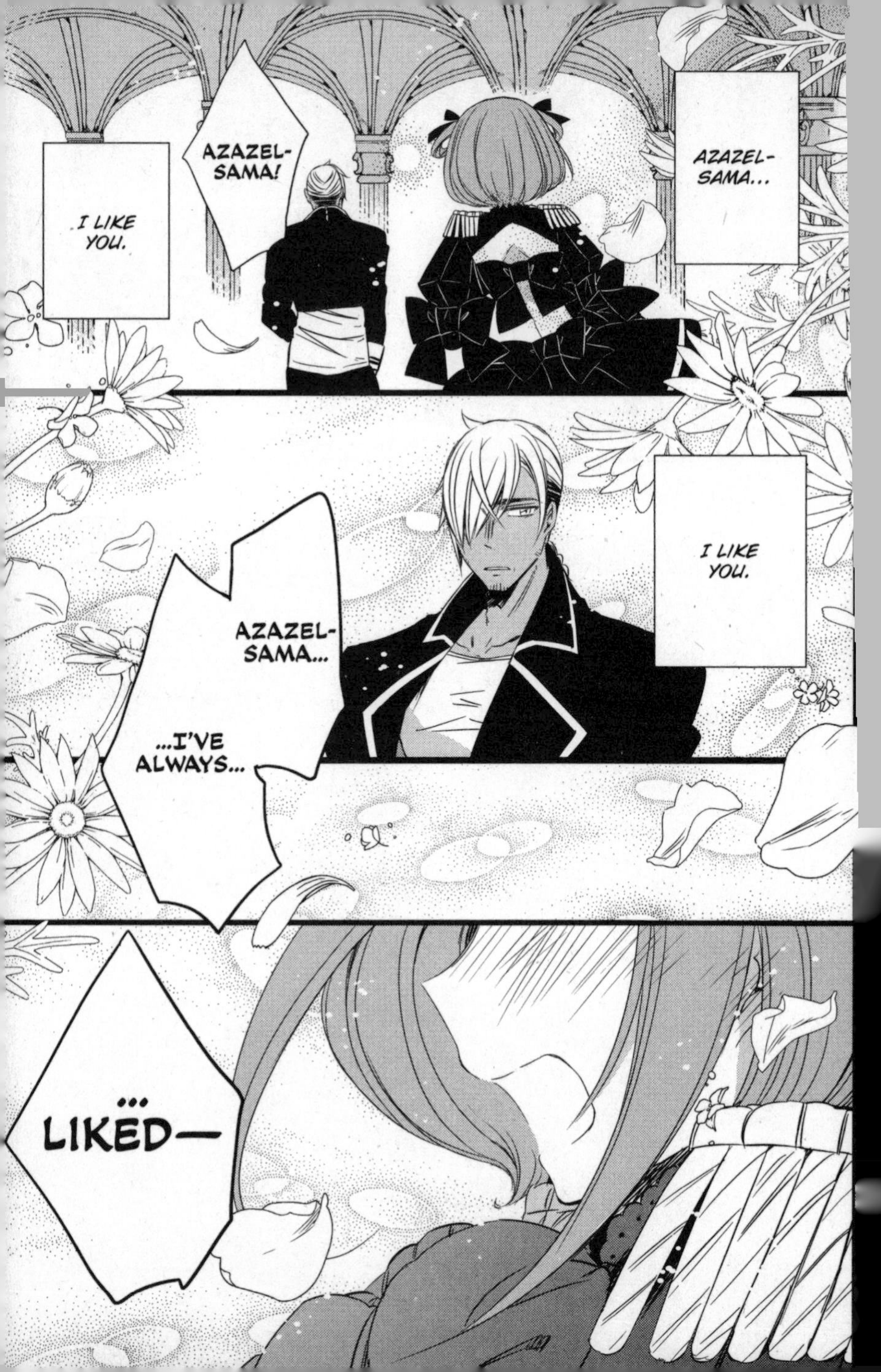
AZAZEL-SAMA...
AZAZEL-SAMA!
I LIKE YOU.
I LIKE YOU.
AZAZEL-SAMA...
...I'VE ALWAYS...
...LIKED—

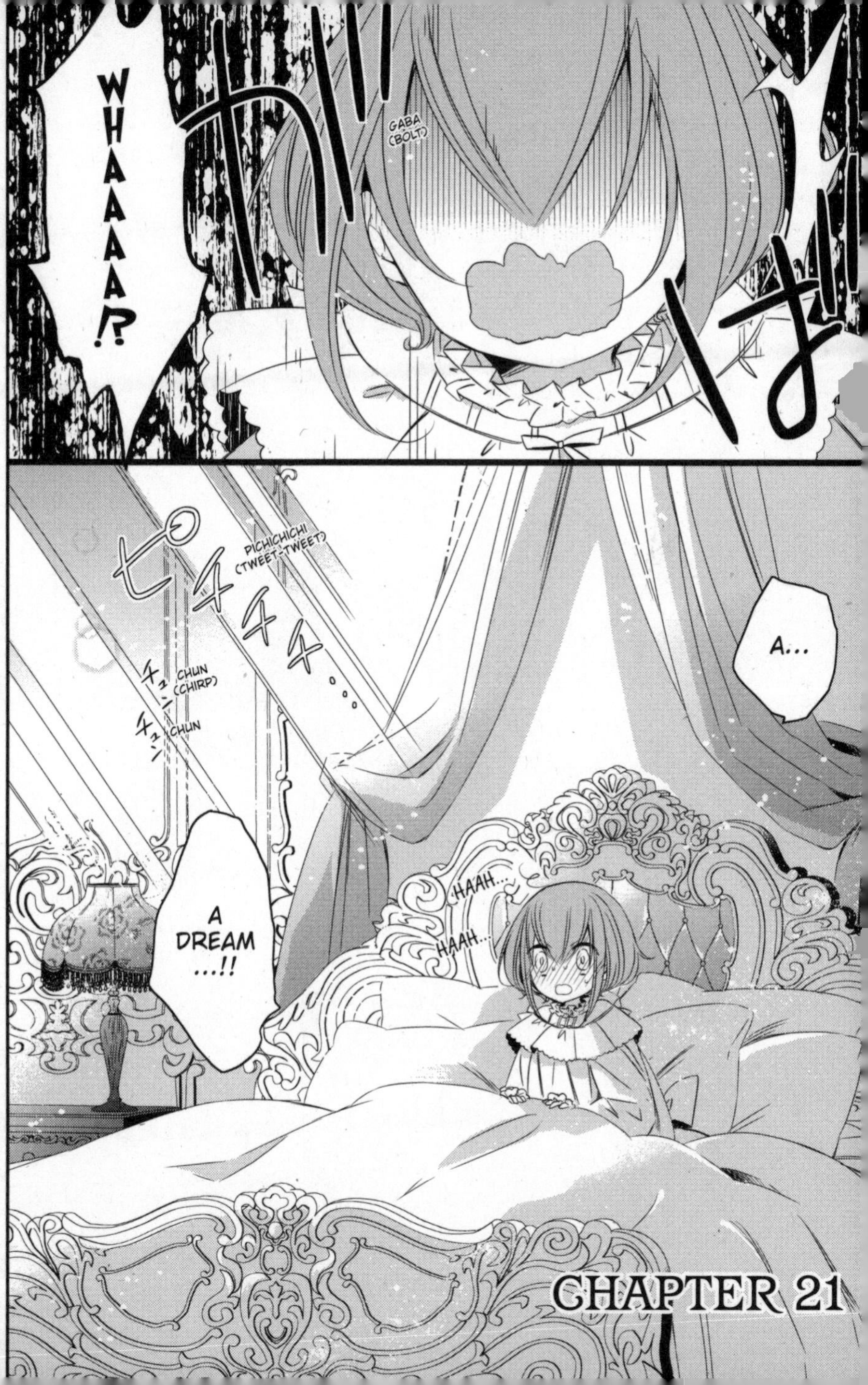
GABA (BOLT)
WHAAAAA!?
A...
PICHICHICHI (TWEET-TWEET)
CHUN (CHIRP)
CHUN
HAAH...
HAAH...
A DREAM ...!!
CHAPTER 21

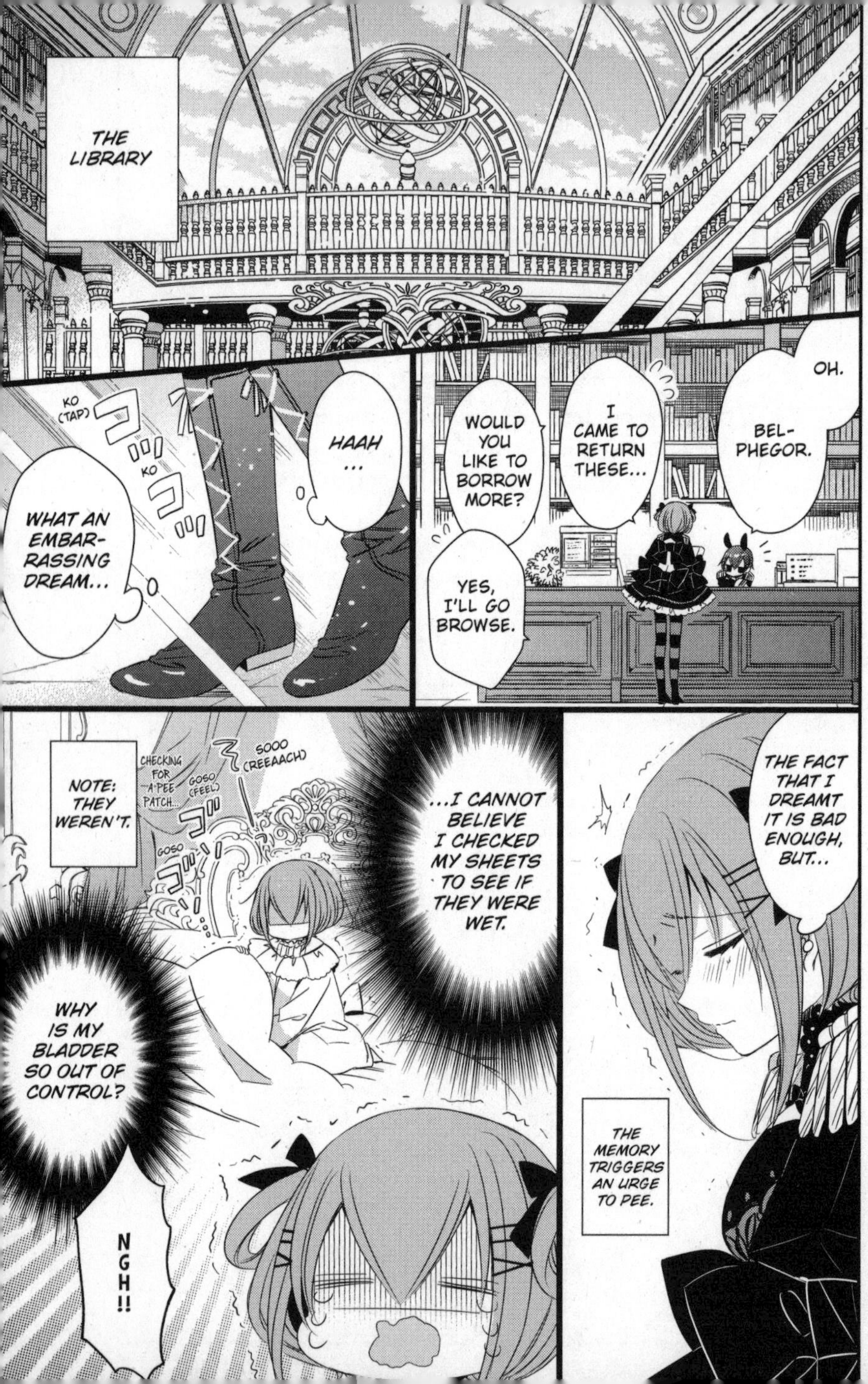
THE LIBRARY
OH.
BEL-PHEGOR.
I CAME TO RETURN THESE...
WOULD YOU LIKE TO BORROW MORE?
YES, I'LL GO BROWSE.
HAAH...
KO (TAP)
KO
WHAT AN EMBAR-RASSING DREAM...
THE FACT THAT I DREAMT IT IS BAD ENOUGH, BUT...
THE MEMORY TRIGGERS AN URGE TO PEE.
...I CANNOT BELIEVE I CHECKED MY SHEETS TO SEE IF THEY WERE WET.
SOOO (REEAACH)
CHECKING FOR A PEE PATCH...
GOSO (FEEL)
GOSO
NOTE: THEY WEREN'T.
WHY IS MY BLADDER SO OUT OF CONTROL?
NGH!!

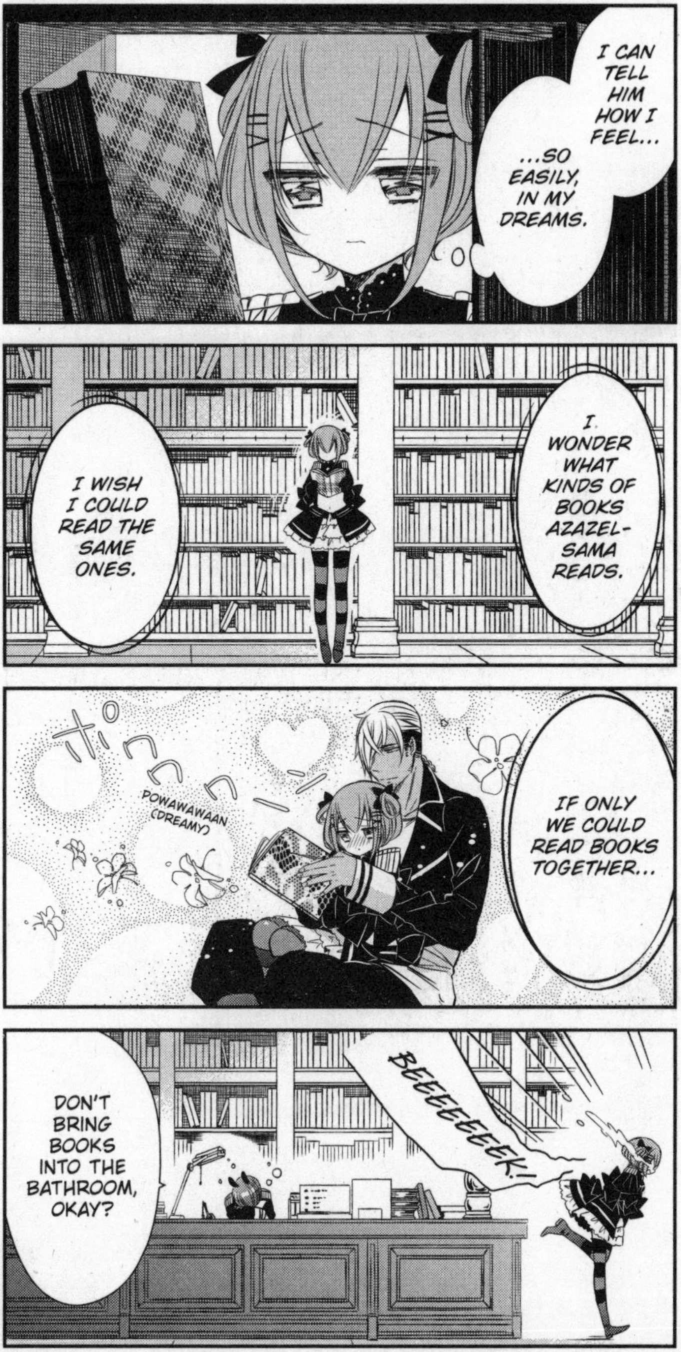
I CAN TELL HIM HOW I FEEL...
...SO EASILY, IN MY DREAMS.
I WONDER WHAT KINDS OF BOOKS AZAZEL-SAMA READS.
I WISH I COULD READ THE SAME ONES.
IF ONLY WE COULD READ BOOKS TOGETHER...
POWAWAWAAN (DREAMY)
BEEEEEEK!
DON'T BRING BOOKS INTO THE BATHROOM, OKAY?

TOGETHER

FOREVER UNABLE TO MEET

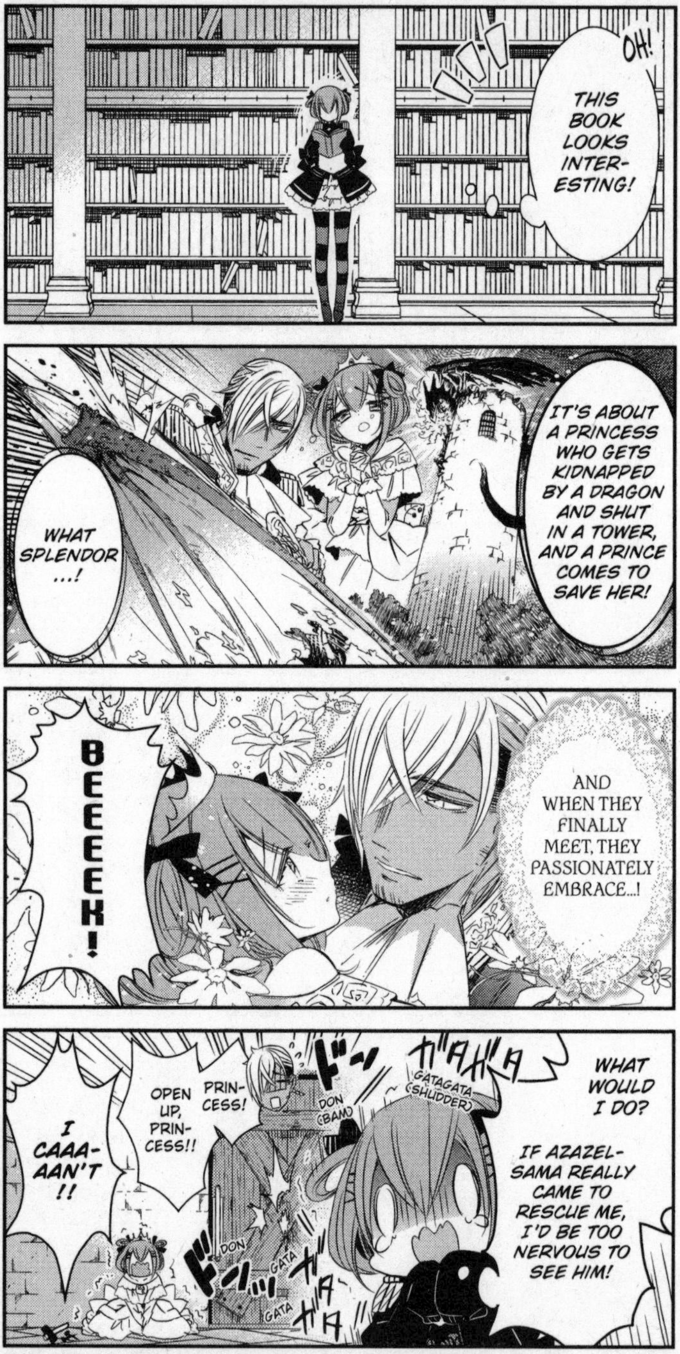
OH! THIS BOOK LOOKS INTER-ESTING!
IT'S ABOUT A PRINCESS WHO GETS KIDNAPPED BY A DRAGON AND SHUT IN A TOWER, AND A PRINCE COMES TO SAVE HER!
WHAT SPLENDOR ...!
AND WHEN THEY FINALLY MEET, THEY PASSIONATELY EMBRACE...!
BEEEEEK!
WHAT WOULD I DO?
IF AZAZEL-SAMA REALLY CAME TO RESCUE ME, I'D BE TOO NERVOUS TO SEE HIM!
GATAGATA (SHUDDER)
DON (BAM)
PRIN-CESS!
OPEN UP, PRIN-CESS!!
I CAAAA-AAN'T !!
DON
GATA
GATA

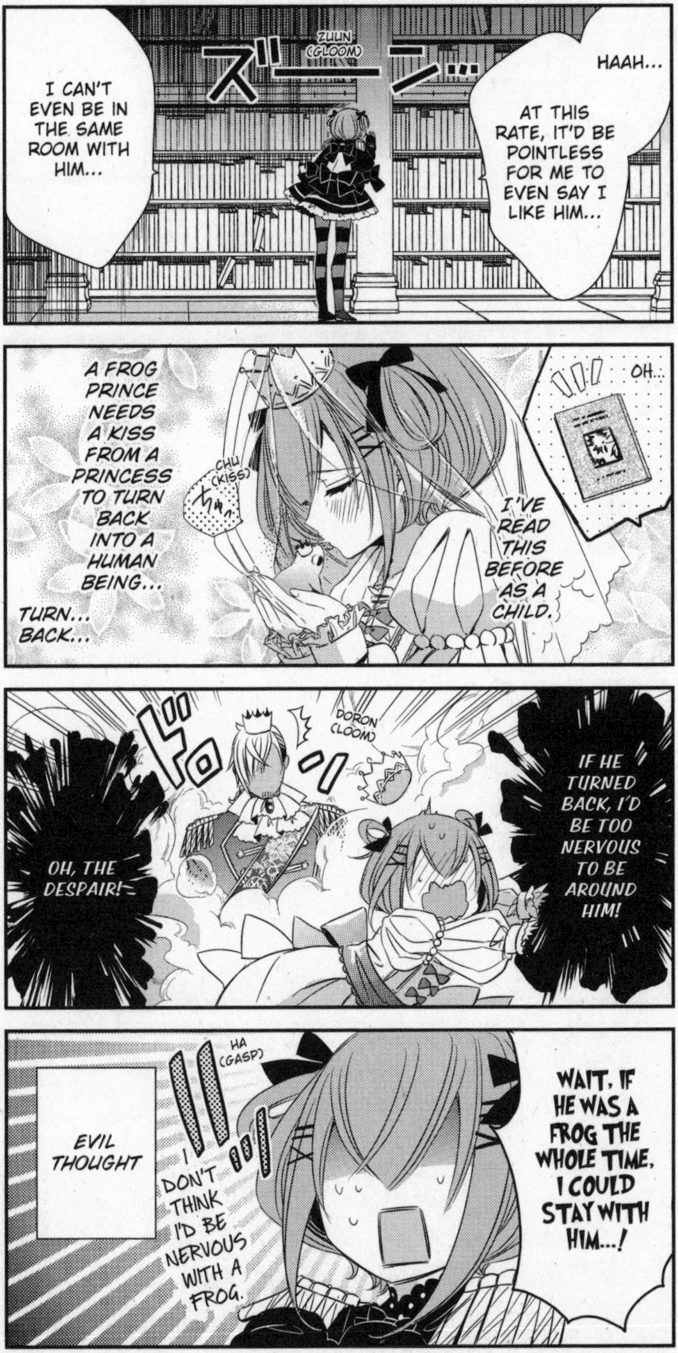
HAAH...
AT THIS RATE, IT'D BE POINTLESS FOR ME TO EVEN SAY I LIKE HIM...
ZUUN (GLOOM)
I CAN'T EVEN BE IN THE SAME ROOM WITH HIM...
OH...
I'VE READ THIS BEFORE AS A CHILD.
CHU (KISS)
A FROG PRINCE NEEDS A KISS FROM A PRINCESS TO TURN BACK INTO A HUMAN BEING...
TURN... BACK...
IF HE TURNED BACK, I'D BE TOO NERVOUS TO BE AROUND HIM!
DORON (LOOM)
OH, THE DESPAIR!
WAIT, IF HE WAS A FROG THE WHOLE TIME, I COULD STAY WITH HIM...!
HA (GASP)
I DON'T THINK I'D BE NERVOUS WITH A FROG.
EVIL THOUGHT

BESIDES, I DON'T THINK GOCCHIN COULD KISS A FROG

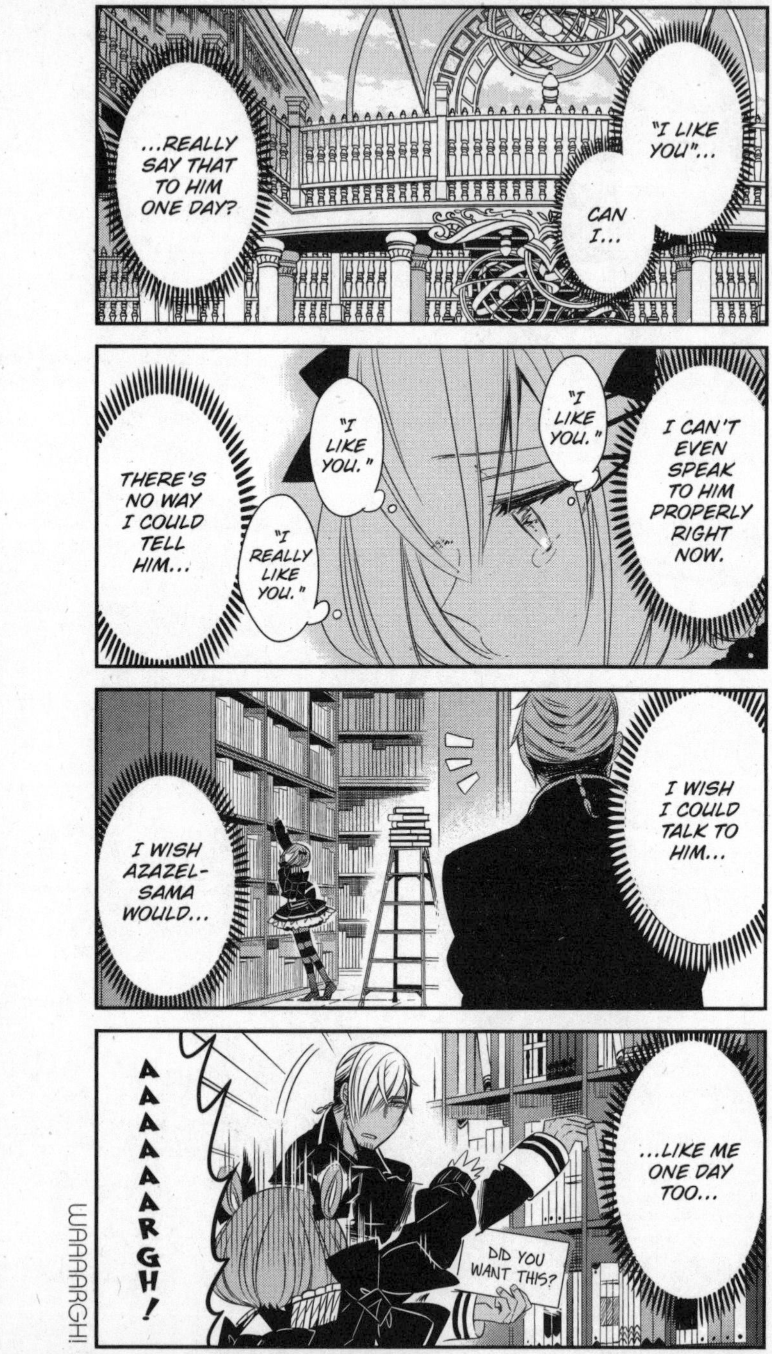
"I LIKE YOU"...
CAN I...
...REALLY SAY THAT TO HIM ONE DAY?
I CAN'T EVEN SPEAK TO HIM PROPERLY RIGHT NOW.
"I LIKE YOU."
"I LIKE YOU."
"I REALLY LIKE YOU."
THERE'S NO WAY I COULD TELL HIM...
I WISH I COULD TALK TO HIM...
I WISH AZAZEL-SAMA WOULD...
...LIKE ME ONE DAY TOO...
DID YOU WANT THIS?
AAAAAAARGH!
WAAAARGH!

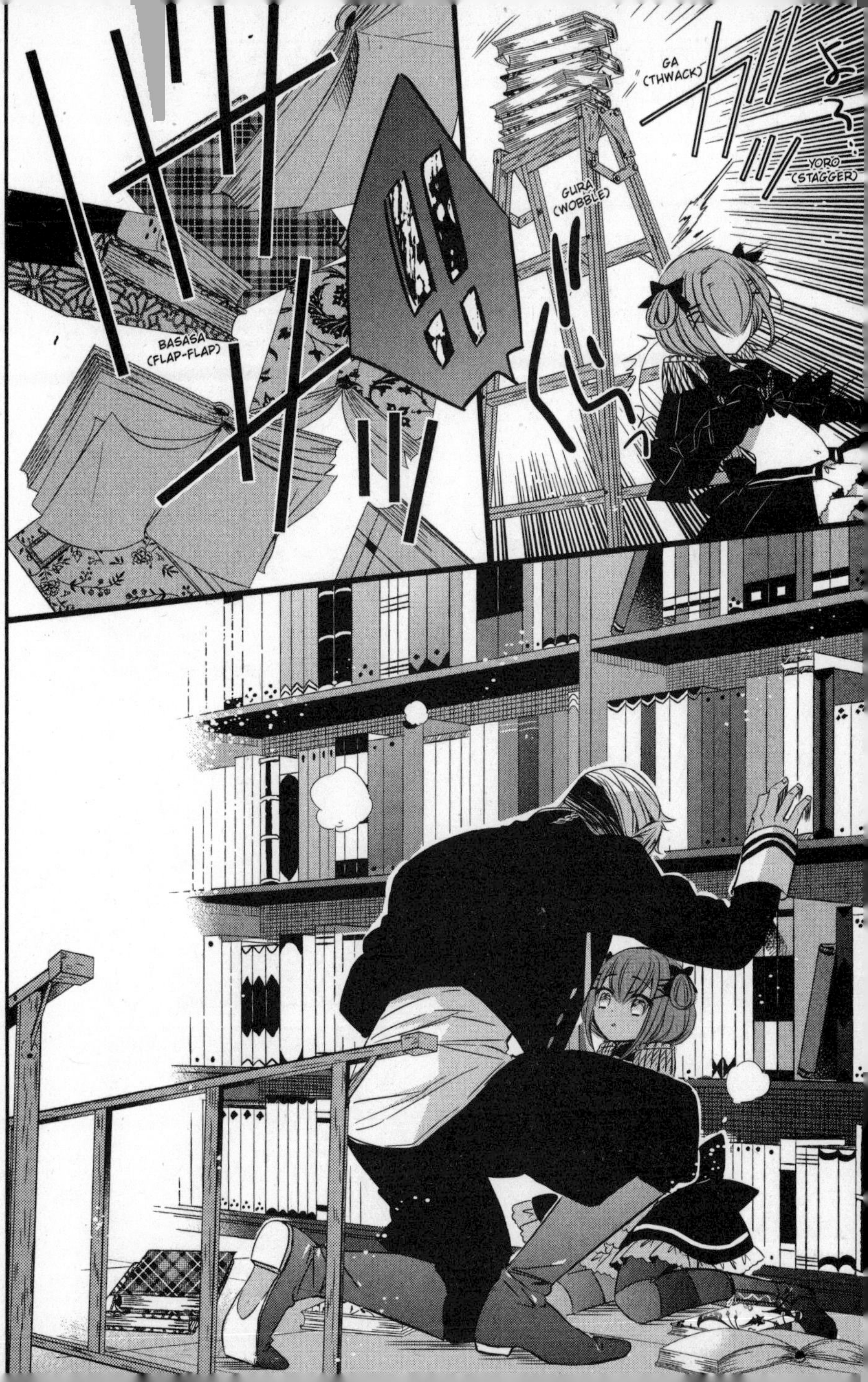
GA
(THWACK)
YORO
(STAGGER)
GURA
(WOBBLE)
BASASA
(FLAP-FLAP)

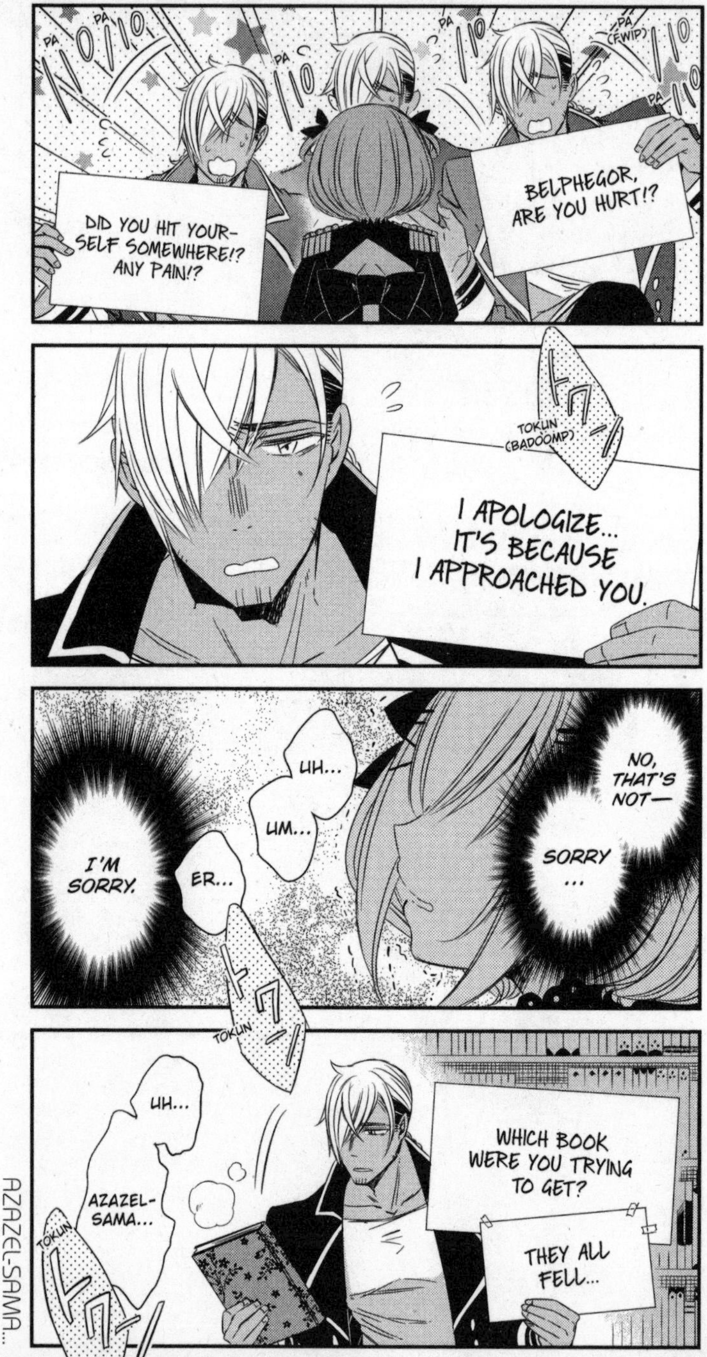
PA
PA (FWIP)
PA
PA
PA
PA
BELPHEGOR, ARE YOU HURT!?
DID YOU HIT YOURSELF SOMEWHERE!? ANY PAIN!?
TOKUN (BADOOMP)
I APOLOGIZE... IT'S BECAUSE I APPROACHED YOU.
NO, THAT'S NOT—
SORRY...
UH...
UM...
ER...
I'M SORRY.
TOKUN
WHICH BOOK WERE YOU TRYING TO GET?
THEY ALL FELL...
UH...
AZAZEL-SAMA...
TOKUN
AZAZEL-SAMA...

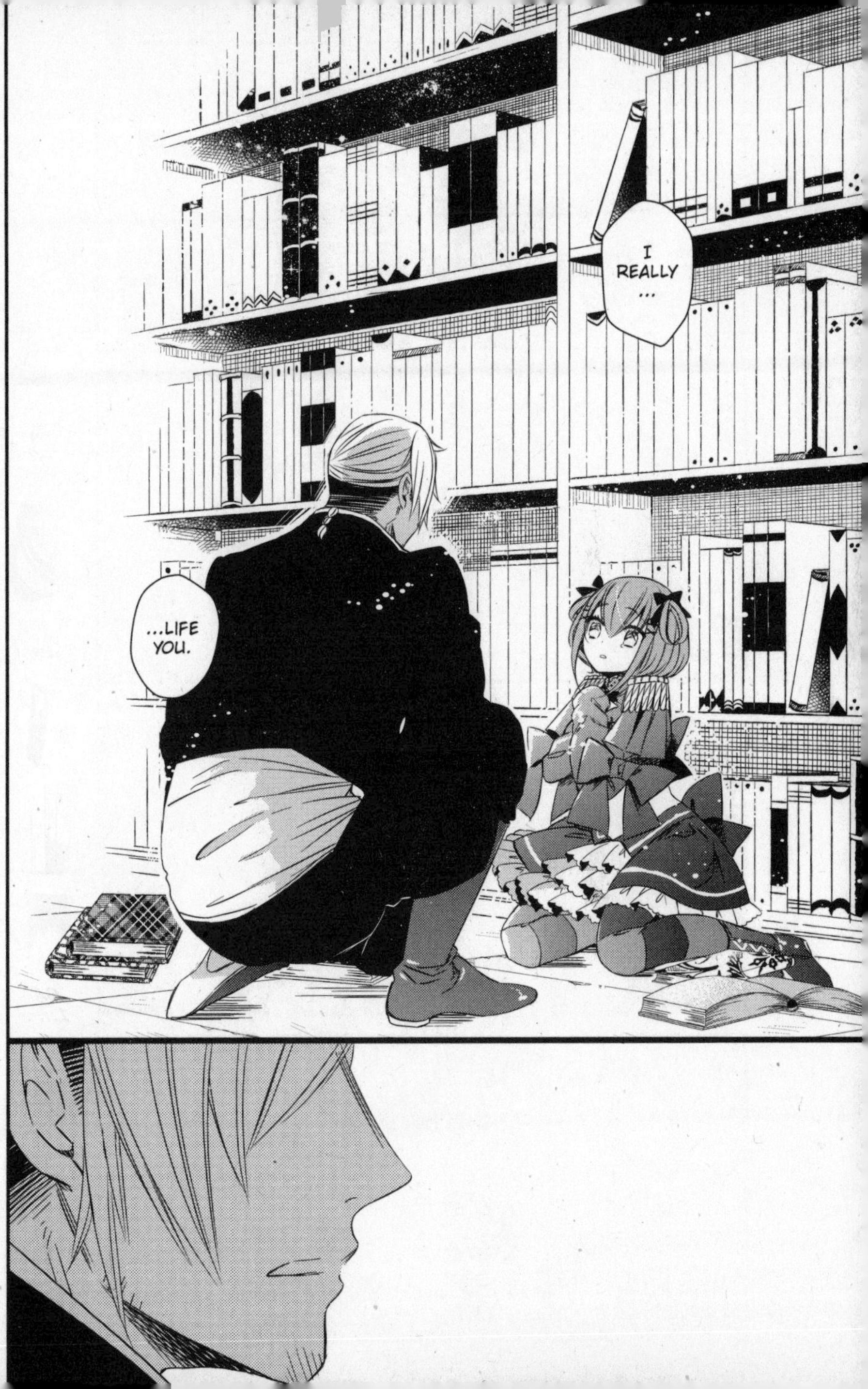
I REALLY ...
...LIFE YOU.

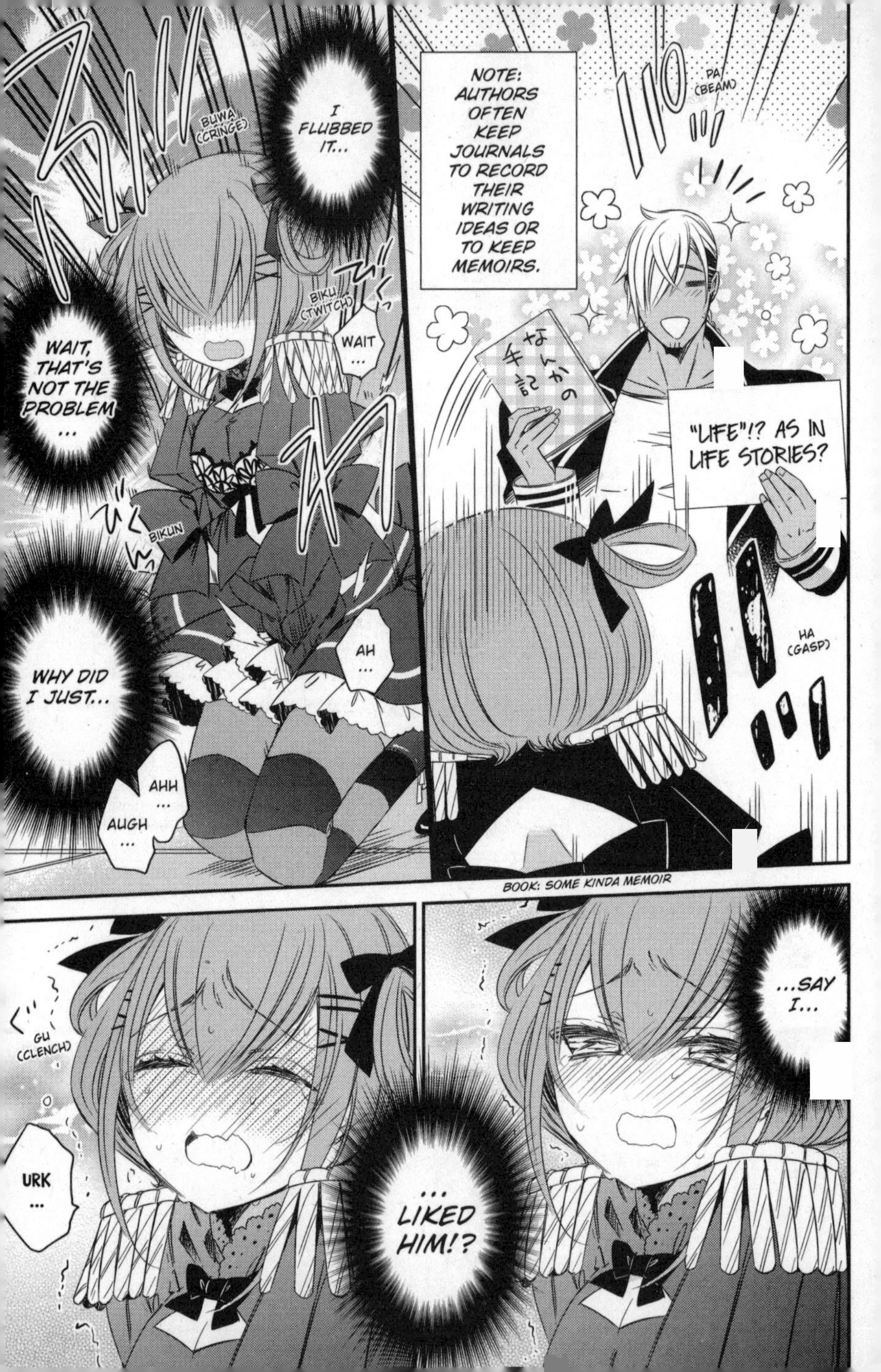
PA (BEAM)
NOTE: AUTHORS OFTEN KEEP JOURNALS TO RECORD THEIR WRITING IDEAS OR TO KEEP MEMOIRS.
なんかの手記
"LIFE"!? AS IN LIFE STORIES?
HA (GASP)
BOOK: SOME KINDA MEMOIR
I FLUBBED IT...
BUWA (CRINGE)
BIKU (TWITCH)
WAIT...
WAIT, THAT'S NOT THE PROBLEM...
BIKUN
AH...
WHY DID I JUST...
AHH...
AUGH...
...SAY I...
...LIKED HIM!?
GU (CLENCH)
URK...

NO MOOORE (SAID THE COW)

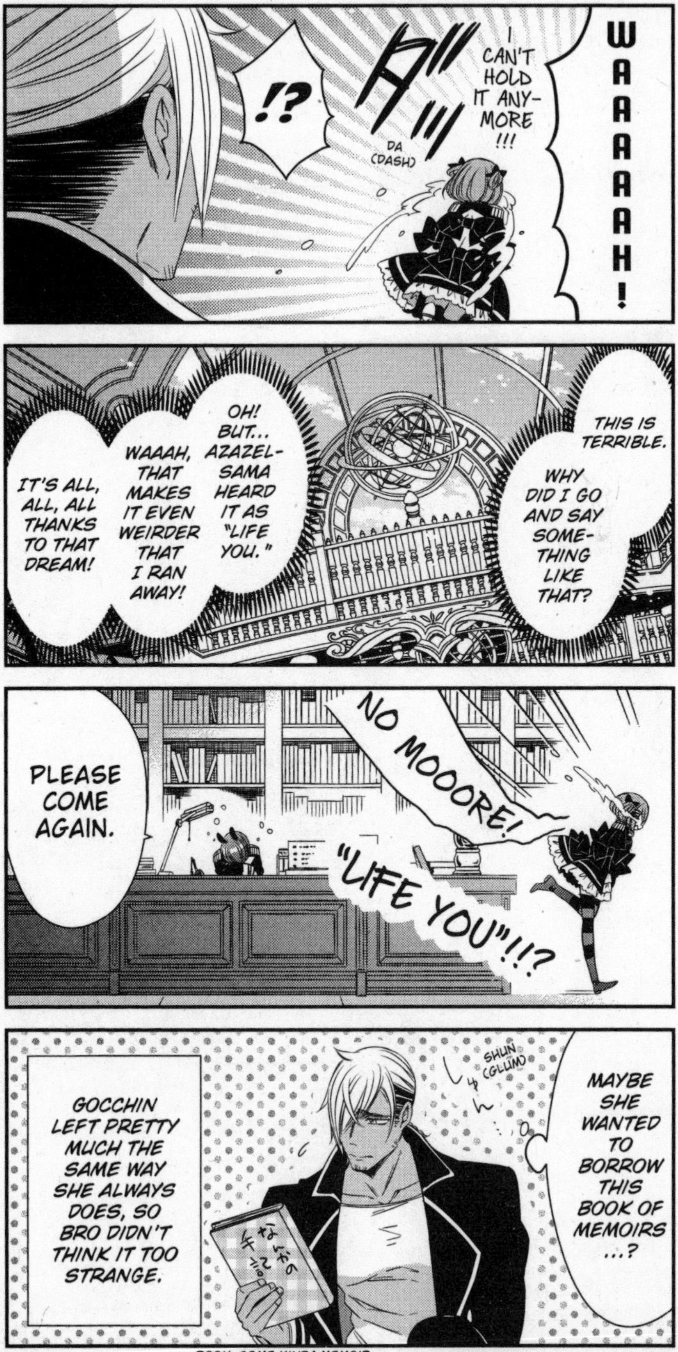
WAAAAAAH!
I CAN'T HOLD IT ANY-MORE!!!
DA (DASH)
!?
THIS IS TERRIBLE.
WHY DID I GO AND SAY SOME-THING LIKE THAT?
OH! BUT... AZAZEL-SAMA HEARD IT AS "LIFE YOU."
WAAAH, THAT MAKES IT EVEN WEIRDER THAT I RAN AWAY!
IT'S ALL, ALL, ALL THANKS TO THAT DREAM!
NO MOOORE!
"LIFE YOU"!!?
PLEASE COME AGAIN.
MAYBE SHE WANTED TO BORROW THIS BOOK OF MEMOIRS ...?
SHUN (GLUM)
なんかの手記
GOCCHIN LEFT PRETTY MUCH THE SAME WAY SHE ALWAYS DOES, SO BRO DIDN'T THINK IT TOO STRANGE.

BOOK: SOME KINDA MEMOIR

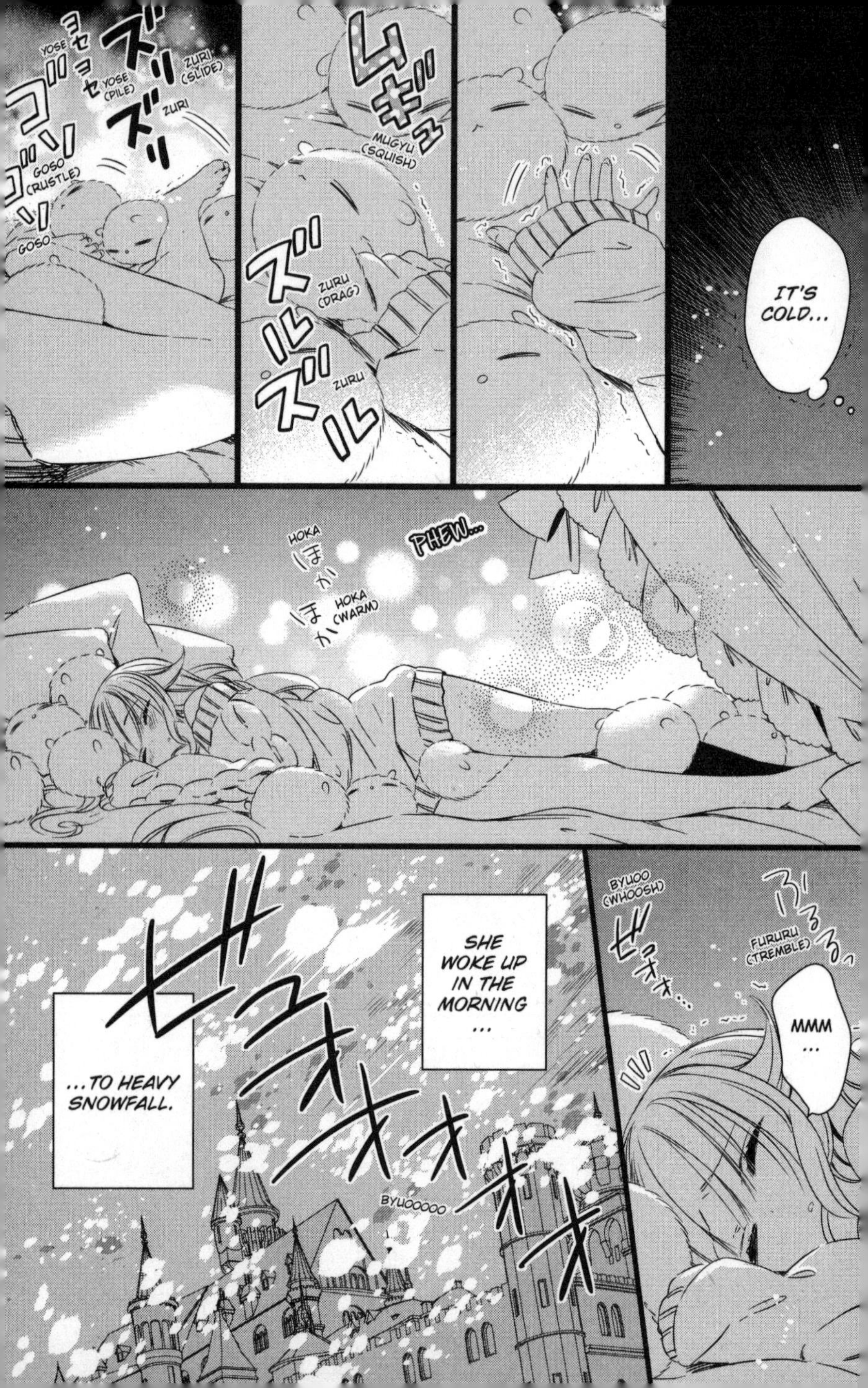
IT'S COLD...
MUGYU (SQUISH)
ZURU (DRAG)
ZURU
ZURI (SLIDE)
ZURI
YOSE
YOSE (PILE)
GOSO (RUSTLE)
GOSO
PHEW...
HOKA
HOKA (WARM)
BYUOO (WHOOSH)
FURURU (TREMBLE)
MMM...
SHE WOKE UP IN THE MORNING...
...TO HEAVY SNOWFALL.
BYUOOOOO

CHAPTER 22

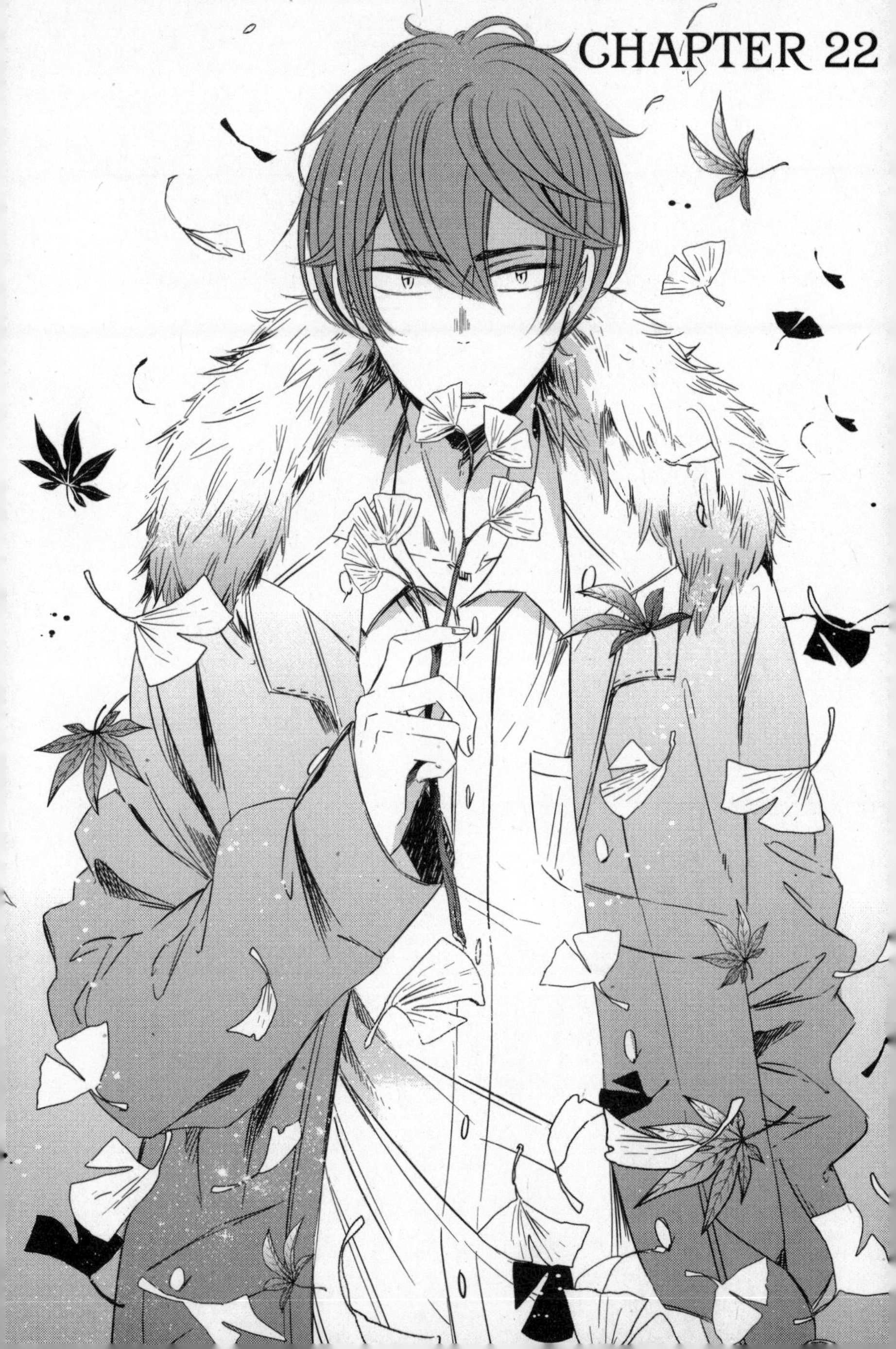

DON'T WANNA GO OUT

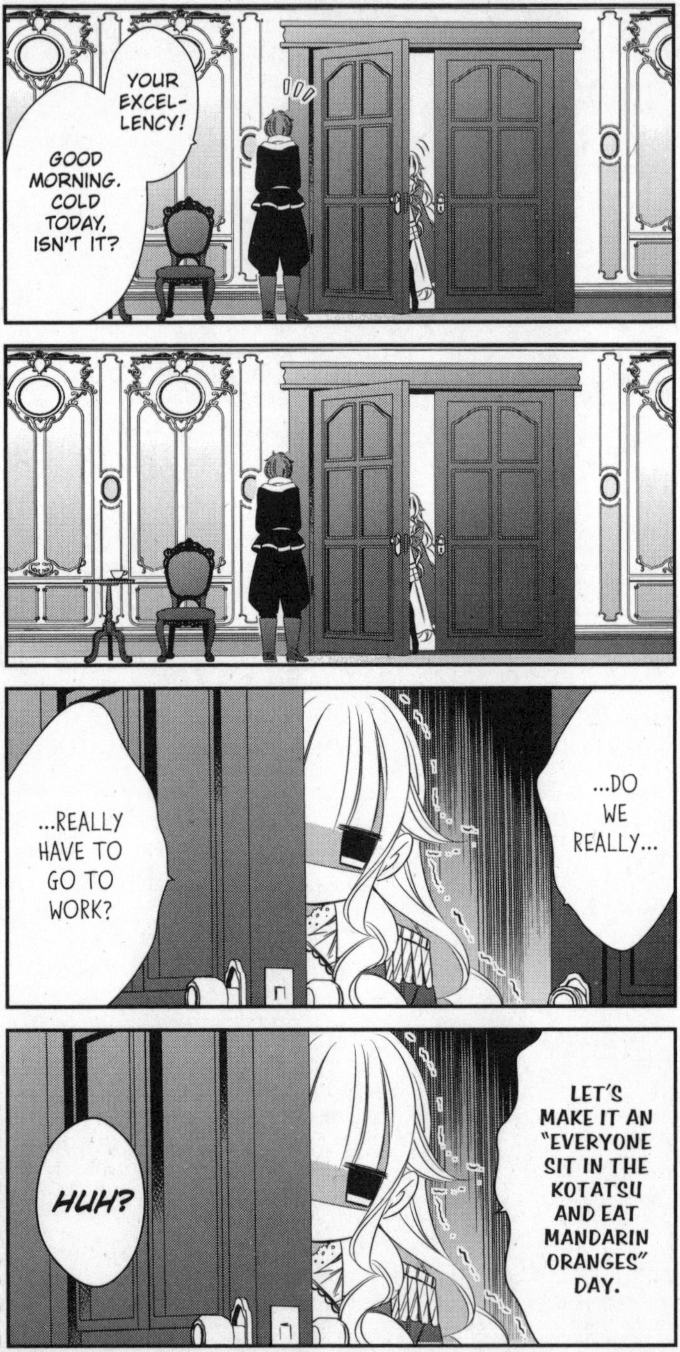
YOUR EXCEL-LENCY!
GOOD MORNING. COLD TODAY, ISN'T IT?
...DO WE REALLY...
...REALLY HAVE TO GO TO WORK?
LET'S MAKE IT AN "EVERYONE SIT IN THE KOTATSU AND EAT MANDARIN ORANGES" DAY.
HUH?

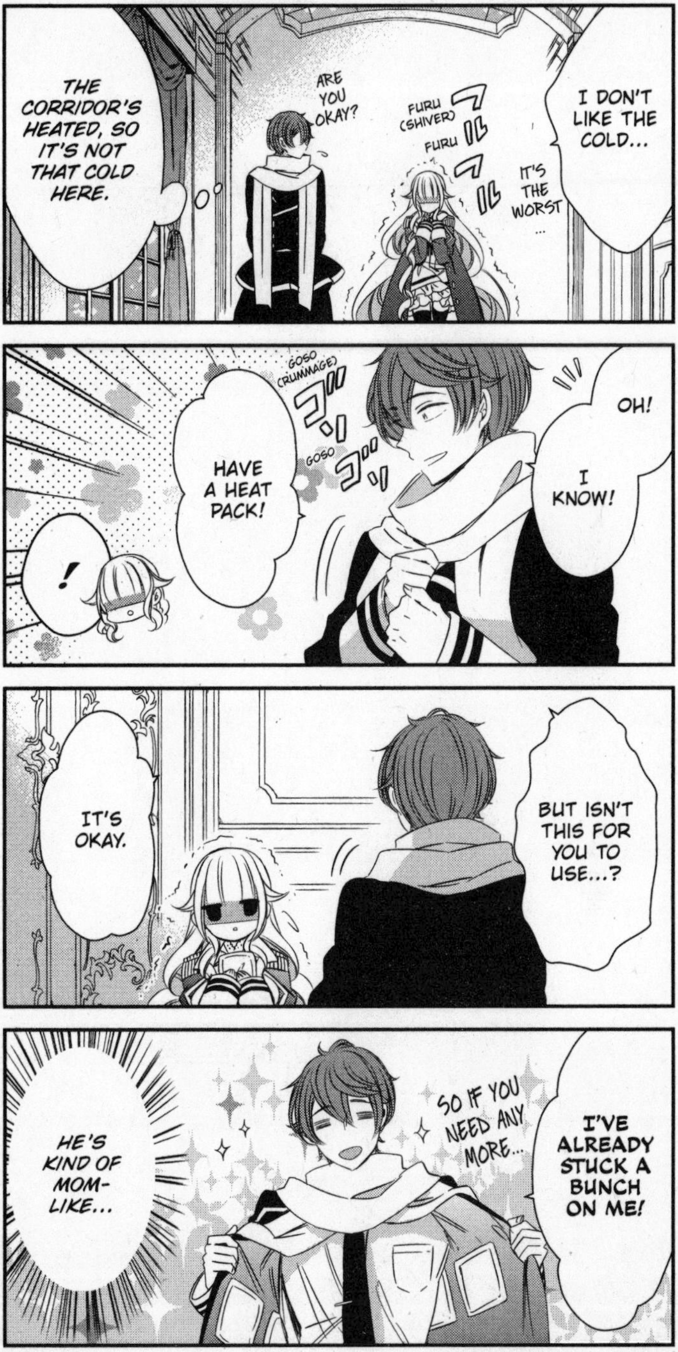
I DON'T LIKE THE COLD...
IT'S THE WORST...
FURU (SHIVER)
FURU
ARE YOU OKAY?
THE CORRIDOR'S HEATED, SO IT'S NOT THAT COLD HERE.
OH!
I KNOW!
GOSO (RUMMAGE)
GOSO
HAVE A HEAT PACK!
!
BUT ISN'T THIS FOR YOU TO USE...?
IT'S OKAY.
I'VE ALREADY STUCK A BUNCH ON ME!
SO IF YOU NEED ANY MORE...
HE'S KIND OF MOM-LIKE...

STICK THEM TO YOUR STOMACH AND BACK

WHATCHA GONNA DO?

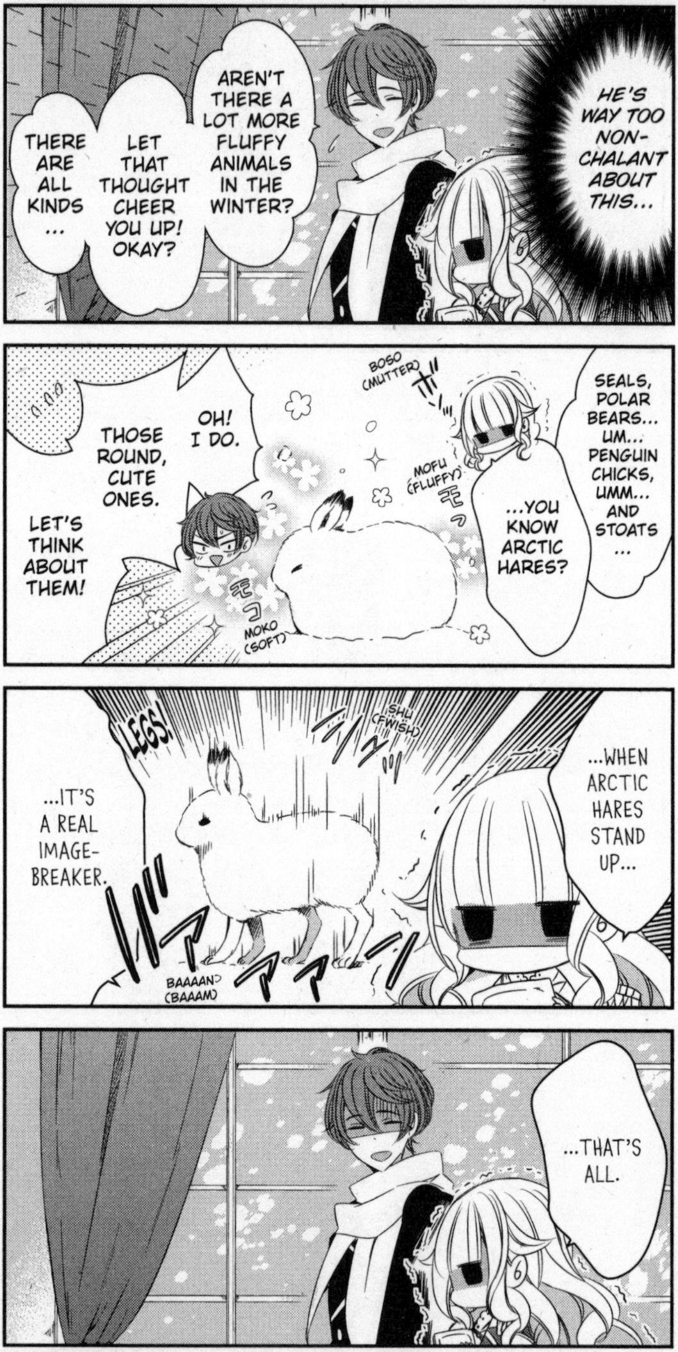
HE'S WAY TOO NON-CHALANT ABOUT THIS...
AREN'T THERE A LOT MORE FLUFFY ANIMALS IN THE WINTER?
LET THAT THOUGHT CHEER YOU UP! OKAY?
THERE ARE ALL KINDS ...
SEALS, POLAR BEARS... UM... PENGUIN CHICKS, UMM... AND STOATS ...
BOSO (MUTTER)
...YOU KNOW ARCTIC HARES?
MOFU (FLUFFY)
OH! I DO.
THOSE ROUND, CUTE ONES.
LET'S THINK ABOUT THEM!
MOKO (SOFT)
...WHEN ARCTIC HARES STAND UP...
SHU (FWISH)
LEGS!
...IT'S A REAL IMAGE-BREAKER.
BAAAAN (BAAAM)
...THAT'S ALL.

YOUR NAME

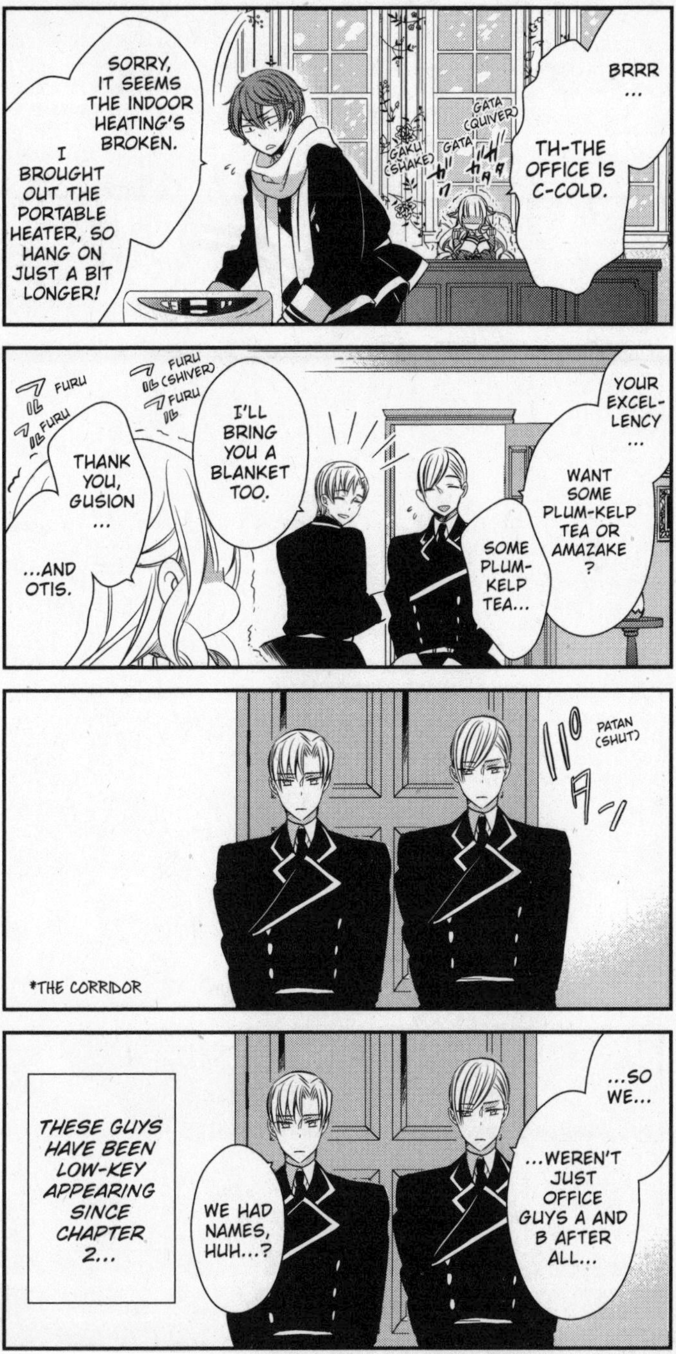
BRRR ...
TH-THE OFFICE IS C-COLD.
GATA (QUIVER)
GAKU (SHAKE) GATA
SORRY, IT SEEMS THE INDOOR HEATING'S BROKEN.
I BROUGHT OUT THE PORTABLE HEATER, SO HANG ON JUST A BIT LONGER!
YOUR EXCELLENCY ...
WANT SOME PLUM-KELP TEA OR AMAZAKE?
SOME PLUM-KELP TEA...
I'LL BRING YOU A BLANKET TOO.
FURU (SHIVER) FURU
FURU FURU
THANK YOU, GUSION ...
...AND OTIS.
PATAN (SHUT)
*THE CORRIDOR
...SO WE...
...WEREN'T JUST OFFICE GUYS A AND B AFTER ALL...
WE HAD NAMES, HUH...?
THESE GUYS HAVE BEEN LOW-KEY APPEARING SINCE CHAPTER 2...

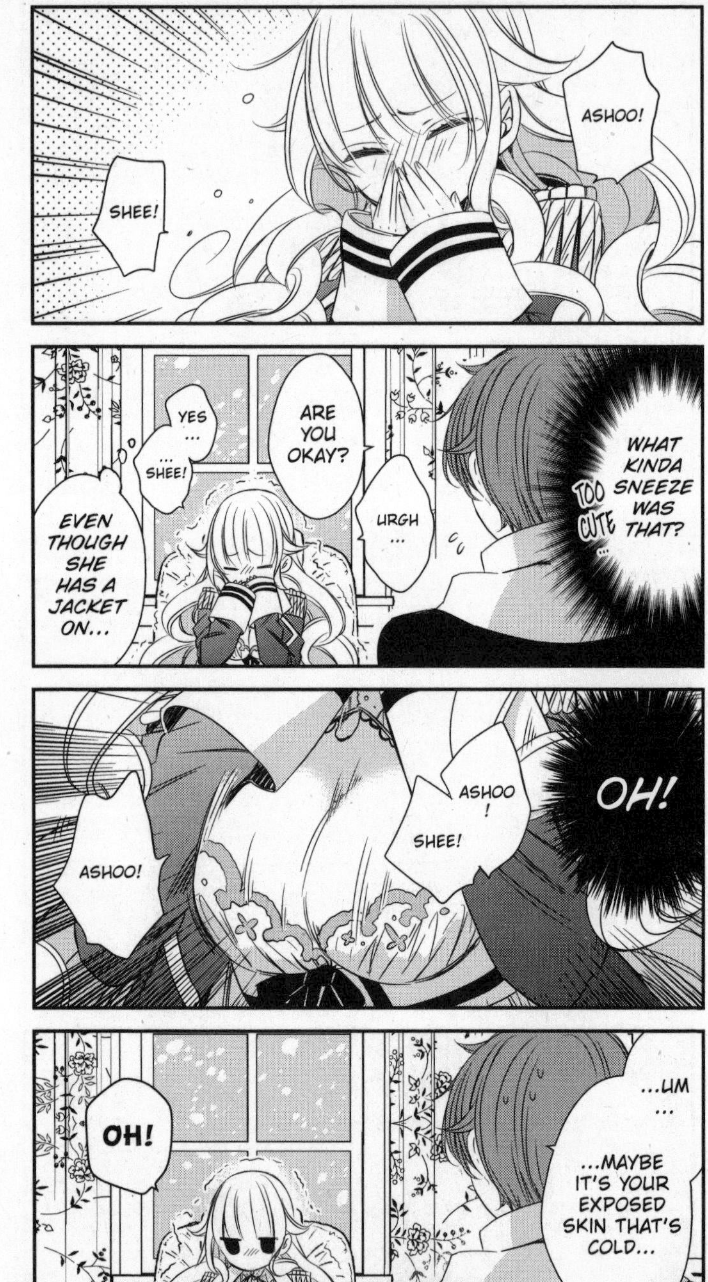
ASHOO!
SHEE!
WHAT KINDA SNEEZE WAS THAT?
TOO CUTE...
URGH...
ARE YOU OKAY?
YES... ...SHEE!
EVEN THOUGH SHE HAS A JACKET ON...
OH!
ASHOO! SHEE!
ASHOO!
...UM...
...MAYBE IT'S YOUR EXPOSED SKIN THAT'S COLD...
OH!
SHEE

COUPLES KEEP AT IT EVEN IN THE COLD

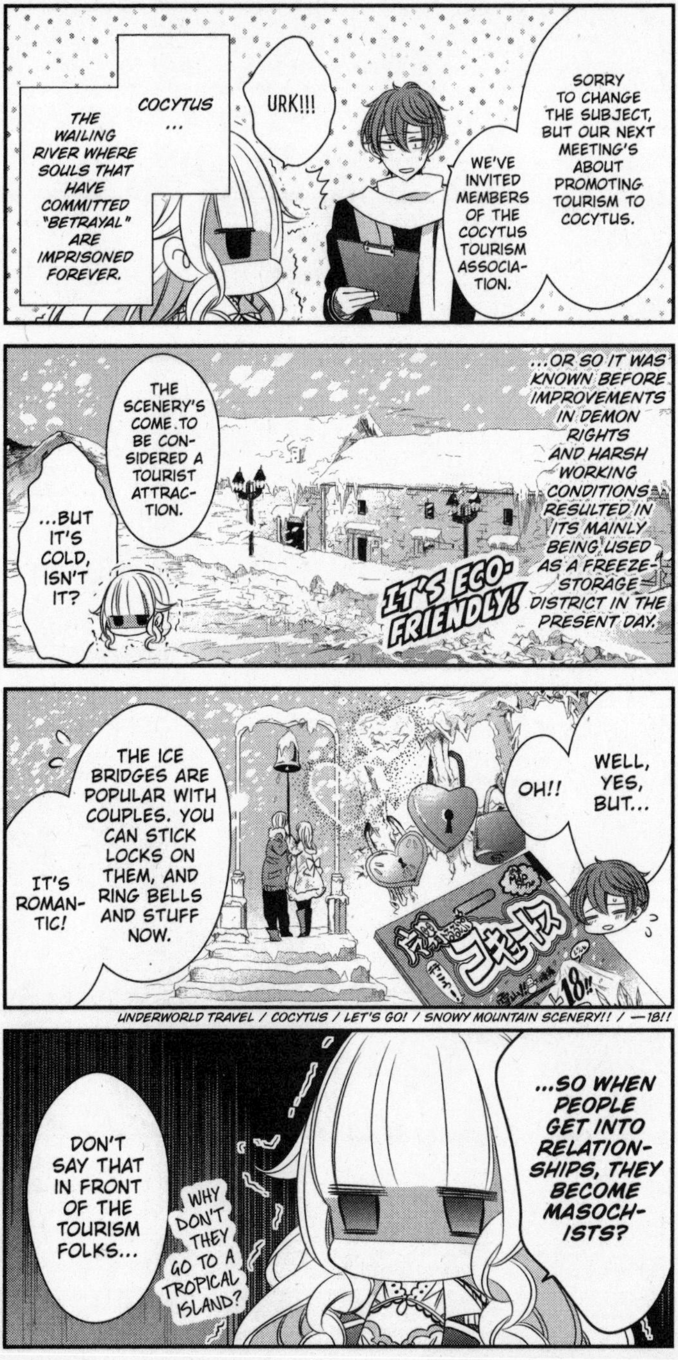
SORRY TO CHANGE THE SUBJECT, BUT OUR NEXT MEETING'S ABOUT PROMOTING TOURISM TO COCYTUS.
WE'VE INVITED MEMBERS OF THE COCYTUS TOURISM ASSOCIATION.
URK!!!
COCYTUS ...
THE WAILING RIVER WHERE SOULS THAT HAVE COMMITTED "BETRAYAL" ARE IMPRISONED FOREVER.
...OR SO IT WAS KNOWN BEFORE IMPROVEMENTS IN DEMON RIGHTS AND HARSH WORKING CONDITIONS RESULTED IN ITS MAINLY BEING USED AS A FREEZE-STORAGE DISTRICT IN THE PRESENT DAY.
IT'S ECO-FRIENDLY!
THE SCENERY'S COME TO BE CONSIDERED A TOURIST ATTRACTION.
...BUT IT'S COLD, ISN'T IT?
WELL, YES, BUT...
OH!!
THE ICE BRIDGES ARE POPULAR WITH COUPLES. YOU CAN STICK LOCKS ON THEM, AND RING BELLS AND STUFF NOW.
IT'S ROMANTIC!
18!!
UNDERWORLD TRAVEL / COCYTUS / LET'S GO! / SNOWY MOUNTAIN SCENERY!! / —18!!
...SO WHEN PEOPLE GET INTO RELATIONSHIPS, THEY BECOME MASOCHISTS?
WHY DON'T THEY GO TO A TROPICAL ISLAND?
DON'T SAY THAT IN FRONT OF THE TOURISM FOLKS...

IF ONLY WE COULD STRIKE A BALANCE (IN OUR BUST SIZE)... BY SACCHAN

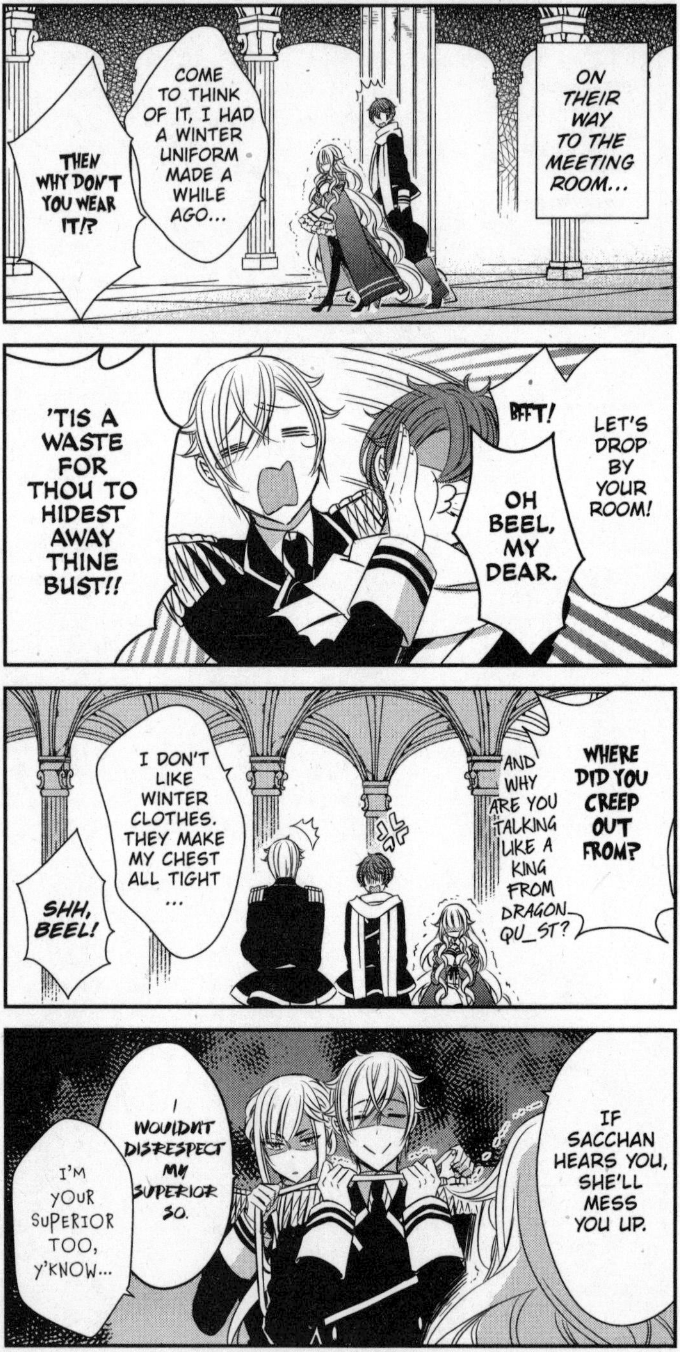
ON THEIR WAY TO THE MEETING ROOM...
COME TO THINK OF IT, I HAD A WINTER UNIFORM MADE A WHILE AGO...
THEN WHY DON'T YOU WEAR IT!?
LET'S DROP BY YOUR ROOM!
BFFT!
OH BEEL, MY DEAR.
'TIS A WASTE FOR THOU TO HIDEST AWAY THINE BUST!!
WHERE DID YOU CREEP OUT FROM?
AND WHY ARE YOU TALKING LIKE A KING FROM DRAGON QU_ST?
I DON'T LIKE WINTER CLOTHES. THEY MAKE MY CHEST ALL TIGHT...
SHH, BEEL!
IF SACCHAN HEARS YOU, SHE'LL MESS YOU UP.
I WOULDN'T DISRESPECT MY SUPERIOR SO.
I'M YOUR SUPERIOR TOO, Y'KNOW...

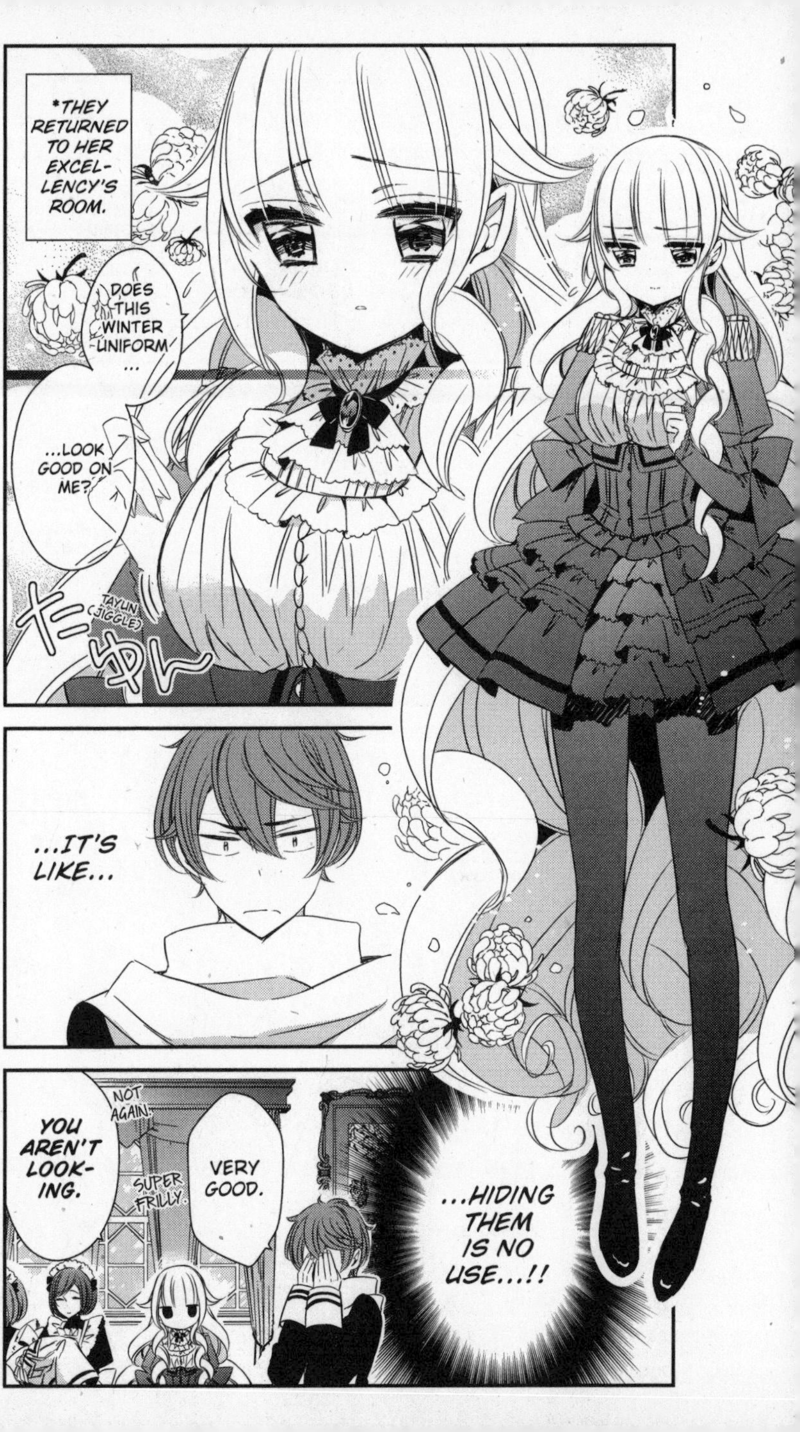
*THEY RETURNED TO HER EXCEL-LENCY'S ROOM.
DOES THIS WINTER UNIFORM ...
...LOOK GOOD ON ME?
たゆん
TAYUN (JIGGLE)
...IT'S LIKE...
...HIDING THEM IS NO USE...!!
VERY GOOD.
SUPER FRILLY.
NOT AGAIN.
YOU AREN'T LOOK-ING.

THE PRESENCE OF SHEER VOLUME

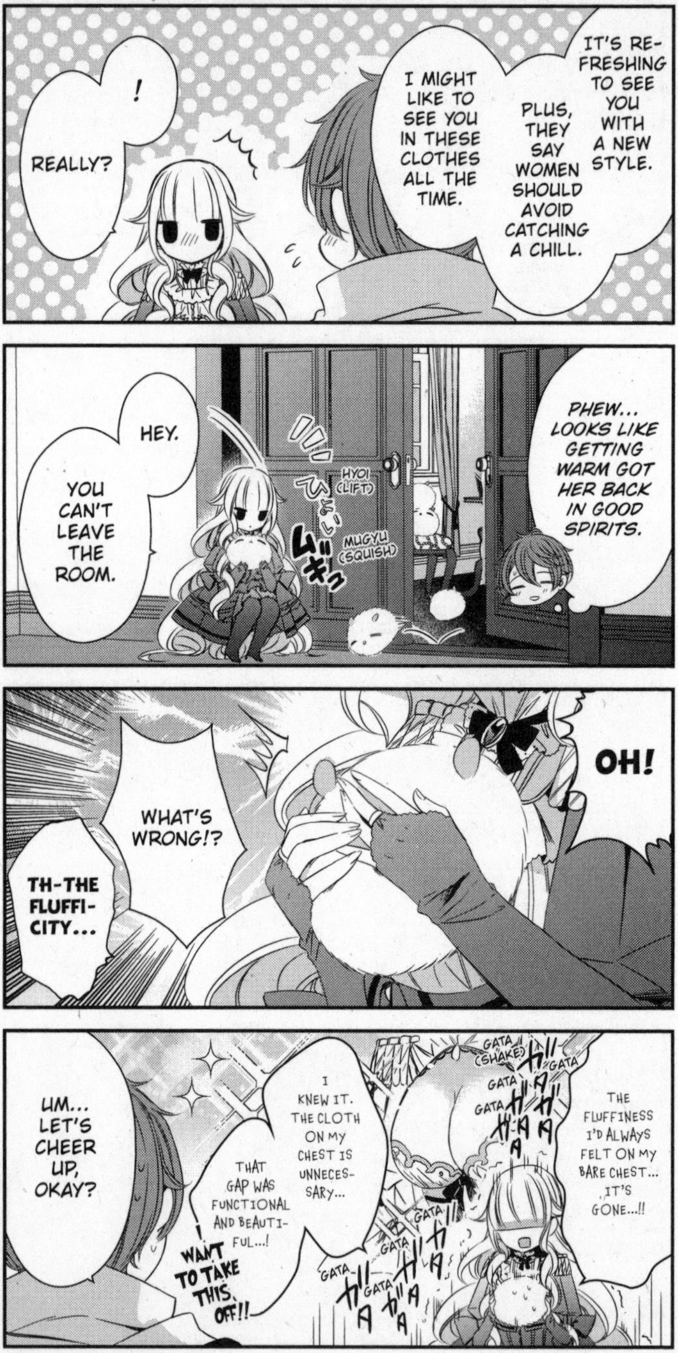
IT'S RE-FRESHING TO SEE YOU WITH A NEW STYLE.
PLUS, THEY SAY WOMEN SHOULD AVOID CATCHING A CHILL.
I MIGHT LIKE TO SEE YOU IN THESE CLOTHES ALL THE TIME.
!
REALLY?
PHEW... LOOKS LIKE GETTING WARM GOT HER BACK IN GOOD SPIRITS.
MUGYU (SQUISH)
HYOI (LIFT)
HEY.
YOU CAN'T LEAVE THE ROOM.
OH!
WHAT'S WRONG!?
TH-THE FLUFFI-CITY...
THE FLUFFINESS I'D ALWAYS FELT ON MY BARE CHEST... IT'S GONE...!!
GATA (SHAKE) GATA GATA GATA
I KNEW IT. THE CLOTH ON MY CHEST IS UNNECES-SARY...
THAT GAP WAS FUNCTIONAL AND BEAUTI-FUL...!
WANT TO TAKE THIS OFF!!
GATA GATA GATA GATA
UM... LET'S CHEER UP, OKAY?

AD-NEESAN'S PERFECT DESIGN

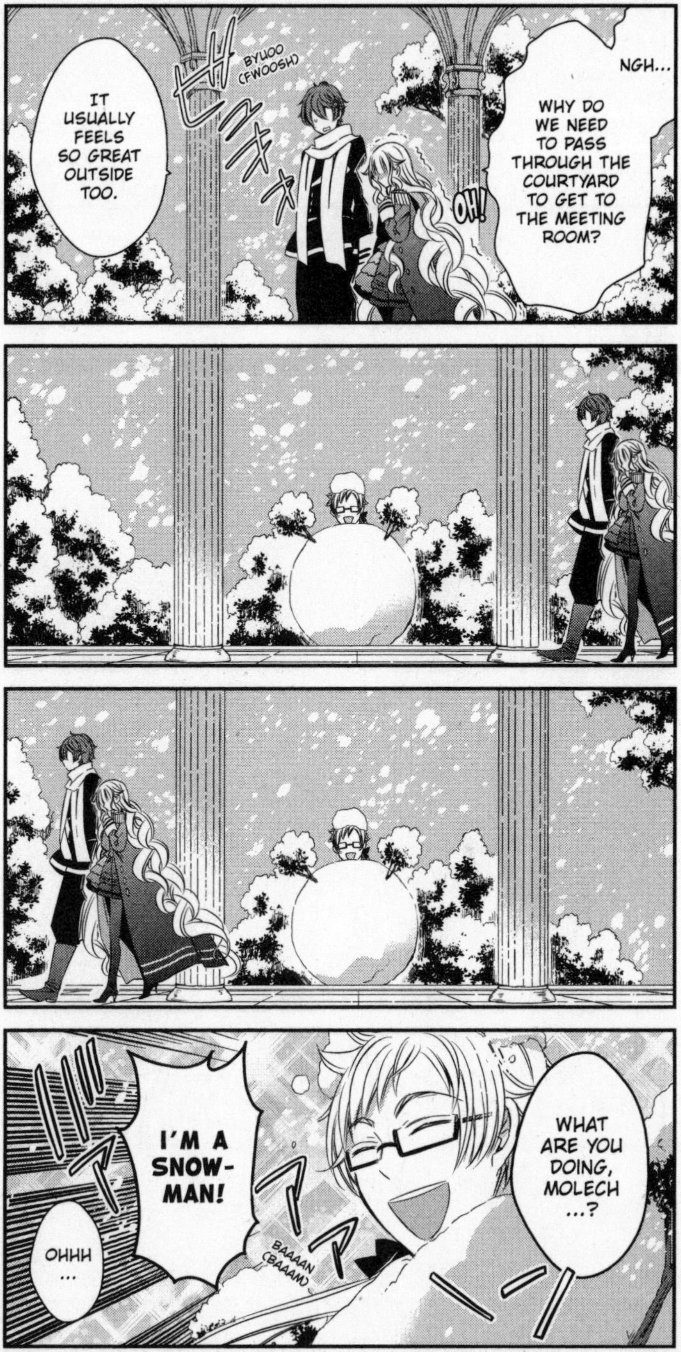
NGH...
WHY DO WE NEED TO PASS THROUGH THE COURTYARD TO GET TO THE MEETING ROOM?
OH!
BYUOO (FWOOSH)
IT USUALLY FEELS SO GREAT OUTSIDE TOO.
WHAT ARE YOU DOING, MOLECH ...?
BAAAAN (BAAAM)
I'M A SNOW-MAN!
OHHH ...

WHAT THE...?

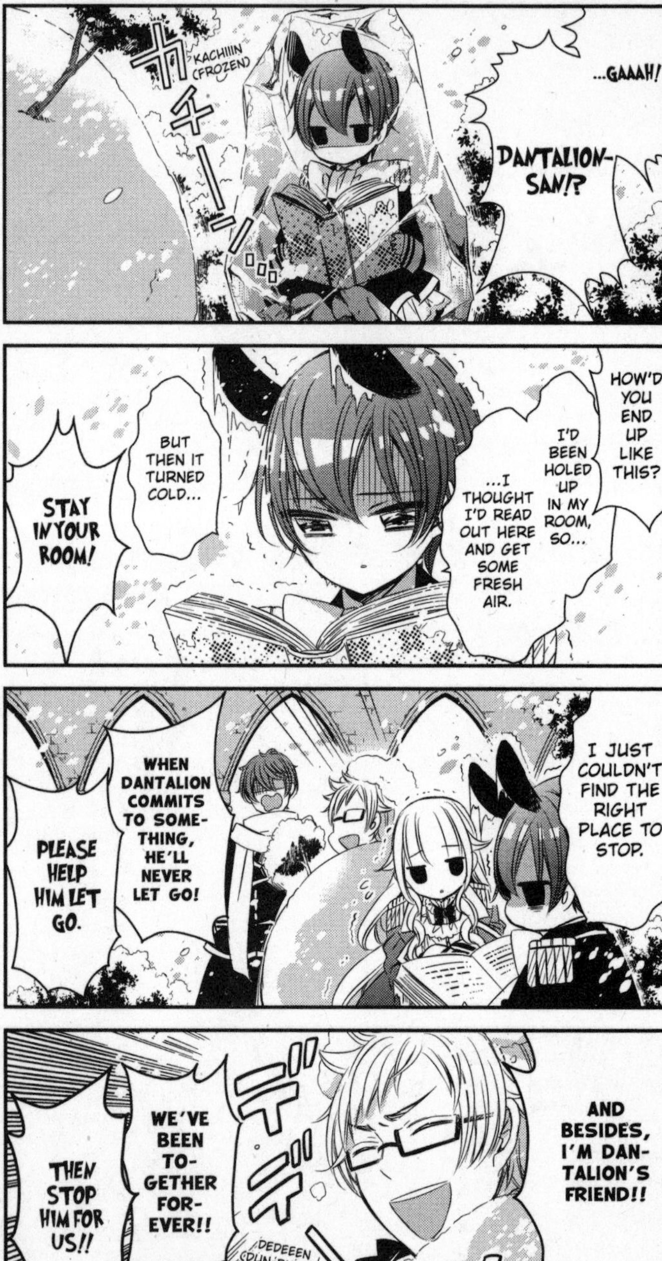
...GAAAH!
DANTALION-SAN!?
KACHIIIN (FROZEN)
HOW'D YOU END UP LIKE THIS?
I'D BEEN HOLED UP IN MY ROOM, SO...
...I THOUGHT I'D READ OUT HERE AND GET SOME FRESH AIR.
BUT THEN IT TURNED COLD...
STAY IN YOUR ROOM!
I JUST COULDN'T FIND THE RIGHT PLACE TO STOP.
WHEN DANTALION COMMITS TO SOME-THING, HE'LL NEVER LET GO!
PLEASE HELP HIM LET GO.
AND BESIDES, I'M DAN-TALION'S FRIEND!!
DEDEEEN (DUN-DUUUN)
WE'VE BEEN TO-GETHER FOR-EVER!!
THEN STOP HIM FOR US!!

SENPAI, YOU'RE NOT HIS FRIEND

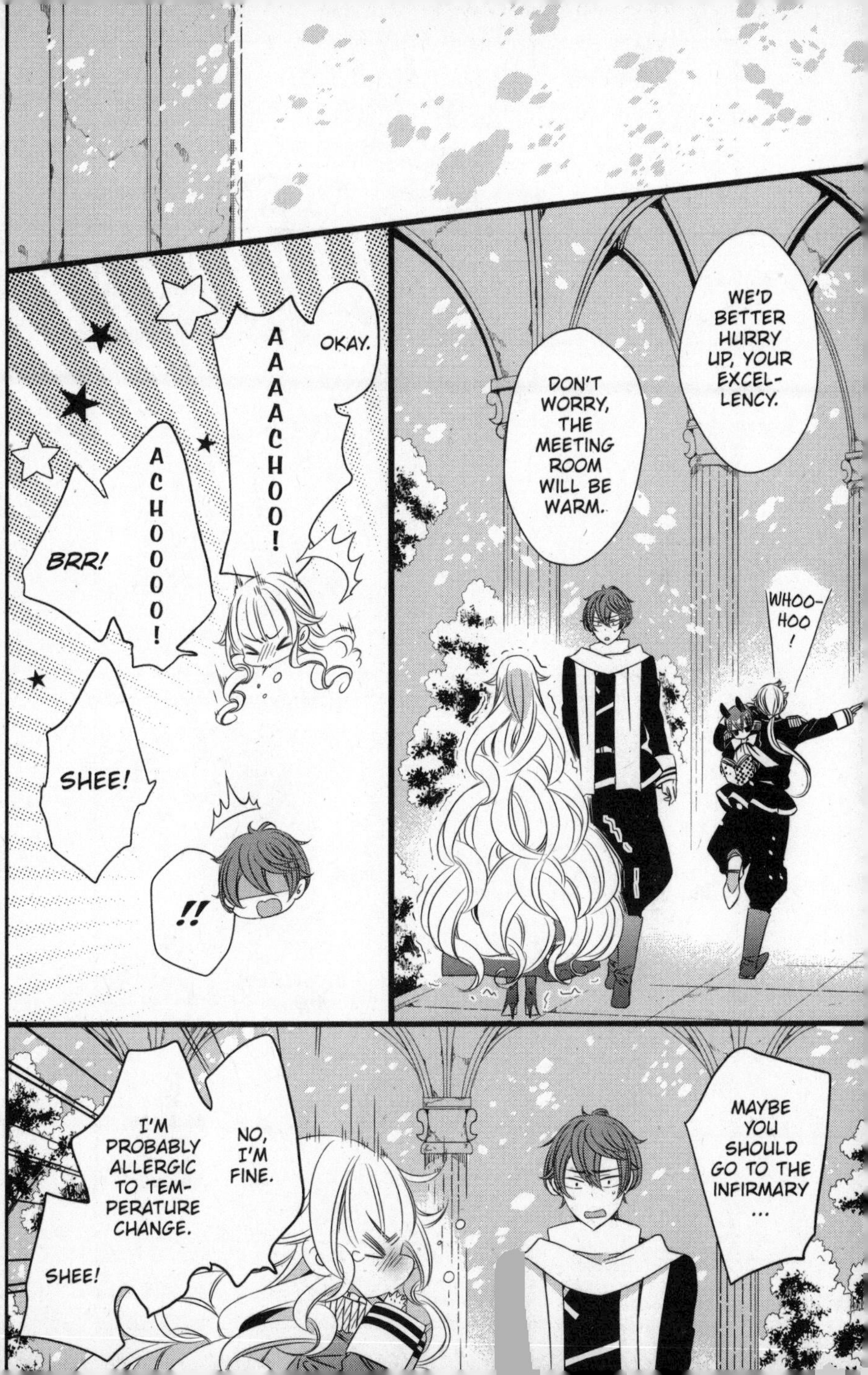
WE'D BETTER HURRY UP, YOUR EXCEL-LENCY.
DON'T WORRY, THE MEETING ROOM WILL BE WARM.
WHOO-HOO!
OKAY.
AAAACHOO!
ACHOOOOOO!
BRR!
SHEE!
!!
MAYBE YOU SHOULD GO TO THE INFIRMARY...
NO, I'M FINE.
I'M PROBABLY ALLERGIC TO TEM-PERATURE CHANGE.
SHEE!

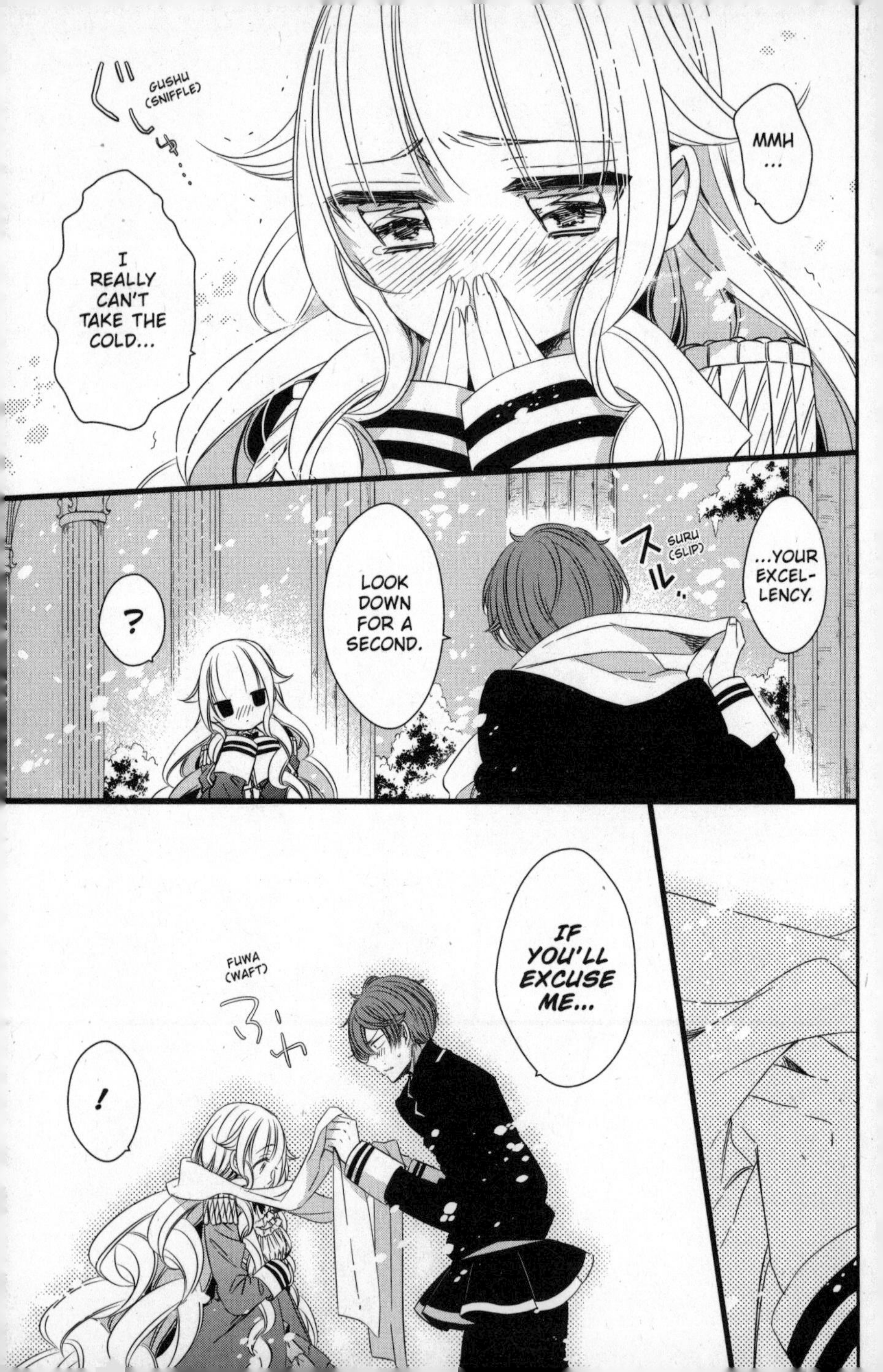
MMH ...
GUSHU (SNIFFLE)
I REALLY CAN'T TAKE THE COLD...
...YOUR EXCEL-LENCY.
SURU (SLIP)
LOOK DOWN FOR A SECOND.
?
IF YOU'LL EXCUSE ME...
FUWA (WAFT)
!

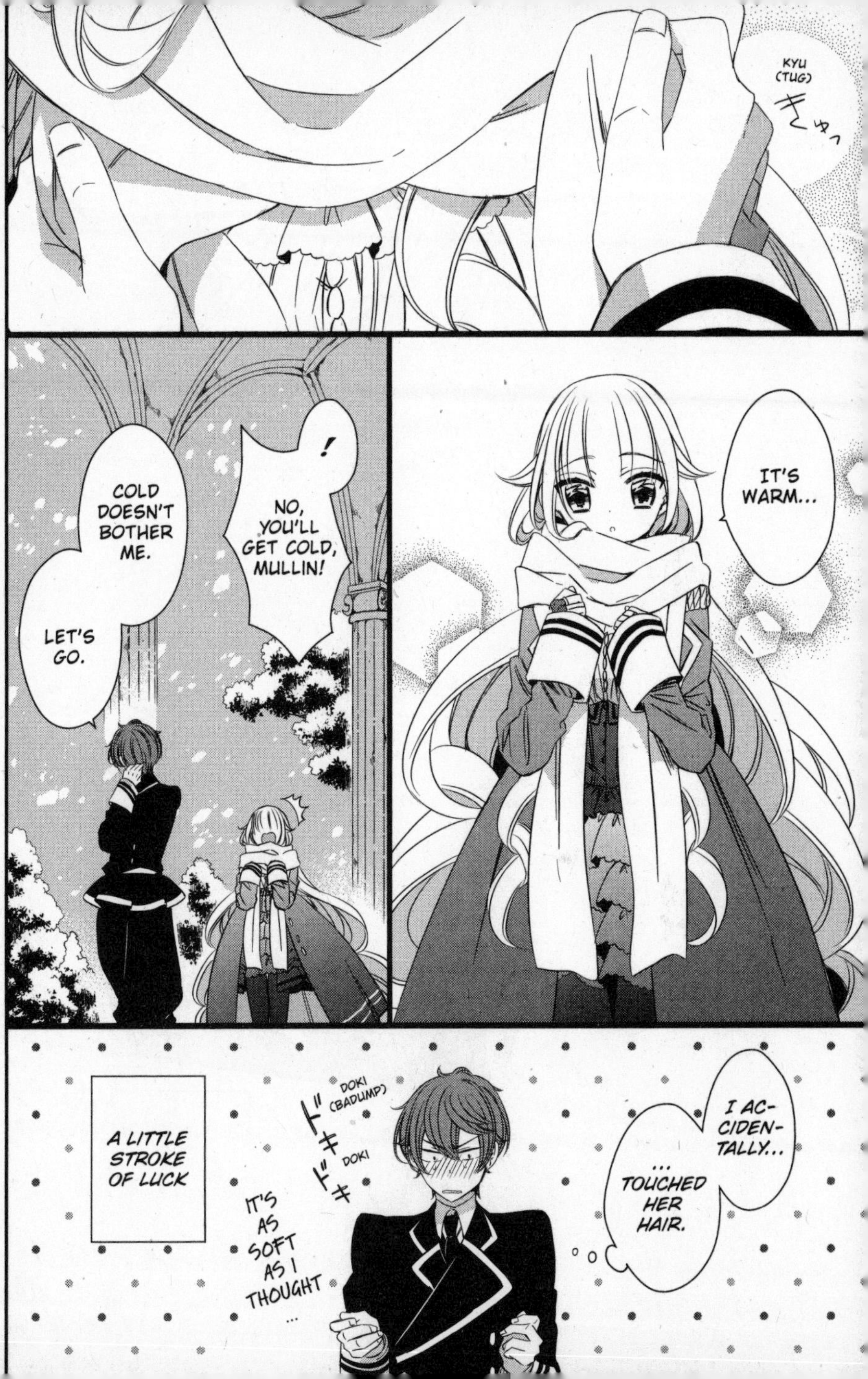
KYU (TUG)
きゅっ
IT'S WARM...
!
NO, YOU'LL GET COLD, MULLIN!
COLD DOESN'T BOTHER ME.
LET'S GO.
I AC-CIDEN-TALLY...
...TOUCHED HER HAIR.
DOKI (BADUMP)
ドキ
ドキ
DOKI
IT'S AS SOFT AS I THOUGHT...
A LITTLE STROKE OF LUCK

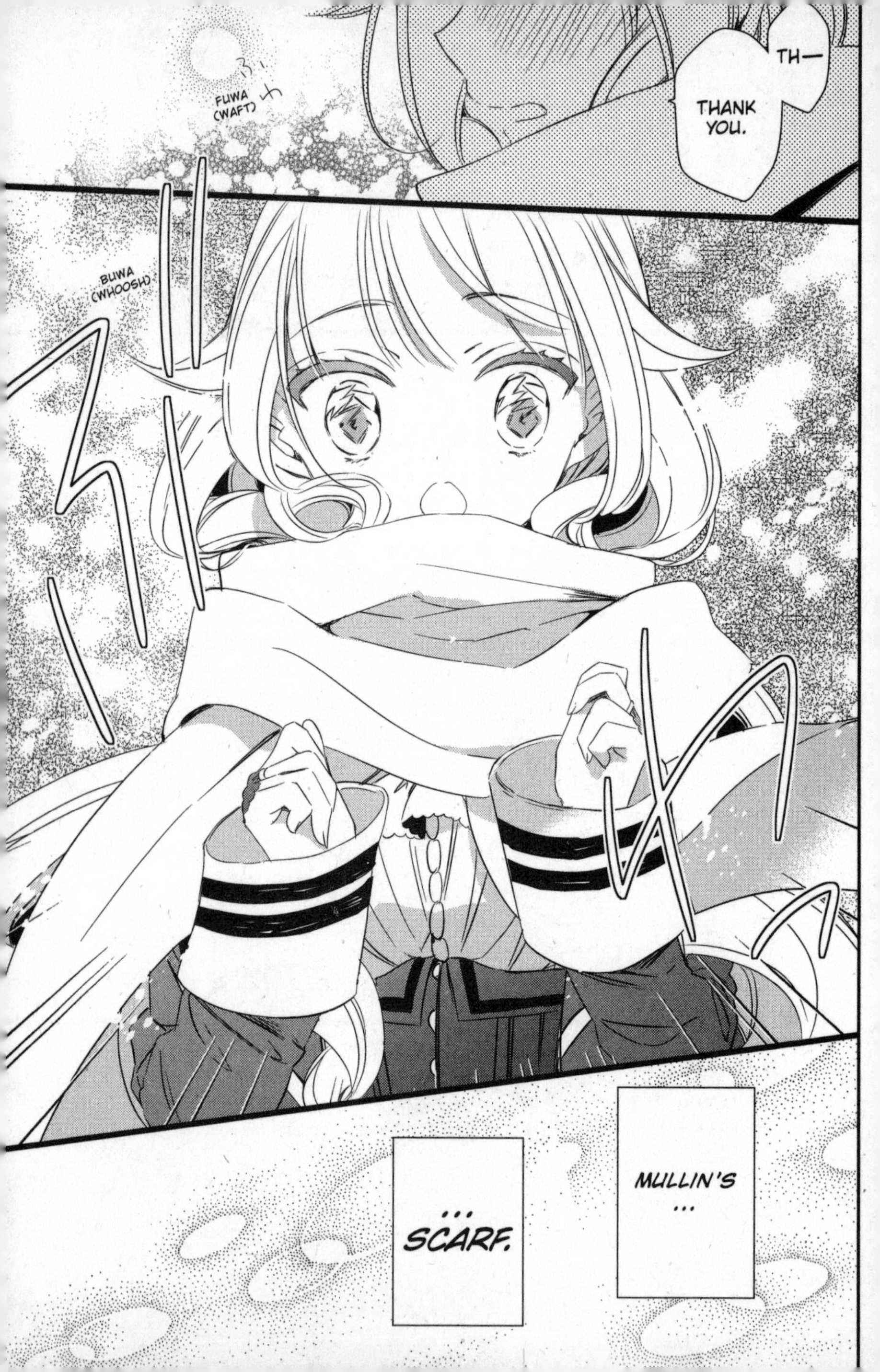
TH—
THANK YOU.
FUWA (WAFT)
BUWA (WHOOSH)
MULLIN'S ...
... SCARF.

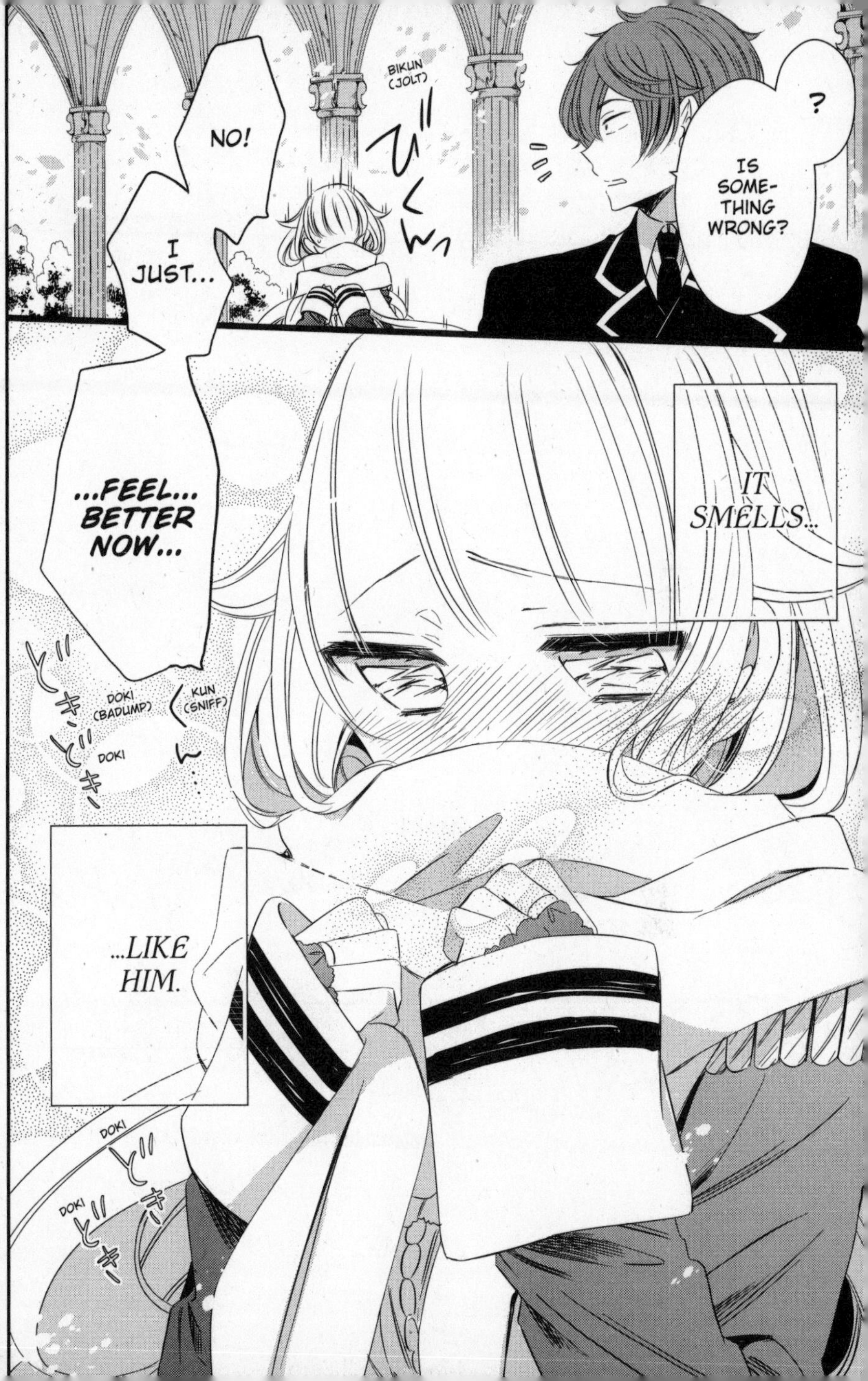
?
IS SOMETHING WRONG?
BIKUN (JOLT)
NO!
I JUST...
...FEEL... BETTER NOW...
IT SMELLS...
KUN (SNIFF)
DOKI (BADUMP)
DOKI
...LIKE HIM.
DOKI
DOKI

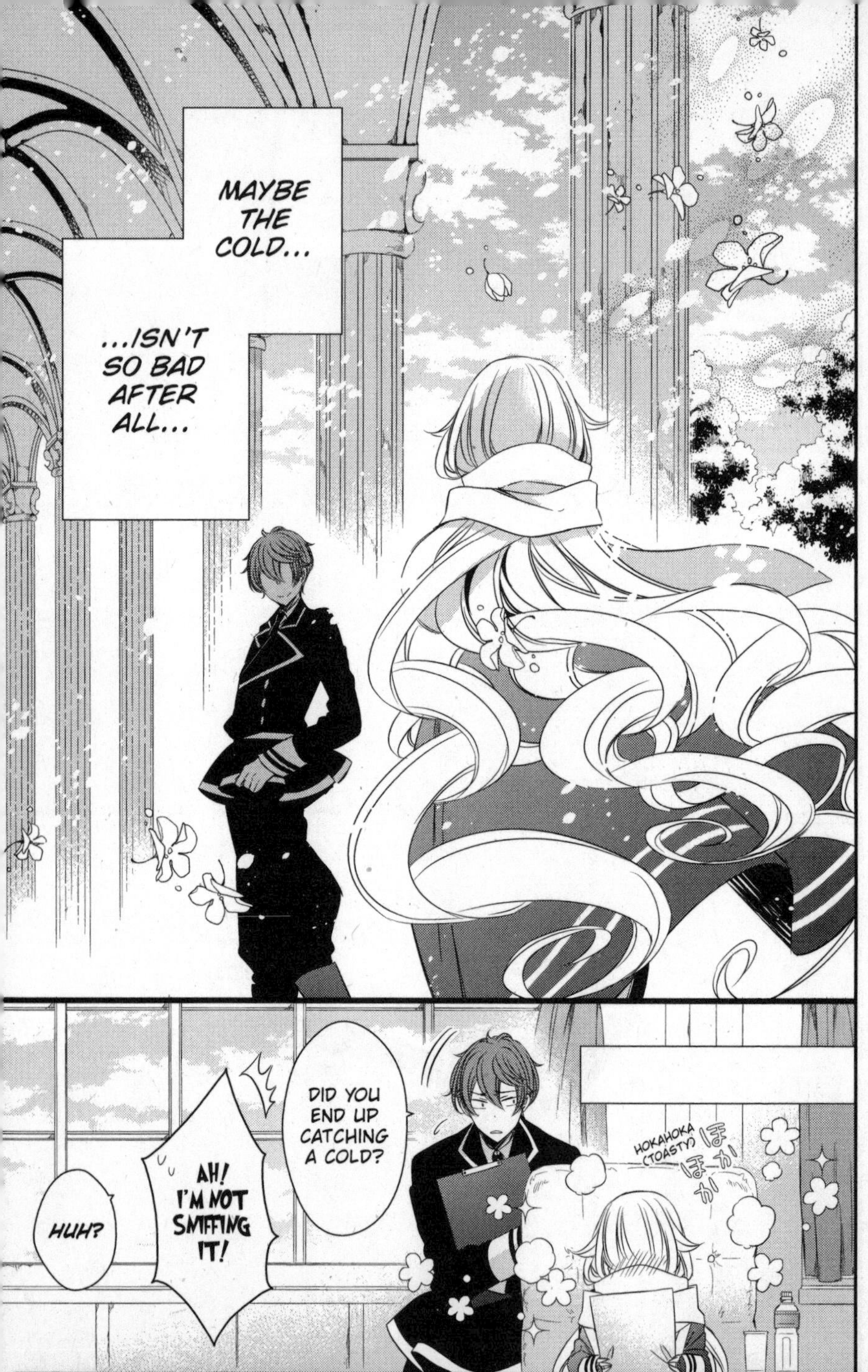
MAYBE THE COLD...
...ISN'T SO BAD AFTER ALL...
HOKAHOKA (TOASTY)
ほかほか
DID YOU END UP CATCHING A COLD?
AH! I'M NOT SNIFFING IT!
HUH?

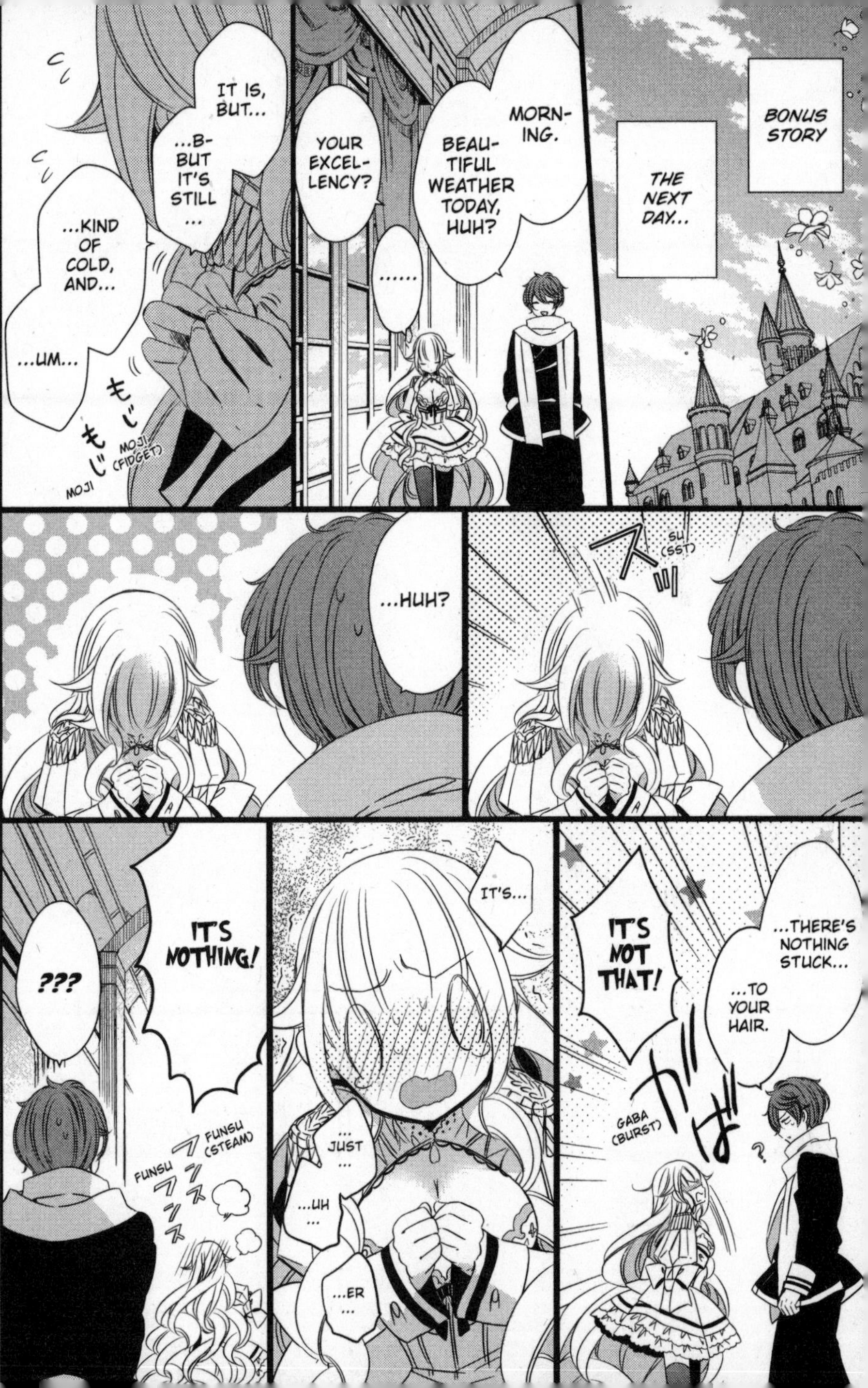
BONUS STORY
THE NEXT DAY...
MORNING.
BEAUTIFUL WEATHER TODAY, HUH?
YOUR EXCELLENCY?
......
IT IS, BUT...
...B-BUT IT'S STILL...
...KIND OF COLD, AND...
...UM...
MOJI (FIDGET)
MOJI
SU (SST)
...HUH?
...THERE'S NOTHING STUCK...
...TO YOUR HAIR.
IT'S NOT THAT!
GABA (BURST)
IT'S...
...JUST...
...UH...
...ER...
IT'S NOTHING!
???
FUNSU (STEAM)
FUNSU

AS MISS BEELZEBUB LIKES VOLUME 3 END

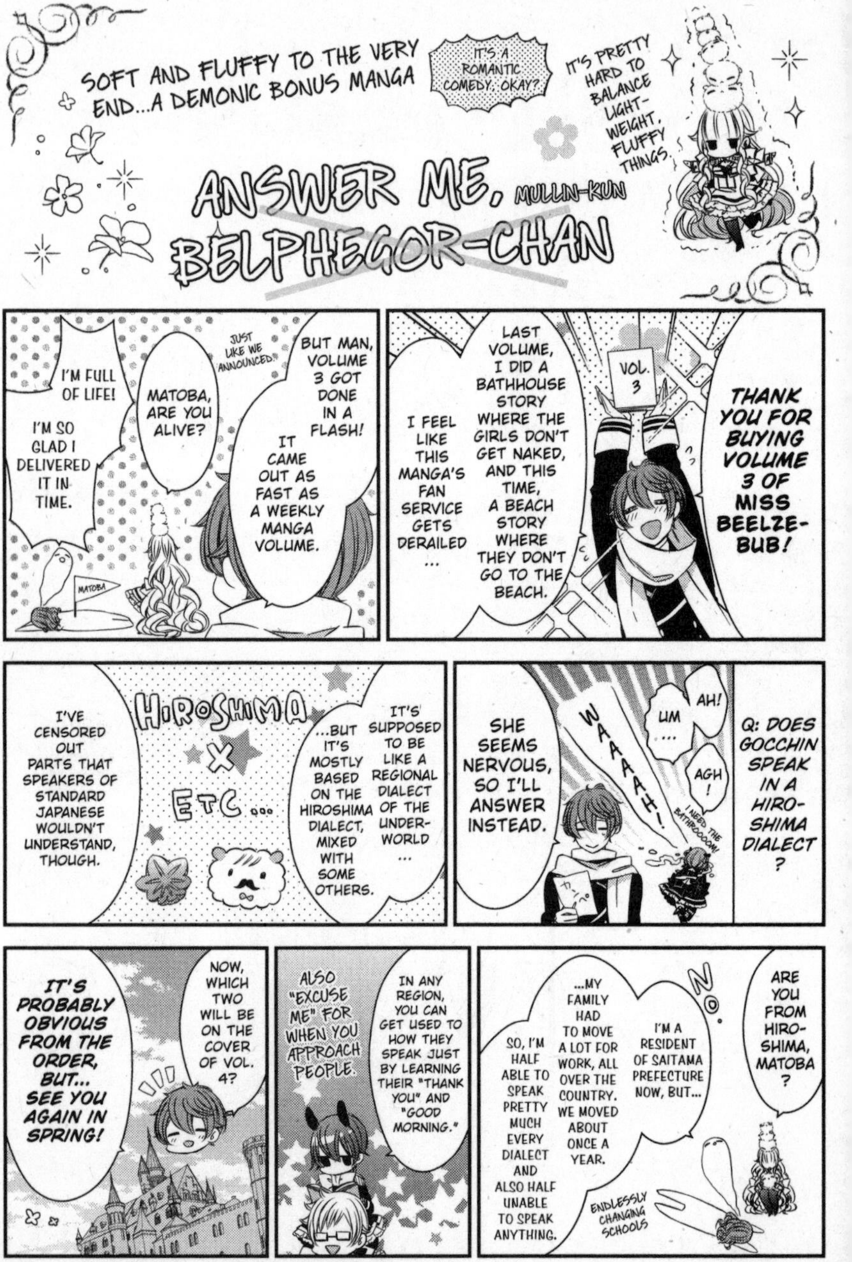
IT'S PRETTY HARD TO BALANCE LIGHT-WEIGHT, FLUFFY THINGS.
IT'S A ROMANTIC COMEDY, OKAY?
SOFT AND FLUFFY TO THE VERY END...A DEMONIC BONUS MANGA
ANSWER ME, MULLIN-KUN BELPHEGOR-CHAN
THANK YOU FOR BUYING VOLUME 3 OF MISS BEELZE-BUB!
VOL. 3
LAST VOLUME, I DID A BATHHOUSE STORY WHERE THE GIRLS DON'T GET NAKED, AND THIS TIME, A BEACH STORY WHERE THEY DON'T GO TO THE BEACH.
I FEEL LIKE THIS MANGA'S FAN SERVICE GETS DERAILED...
BUT MAN, VOLUME 3 GOT DONE IN A FLASH!
IT CAME OUT AS FAST AS A WEEKLY MANGA VOLUME.
JUST LIKE WE ANNOUNCED.
MATOBA, ARE YOU ALIVE?
I'M FULL OF LIFE!
I'M SO GLAD I DELIVERED IT IN TIME.
MATOBA
Q: DOES GOCCHIN SPEAK IN A HIRO-SHIMA DIALECT?
AH!
UM...
AGH!
WAAAAAH!
I NEED THE BATHROOOOM!
SHE SEEMS NERVOUS, SO I'LL ANSWER INSTEAD.
IT'S SUPPOSED TO BE LIKE A REGIONAL DIALECT OF THE UNDER-WORLD...
...BUT IT'S MOSTLY BASED ON THE HIROSHIMA DIALECT, MIXED WITH SOME OTHERS.
HIROSHIMA X ETC...
I'VE CENSORED OUT PARTS THAT SPEAKERS OF STANDARD JAPANESE WOULDN'T UNDERSTAND, THOUGH.
ARE YOU FROM HIRO-SHIMA, MATOBA?
NO.
I'M A RESIDENT OF SAITAMA PREFECTURE NOW, BUT...
...MY FAMILY HAD TO MOVE A LOT FOR WORK, ALL OVER THE COUNTRY. WE MOVED ABOUT ONCE A YEAR.
SO, I'M HALF ABLE TO SPEAK PRETTY MUCH EVERY DIALECT AND ALSO HALF UNABLE TO SPEAK ANYTHING.
ENDLESSLY CHANGING SCHOOLS
IN ANY REGION, YOU CAN GET USED TO HOW THEY SPEAK JUST BY LEARNING THEIR "THANK YOU" AND "GOOD MORNING."
ALSO "EXCUSE ME" FOR WHEN YOU APPROACH PEOPLE.
NOW, WHICH TWO WILL BE ON THE COVER OF VOL. 4?
IT'S PROBABLY OBVIOUS FROM THE ORDER, BUT... SEE YOU AGAIN IN SPRING!

IT MIGHT BE THE PERSON ON THE INSIDE COVER, AND DANTALION...

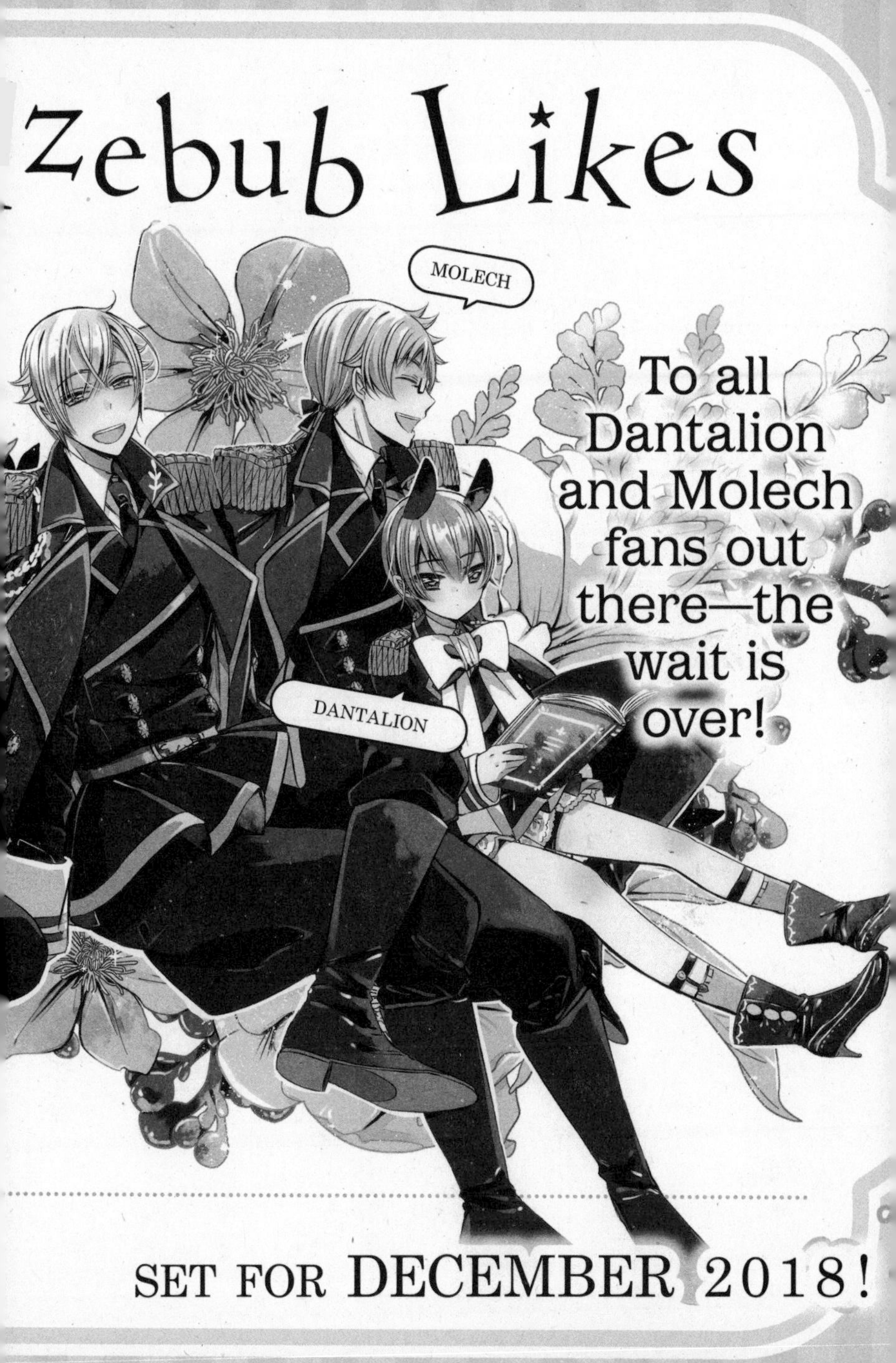
Zebub Likes
MOLECH
DANTALION
To all Dantalion and Molech fans out there—the wait is over!
SET FOR DECEMBER 2018!